DARKSEID
WAR
PART 1

JUSTICE LEAGUE

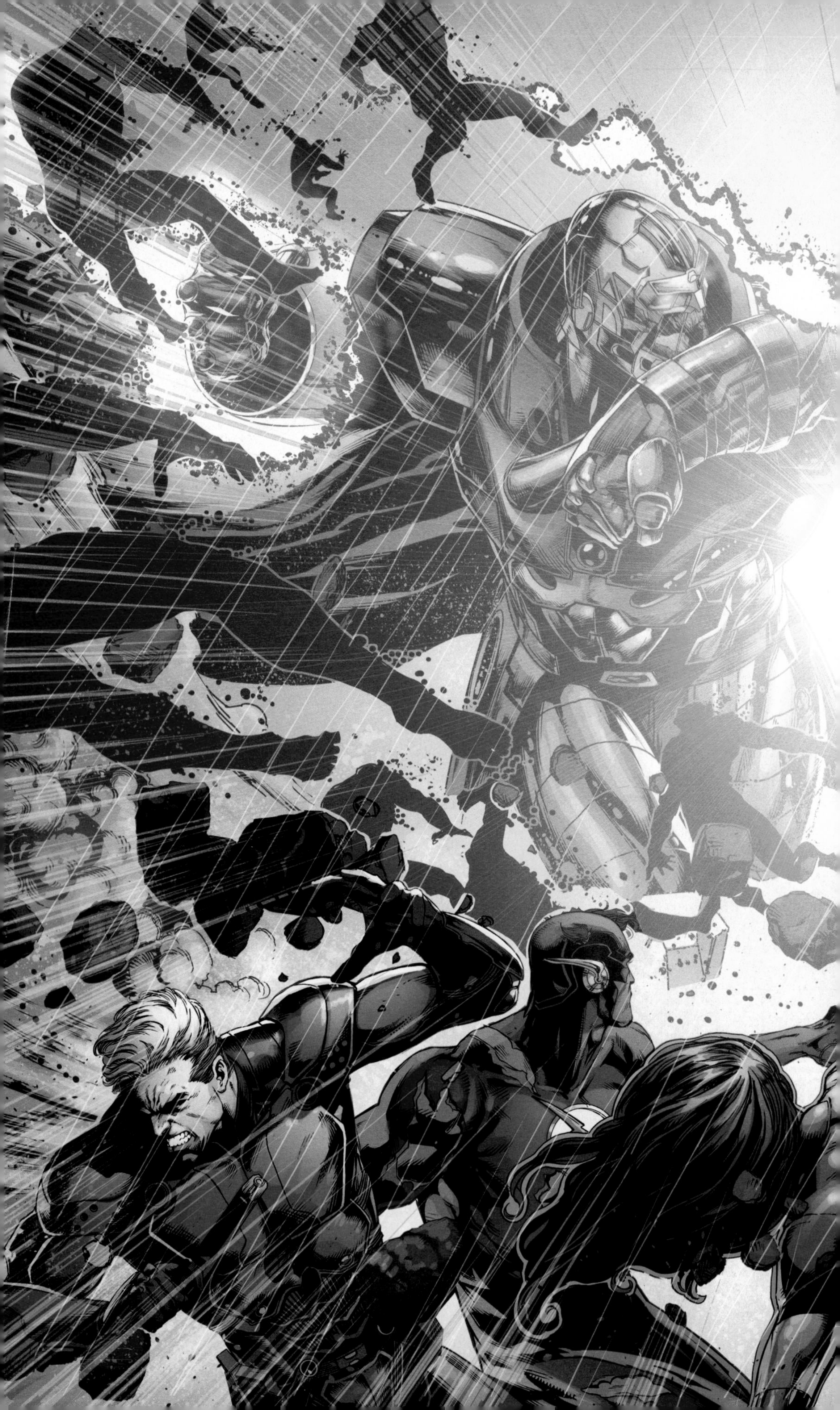

JUSTICE LEAGUE

VOLUME 7
DARKSEID
WAR
PART 1

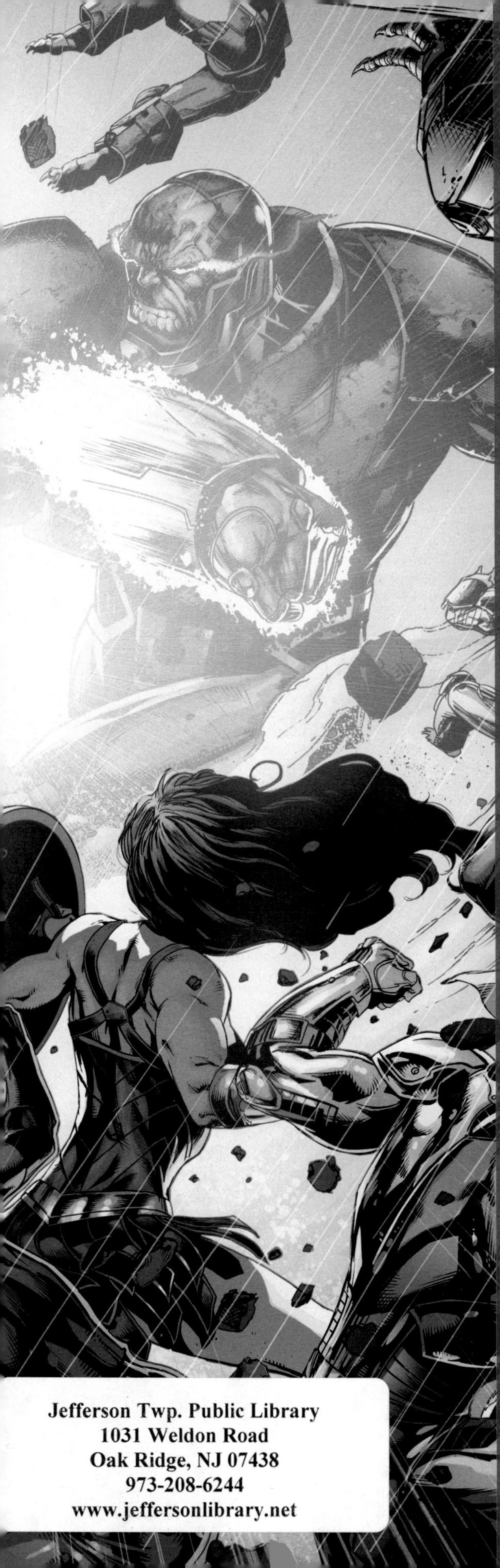

WRITTEN BY
GEOFF JOHNS

ART BY
JASON FABOK
KEVIN MAGUIRE
PHIL JIMENEZ
DAN JURGENS
JERRY ORDWAY
SCOTT KOLINS
JIM LEE
SCOTT WILLIAMS

COLOR BY
BRAD ANDERSON
ALEX SINCLAIR

LETTERS BY
ROB LEIGH

COLLECTION COVER ART BY
JASON FABOK &
BRAD ANDERSON

SUPERMAN CREATED BY
JERRY SIEGEL &
JOE SHUSTER
BY SPECIAL ARRANGEMENT
WITH THE JERRY SIEGEL FAMILY

THE NEW GODS CREATED BY
JACK KIRBY

BRIAN CUNNINGHAM Editor – Original Series
AMEDEO TURTURRO Assistant Editor – Original Series
JEB WOODARD Group Editor – Collected Editions
ROBIN WILDMAN Editor – Collected Edition
STEVE COOK Design Director – Books
DAMIAN RYLAND Publication Design

BOB HARRAS Senior VP – Editor-in-Chief, DC Comics

DIANE NELSON President
DAN DIDIO and JIM LEE Co-Publishers
GEOFF JOHNS Chief Creative Officer
AMIT DESAI Senior VP – Marketing & Global Franchise Management
NAIRI GARDINER Senior VP – Finance
SAM ADES VP – Digital Marketing
BOBBIE CHASE VP – Talent Development
MARK CHIARELLO Senior VP – Art, Design & Collected Editions
JOHN CUNNINGHAM VP – Content Strategy
ANNE DEPIES VP – Strategy Planning & Reporting
DON FALLETTI VP – Manufacturing Operations
LAWRENCE GANEM VP – Editorial Administration & Talent Relations
ALISON GILL Senior VP – Manufacturing & Operations
HANK KANALZ Senior VP – Editorial Strategy & Administration
JAY KOGAN VP – Legal Affairs
DEREK MADDALENA Senior VP – Sales & Business Development
JACK MAHAN VP – Business Affairs
DAN MIRON VP – Sales Planning & Trade Development
NICK NAPOLITANO VP – Manufacturing Administration
CAROL ROEDER VP – Marketing
EDDIE SCANNELL VP – Mass Account & Digital Sales
COURTNEY SIMMONS Senior VP – Publicity & Communications
JIM (SKI) SOKOLOWSKI VP – Comic Book Specialty & Newsstand Sales
SANDY YI Senior VP – Global Franchise Management

JUSTICE LEAGUE VOLUME 7: DARKSEID WAR PART 1

DC Comics, 2900 West Alameda Avenue, Burbank, CA 91505
Printed by RR Donnelley, Salem, VA, USA. 8/19/16. First Printing.
ISBN: 978-1-4012-6452-9

Library of Congress Cataloging-in-Publication Data is available.

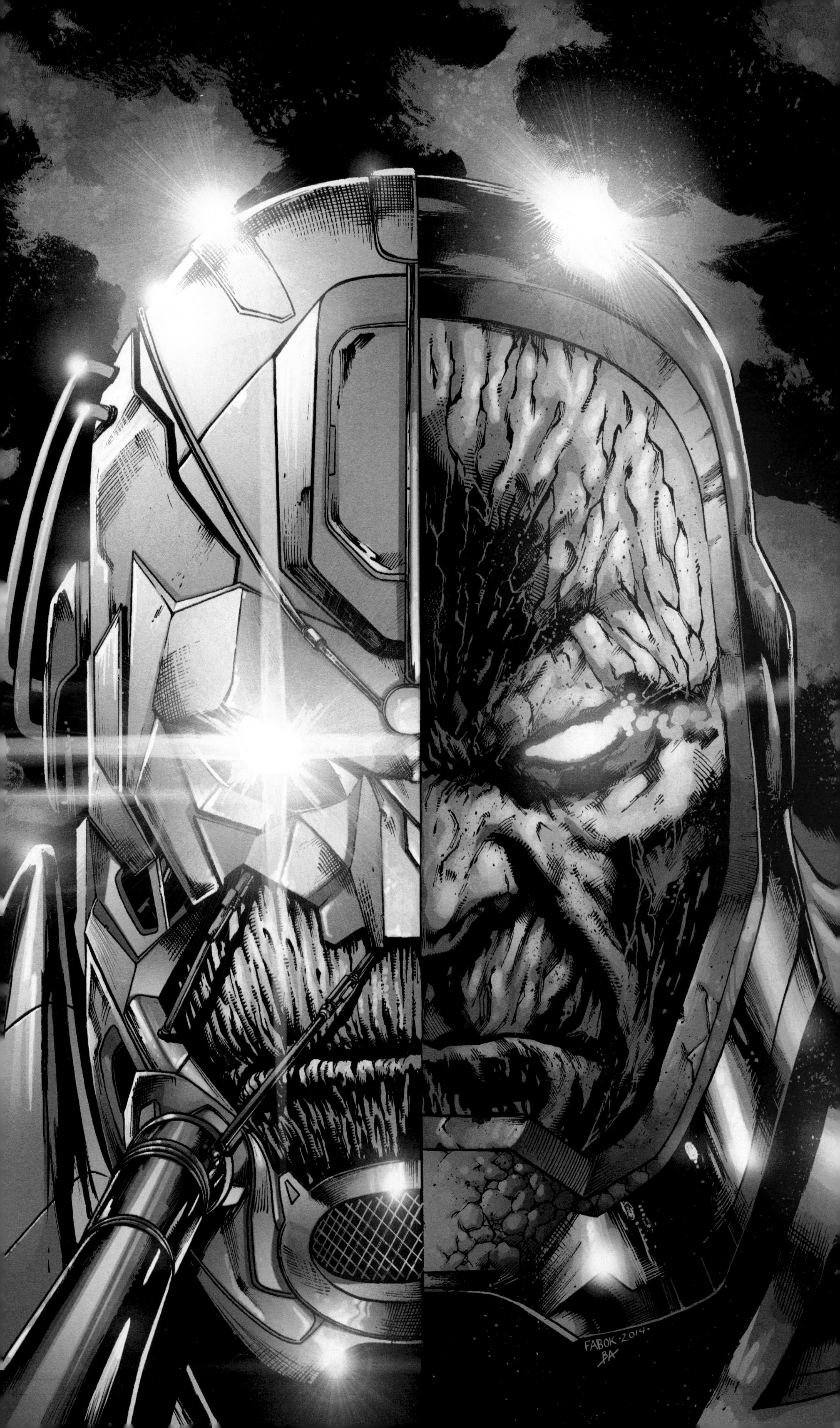
FABOK ·2014·
BA

DARKSEID WAR SNEAK PEEK GEOFF JOHNS writer JASON FABOK artist BRAD ANDERSON colorist ROB LEIGH letterer
DARKSEID WAR PROLOGUE GEOFF JOHNS writer KEVIN MAGUIRE, PHIL JIMENEZ, DAN JURGENS, JERRY ORDWAY, SCOTT KOLINS, JASON FABOK, JIM LEE, SCOTT WILLIAMS artists BRAD ANDERSON, ALEX SINCLAIR colorists ROB LEIGH letterer cover by JASON FABOK & BRAD ANDERSON

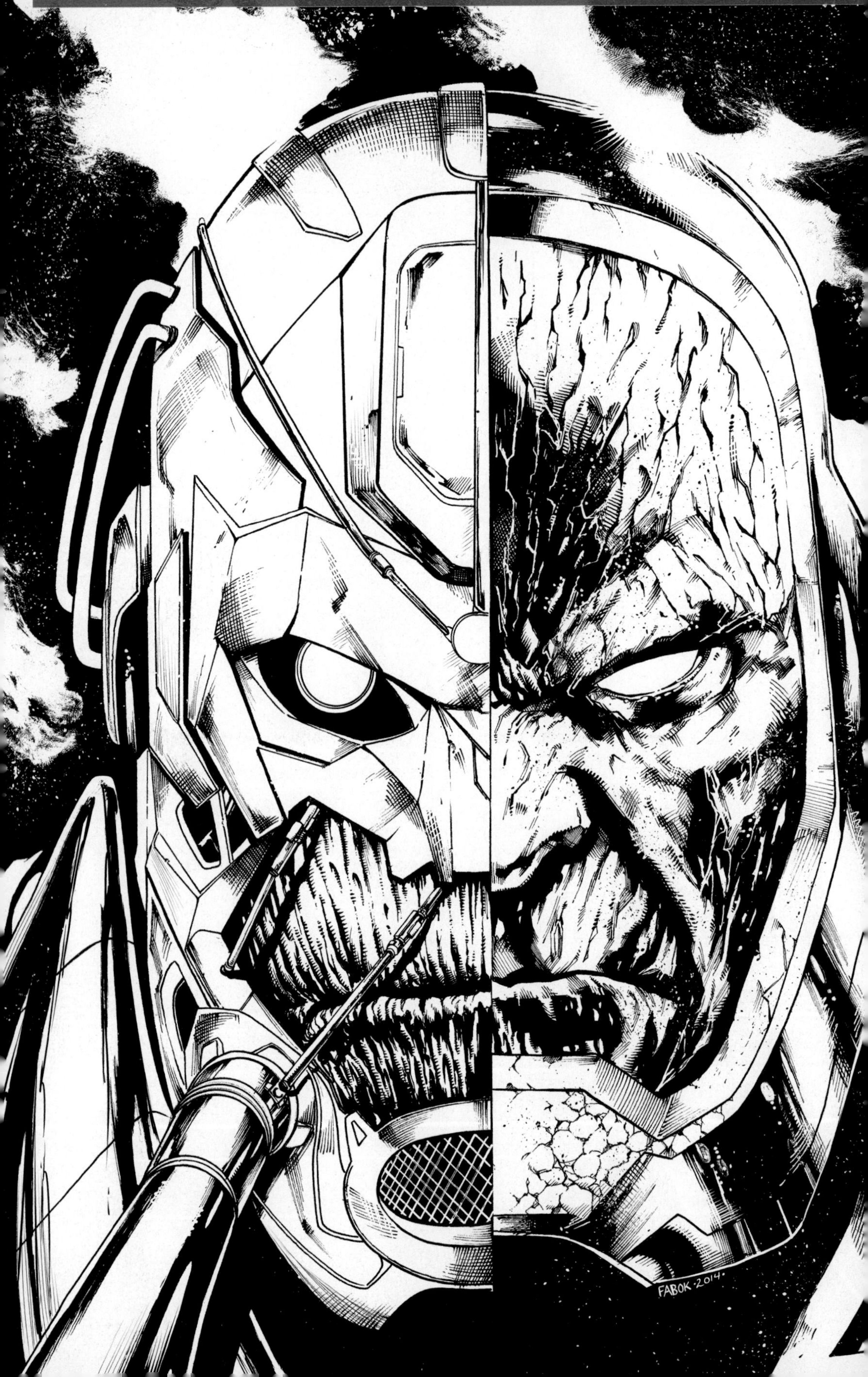
FABOK 2014

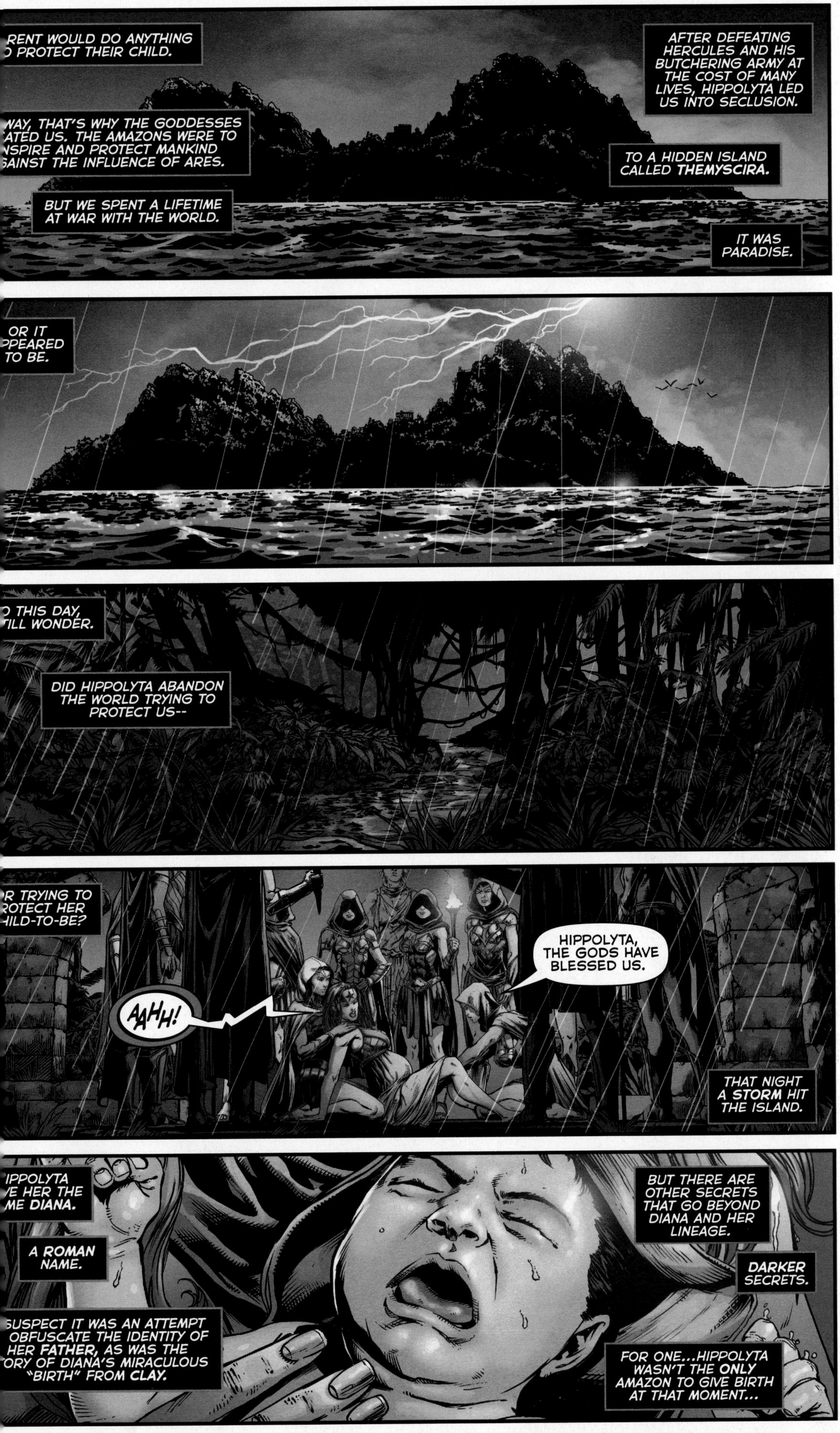

RENT WOULD DO ANYTHING
O PROTECT THEIR CHILD.
WAY, THAT'S WHY THE GODDESSES
ATED US. THE AMAZONS WERE TO
NSPIRE AND PROTECT MANKIND
GAINST THE INFLUENCE OF ARES.
BUT WE SPENT A LIFETIME AT WAR WITH THE WORLD.
AFTER DEFEATING HERCULES AND HIS BUTCHERING ARMY AT THE COST OF MANY LIVES, HIPPOLYTA LED US INTO SECLUSION.
TO A HIDDEN ISLAND CALLED **THEMYSCIRA.**
IT WAS PARADISE.
OR IT
PPEARED
TO BE.
O THIS DAY,
TILL WONDER.
DID HIPPOLYTA ABANDON THE WORLD TRYING TO PROTECT US--
R TRYING TO
ROTECT HER
HILD-TO-BE?
AAHH!
HIPPOLYTA, THE GODS HAVE BLESSED US.
THAT NIGHT A **STORM** HIT THE ISLAND.
IPPOLYTA
VE HER THE
ME **DIANA.**
A **ROMAN** NAME.
SUSPECT IT WAS AN ATTEMPT
OBFUSCATE THE IDENTITY OF
HER **FATHER,** AS WAS THE
ORY OF DIANA'S MIRACULOUS
"BIRTH" FROM **CLAY.**
BUT THERE ARE OTHER SECRETS THAT GO BEYOND DIANA AND HER LINEAGE.
DARKER SECRETS.
FOR ONE...HIPPOLYTA WASN'T THE **ONLY** AMAZON TO GIVE BIRTH AT THAT MOMENT...

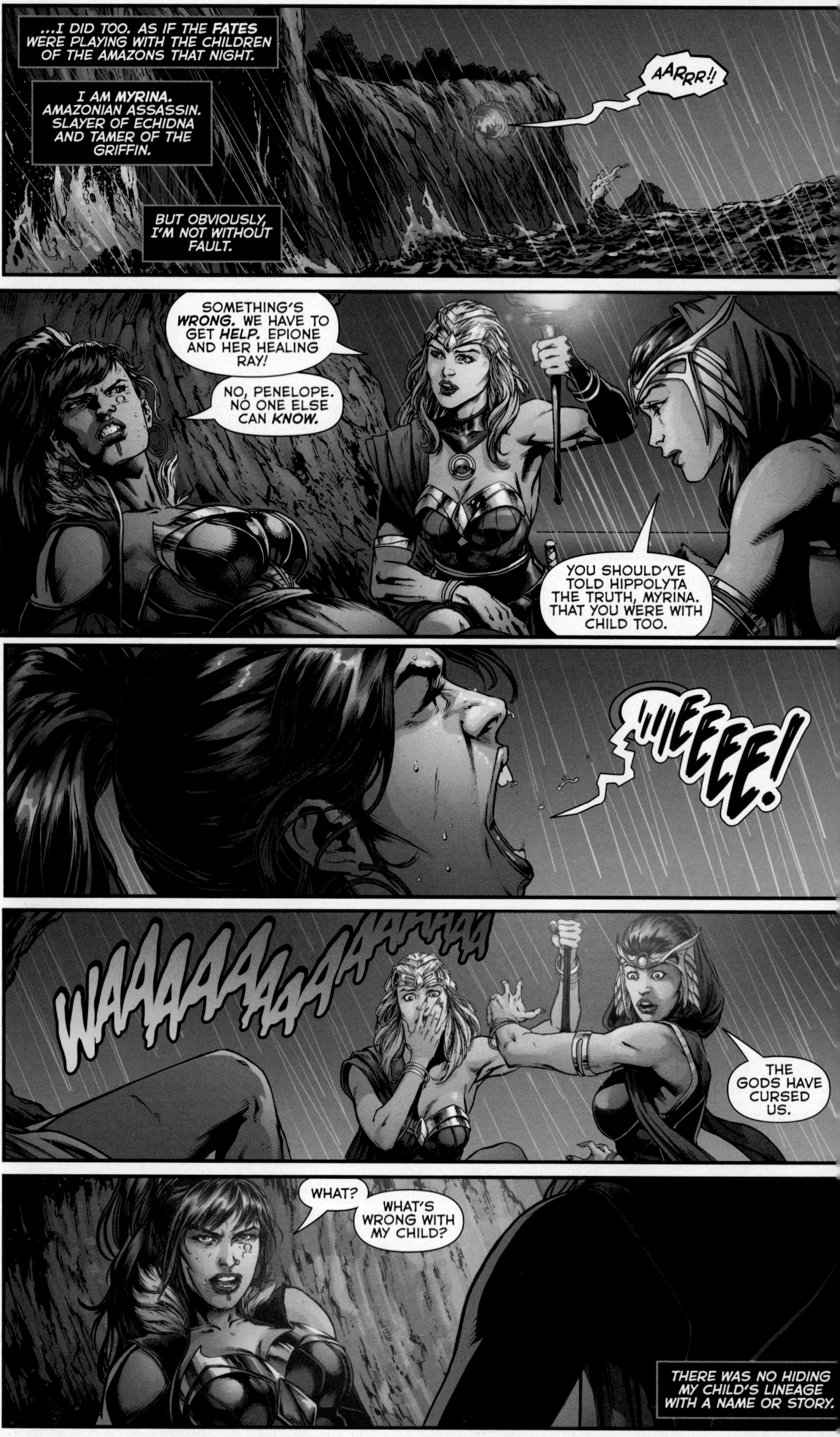
...I DID TOO. AS IF THE FATES WERE PLAYING WITH THE CHILDREN OF THE AMAZONS THAT NIGHT.
I AM MYRINA. AMAZONIAN ASSASSIN. SLAYER OF ECHIDNA AND TAMER OF THE GRIFFIN.
AARRR!!
BUT OBVIOUSLY, I'M NOT WITHOUT FAULT.
SOMETHING'S WRONG. WE HAVE TO GET HELP. EPIONE AND HER HEALING RAY!
NO, PENELOPE. NO ONE ELSE CAN KNOW.
YOU SHOULD'VE TOLD HIPPOLYTA THE TRUTH, MYRINA. THAT YOU WERE WITH CHILD TOO.
IIIEEEE!
WAAAAAAAAAAAAAAAA
THE GODS HAVE CURSED US.
WHAT?
WHAT'S WRONG WITH MY CHILD?
THERE WAS NO HIDING MY CHILD'S LINEAGE WITH A NAME OR STORY.

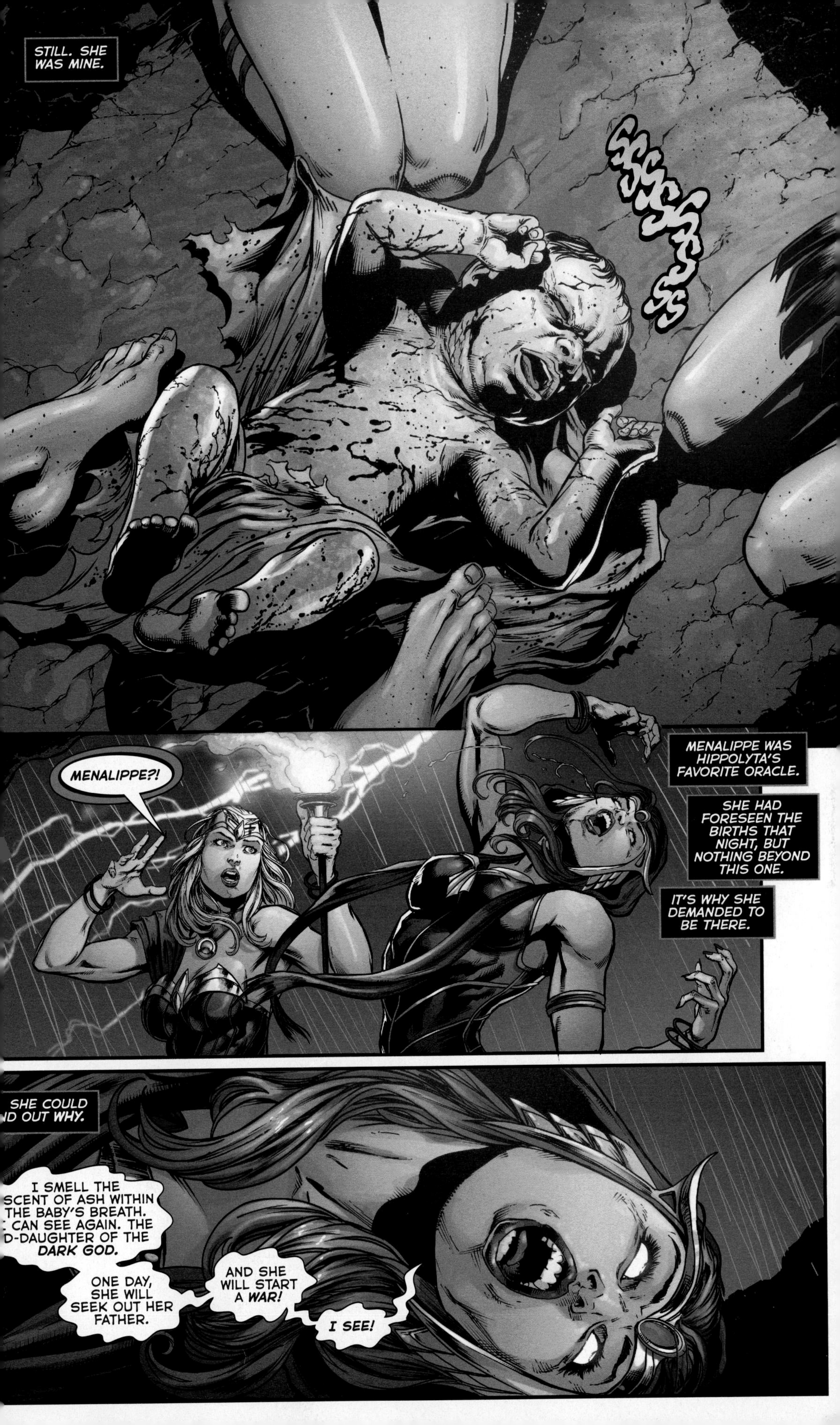
STILL. SHE WAS MINE.
SSSSSSSS
MENALIPPE?!
MENALIPPE WAS HIPPOLYTA'S FAVORITE ORACLE.
SHE HAD FORESEEN THE BIRTHS THAT NIGHT, BUT NOTHING BEYOND THIS ONE.
IT'S WHY SHE DEMANDED TO BE THERE.
SHE COULD
D OUT WHY.
I SMELL THE SCENT OF ASH WITHIN THE BABY'S BREATH. CAN SEE AGAIN. THE D-DAUGHTER OF THE DARK GOD.
ONE DAY, SHE WILL SEEK OUT HER FATHER.
AND SHE WILL START A WAR!
I SEE!

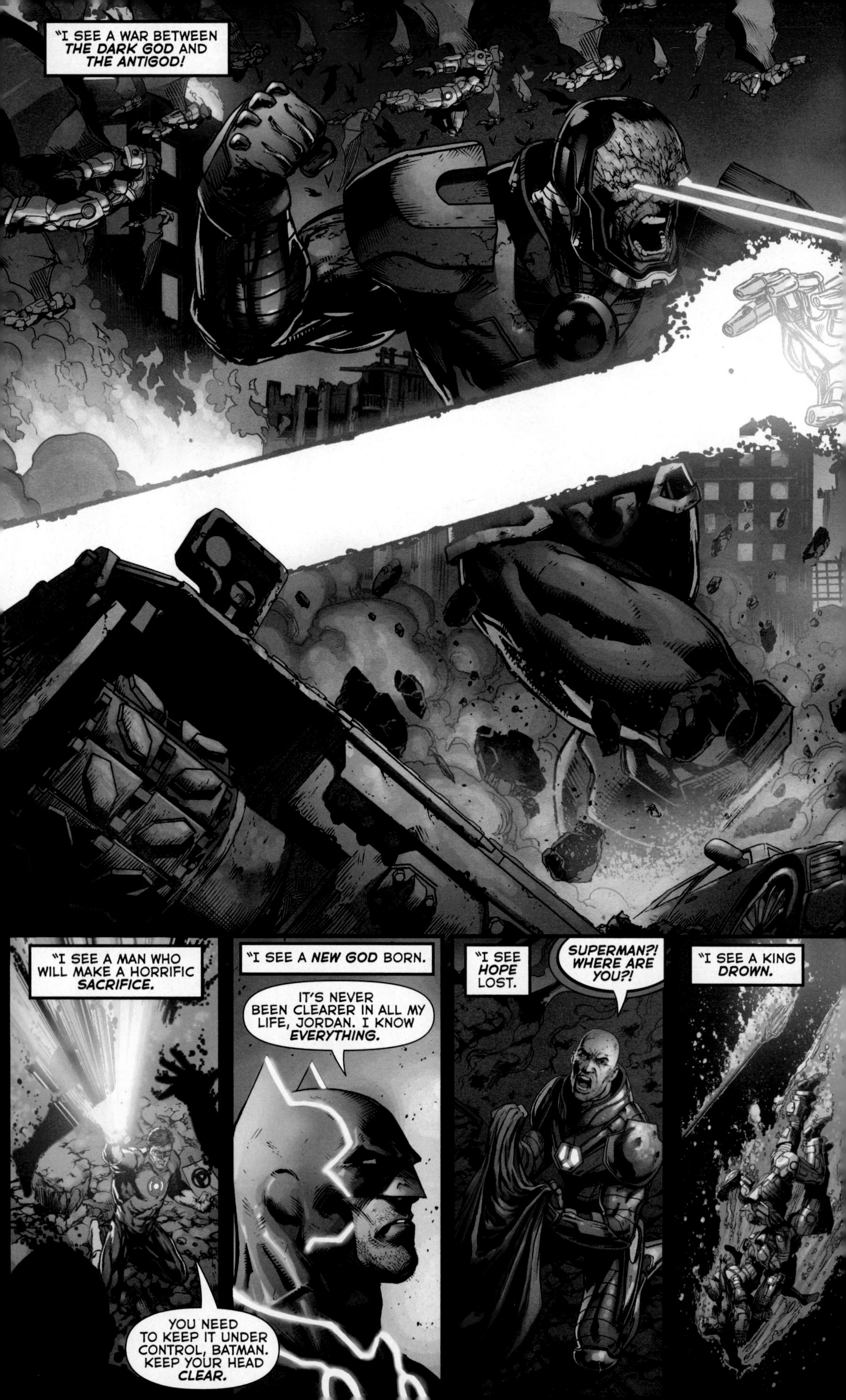
"I SEE A WAR BETWEEN THE DARK GOD AND THE ANTIGOD!
"I SEE A MAN WHO WILL MAKE A HORRIFIC SACRIFICE.
"I SEE A NEW GOD BORN.
IT'S NEVER BEEN CLEARER IN ALL MY LIFE, JORDAN. I KNOW EVERYTHING.
YOU NEED TO KEEP IT UNDER CONTROL, BATMAN. KEEP YOUR HEAD CLEAR.
"I SEE HOPE LOST.
SUPERMAN?! WHERE ARE YOU?!
"I SEE A KING DROWN.

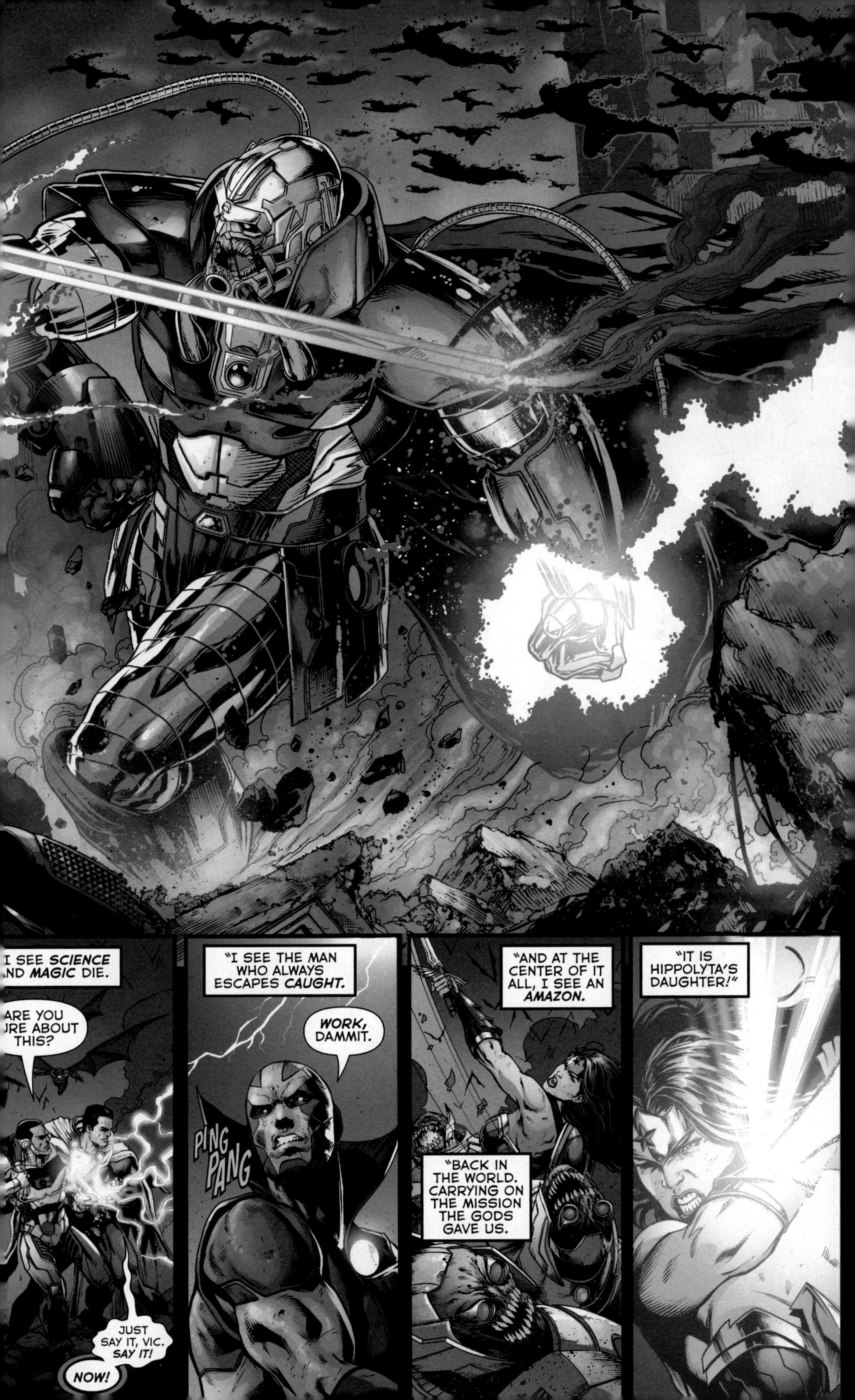

I SEE SCIENCE AND MAGIC DIE.
ARE YOU SURE ABOUT THIS?
JUST SAY IT, VIC. SAY IT!
NOW!
"I SEE THE MAN WHO ALWAYS ESCAPES CAUGHT.
WORK, DAMMIT.
PING
PANG
"AND AT THE CENTER OF IT ALL, I SEE AN AMAZON.
"BACK IN THE WORLD. CARRYING ON THE MISSION THE GODS GAVE US.
"IT IS HIPPOLYTA'S DAUGHTER!"

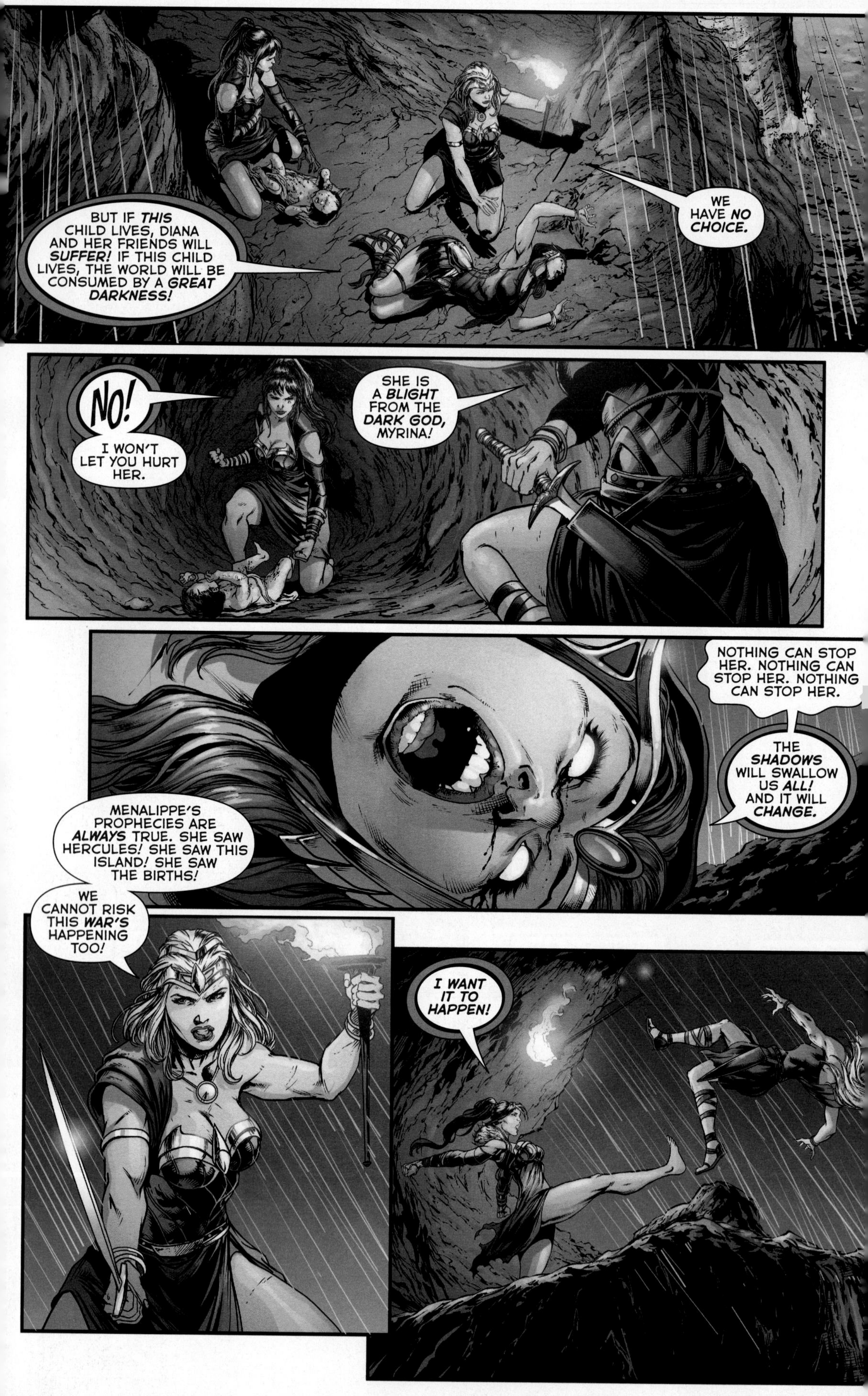

BUT IF THIS CHILD LIVES, DIANA AND HER FRIENDS WILL SUFFER! IF THIS CHILD LIVES, THE WORLD WILL BE CONSUMED BY A GREAT DARKNESS!
WE HAVE NO CHOICE.
NO!
I WON'T LET YOU HURT HER.
SHE IS A BLIGHT FROM THE DARK GOD, MYRINA!
NOTHING CAN STOP HER. NOTHING CAN STOP HER. NOTHING CAN STOP HER.
THE SHADOWS WILL SWALLOW US ALL! AND IT WILL CHANGE.
MENALIPPE'S PROPHECIES ARE ALWAYS TRUE. SHE SAW HERCULES! SHE SAW THIS ISLAND! SHE SAW THE BIRTHS!
WE CANNOT RISK THIS WAR'S HAPPENING TOO!
I WANT IT TO HAPPEN!

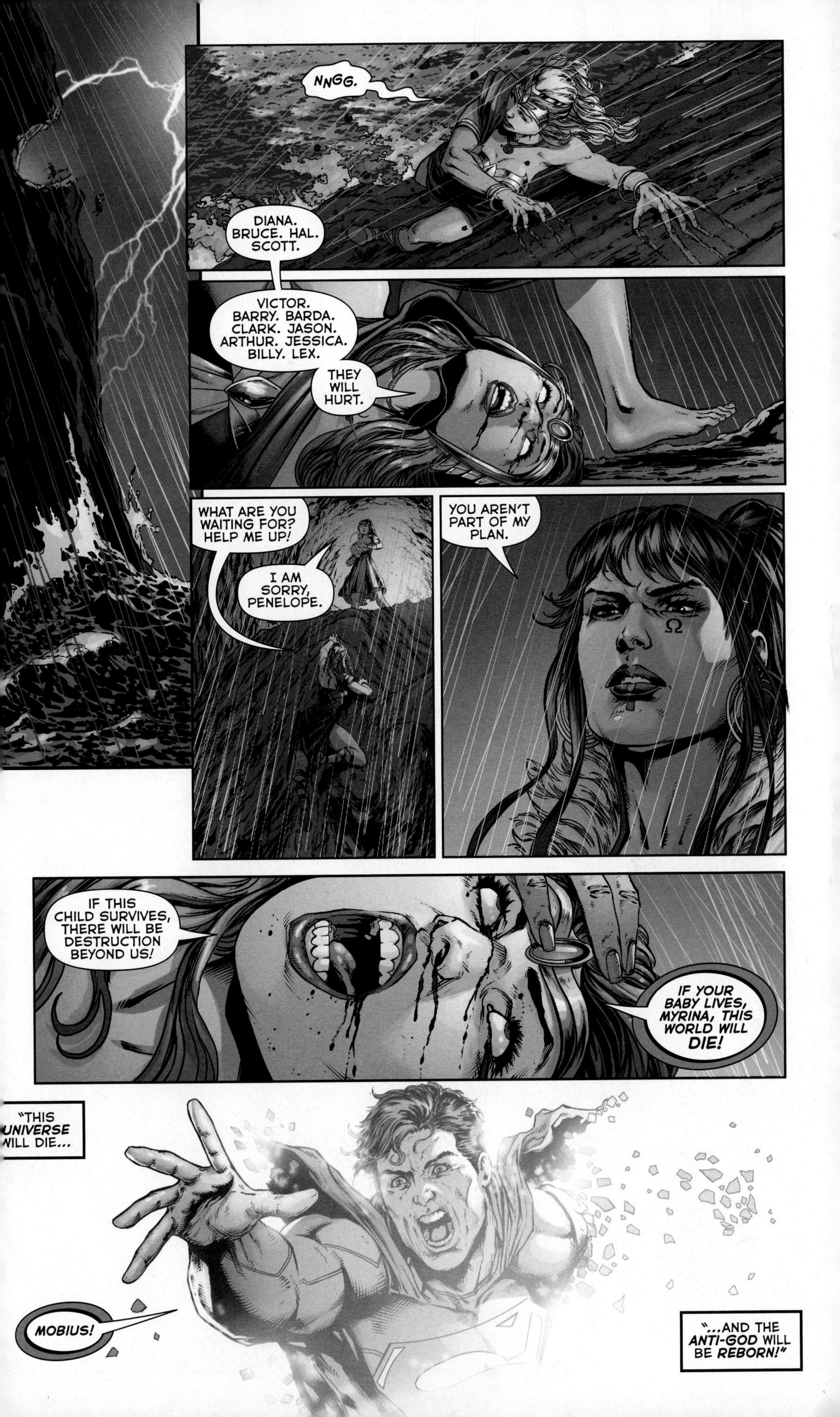
NNGG.
DIANA. BRUCE. HAL. SCOTT.
VICTOR. BARRY. BARDA. CLARK. JASON. ARTHUR. JESSICA. BILLY. LEX.
THEY WILL HURT.
WHAT ARE YOU WAITING FOR? HELP ME UP!
I AM SORRY, PENELOPE.
YOU AREN'T PART OF MY PLAN.
IF THIS CHILD SURVIVES, THERE WILL BE DESTRUCTION BEYOND US!
IF YOUR BABY LIVES, MYRINA, THIS WORLD WILL DIE!
"THIS UNIVERSE WILL DIE...
MOBIUS!
"...AND THE ANTI-GOD WILL BE REBORN!"

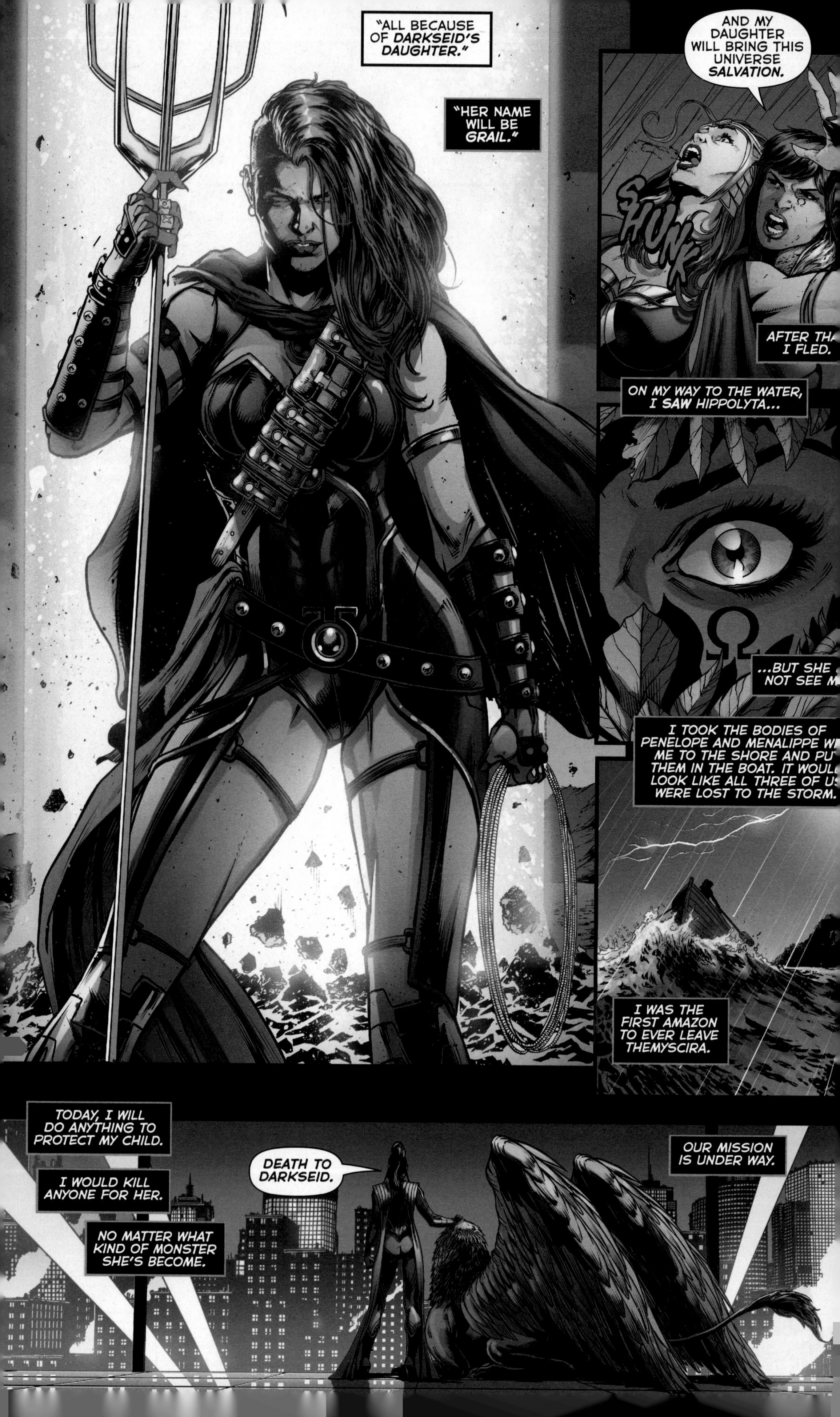
"ALL BECAUSE OF DARKSEID'S DAUGHTER."
"HER NAME WILL BE GRAIL."
AND MY DAUGHTER WILL BRING THIS UNIVERSE SALVATION.
SHUNK
AFTER THA I FLED.
ON MY WAY TO THE WATER, I SAW HIPPOLYTA...
...BUT SHE NOT SEE M
I TOOK THE BODIES OF PENELOPE AND MENALIPPE W ME TO THE SHORE AND PU THEM IN THE BOAT. IT WOUL LOOK LIKE ALL THREE OF U WERE LOST TO THE STORM.
I WAS THE FIRST AMAZON TO EVER LEAVE THEMYSCIRA.
TODAY, I WILL DO ANYTHING TO PROTECT MY CHILD.
I WOULD KILL ANYONE FOR HER.
NO MATTER WHAT KIND OF MONSTER SHE'S BECOME.
DEATH TO DARKSEID.
OUR MISSION IS UNDER WAY.

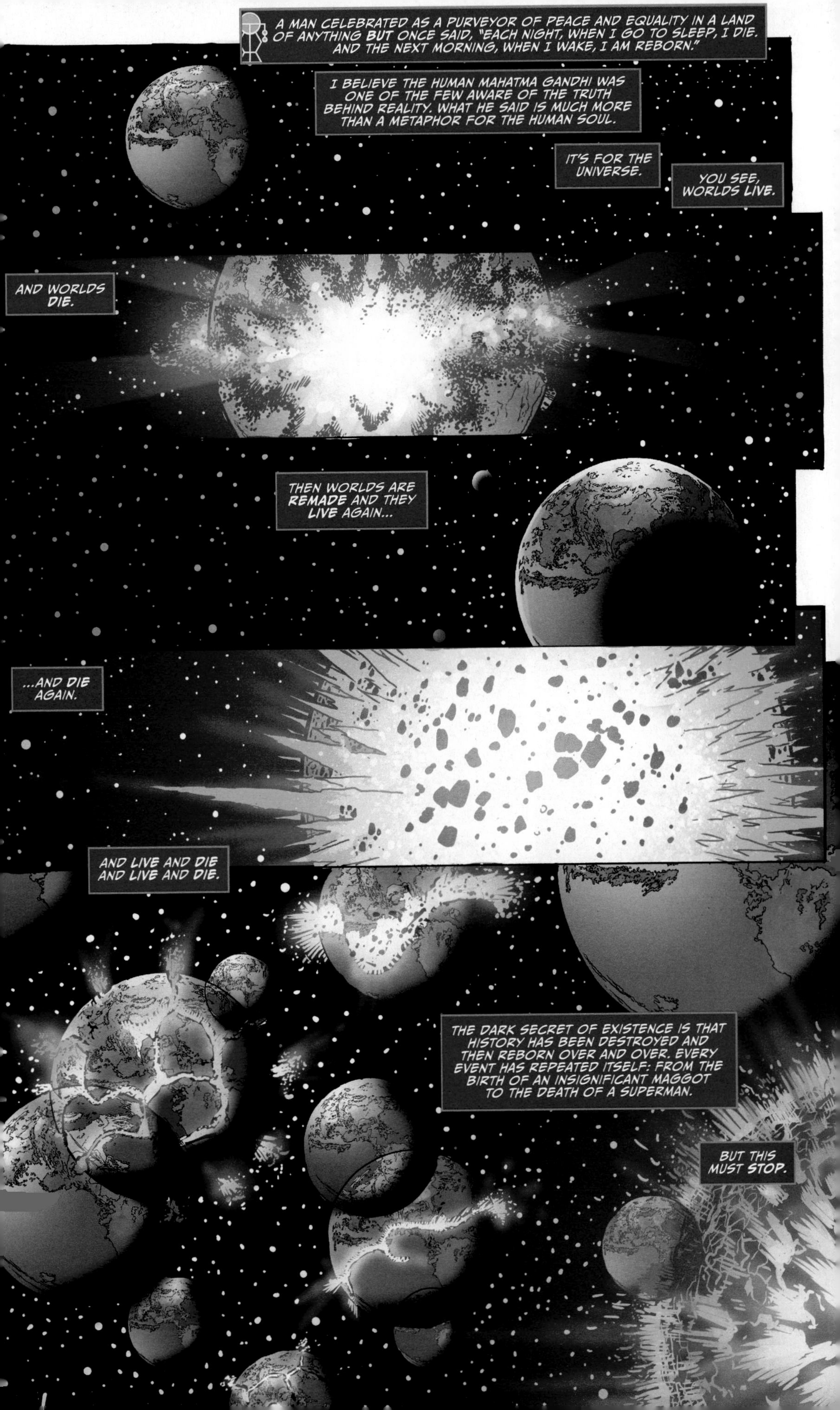
A MAN CELEBRATED AS A PURVEYOR OF PEACE AND EQUALITY IN A LAND OF ANYTHING BUT ONCE SAID, "EACH NIGHT, WHEN I GO TO SLEEP, I DIE. AND THE NEXT MORNING, WHEN I WAKE, I AM REBORN."
I BELIEVE THE HUMAN MAHATMA GANDHI WAS ONE OF THE FEW AWARE OF THE TRUTH BEHIND REALITY. WHAT HE SAID IS MUCH MORE THAN A METAPHOR FOR THE HUMAN SOUL.
IT'S FOR THE UNIVERSE.
YOU SEE, WORLDS LIVE.
AND WORLDS DIE.
THEN WORLDS ARE REMADE AND THEY LIVE AGAIN...
...AND DIE AGAIN.
AND LIVE AND DIE AND LIVE AND DIE.
THE DARK SECRET OF EXISTENCE IS THAT HISTORY HAS BEEN DESTROYED AND THEN REBORN OVER AND OVER. EVERY EVENT HAS REPEATED ITSELF: FROM THE BIRTH OF AN INSIGNIFICANT MAGGOT TO THE DEATH OF A SUPERMAN.
BUT THIS MUST STOP.

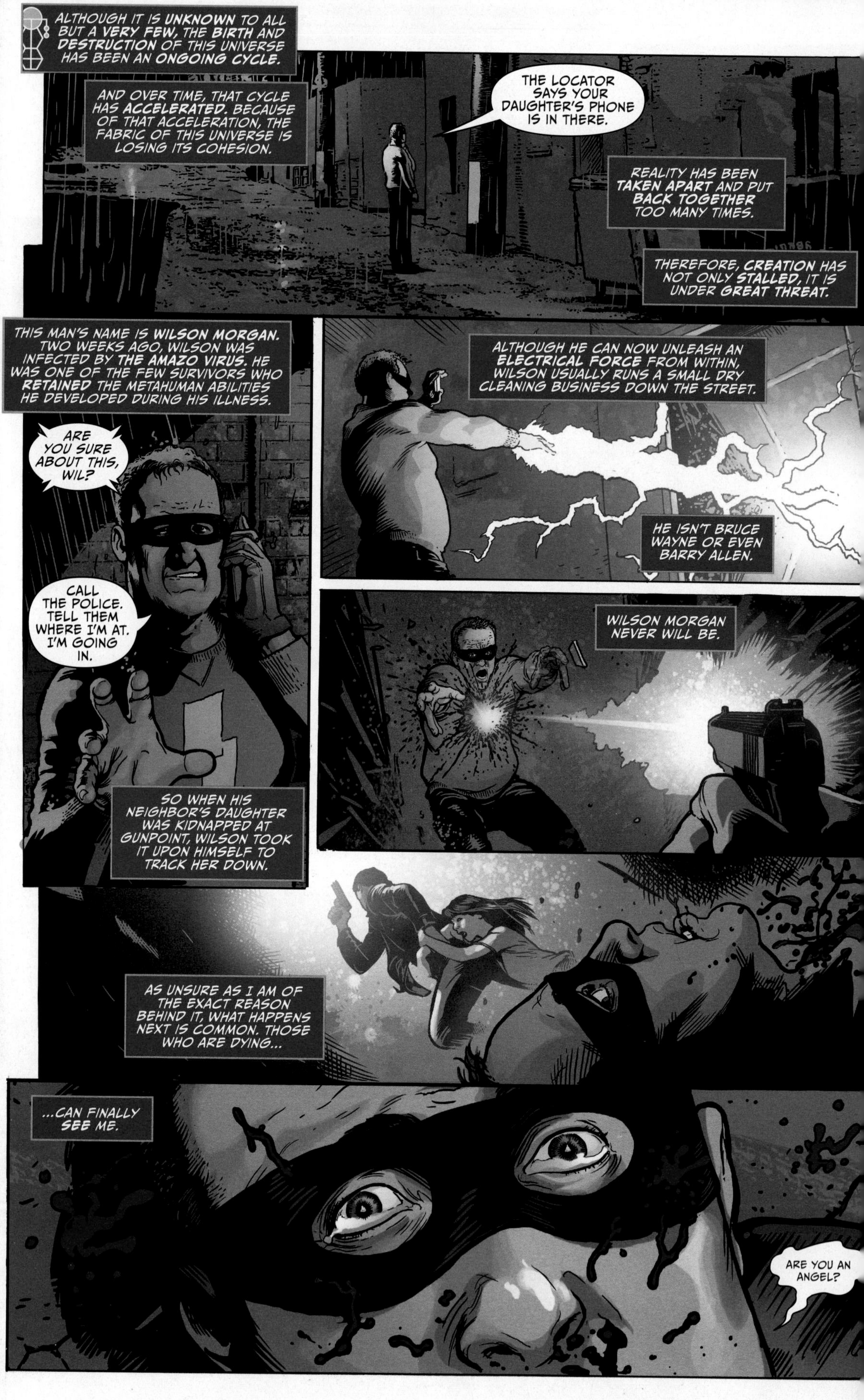
ALTHOUGH IT IS UNKNOWN TO ALL BUT A VERY FEW, THE BIRTH AND DESTRUCTION OF THIS UNIVERSE HAS BEEN AN ONGOING CYCLE.
AND OVER TIME, THAT CYCLE HAS ACCELERATED. BECAUSE OF THAT ACCELERATION, THE FABRIC OF THIS UNIVERSE IS LOSING ITS COHESION.
THE LOCATOR SAYS YOUR DAUGHTER'S PHONE IS IN THERE.
REALITY HAS BEEN TAKEN APART AND PUT BACK TOGETHER TOO MANY TIMES.
THEREFORE, CREATION HAS NOT ONLY STALLED, IT IS UNDER GREAT THREAT.
THIS MAN'S NAME IS WILSON MORGAN. TWO WEEKS AGO, WILSON WAS INFECTED BY THE AMAZO VIRUS. HE WAS ONE OF THE FEW SURVIVORS WHO RETAINED THE METAHUMAN ABILITIES HE DEVELOPED DURING HIS ILLNESS.
ARE YOU SURE ABOUT THIS, WIL?
CALL THE POLICE. TELL THEM WHERE I'M AT. I'M GOING IN.
SO WHEN HIS NEIGHBOR'S DAUGHTER WAS KIDNAPPED AT GUNPOINT, WILSON TOOK IT UPON HIMSELF TO TRACK HER DOWN.
ALTHOUGH HE CAN NOW UNLEASH AN ELECTRICAL FORCE FROM WITHIN, WILSON USUALLY RUNS A SMALL DRY CLEANING BUSINESS DOWN THE STREET.
HE ISN'T BRUCE WAYNE OR EVEN BARRY ALLEN.
WILSON MORGAN NEVER WILL BE.
AS UNSURE AS I AM OF THE EXACT REASON BEHIND IT, WHAT HAPPENS NEXT IS COMMON. THOSE WHO ARE DYING...
...CAN FINALLY SEE ME.
ARE YOU AN ANGEL?

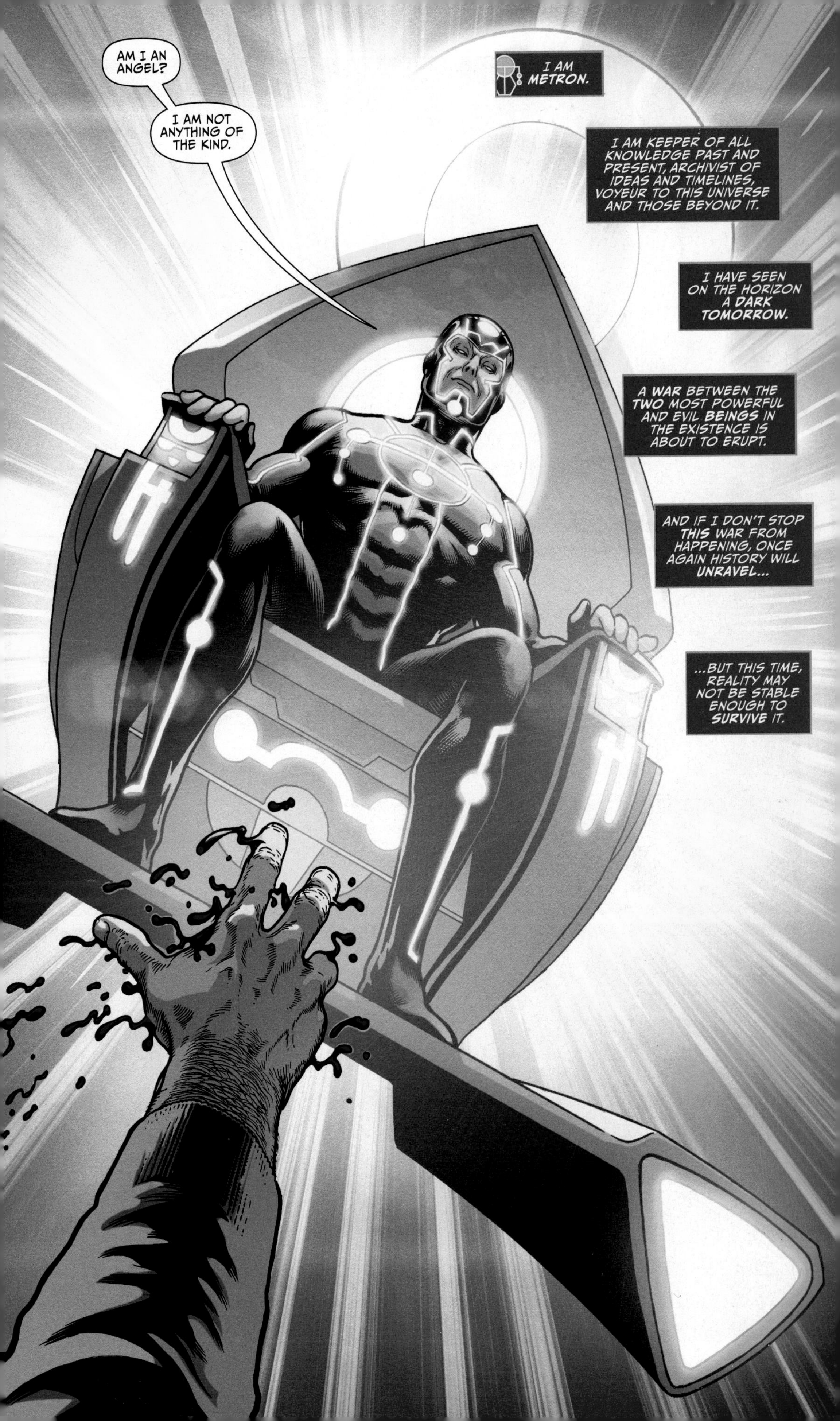

AM I AN ANGEL?
I AM NOT ANYTHING OF THE KIND.
I AM METRON.
I AM KEEPER OF ALL KNOWLEDGE PAST AND PRESENT, ARCHIVIST OF IDEAS AND TIMELINES, VOYEUR TO THIS UNIVERSE AND THOSE BEYOND IT.
I HAVE SEEN ON THE HORIZON A DARK TOMORROW.
A WAR BETWEEN THE TWO MOST POWERFUL AND EVIL BEINGS IN THE EXISTENCE IS ABOUT TO ERUPT.
AND IF I DON'T STOP THIS WAR FROM HAPPENING, ONCE AGAIN HISTORY WILL UNRAVEL...
...BUT THIS TIME, REALITY MAY NOT BE STABLE ENOUGH TO SURVIVE IT.

I HAVE SAT UPON THE MOBIUS CHAIR FOR AS LONG AS EXISTENCE AND BEFORE AND OBSERVED AND REMAINED SILENT.

BECAUSE THE TRUTH IS, WHETHER THESE BEINGS LIVE OR DIE AFFECTS ME VERY LITTLE.

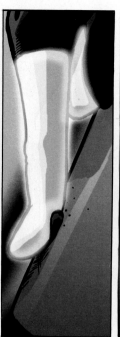

STILL. WITHOUT THEM TO OBSERVE, I LOSE PURPOSE.

I OBSERVE EMPTINESS.

SO ALTHOUGH I HAVE BEEN FORBIDDEN TO USE MY KNOWLEDGE TO INTERFERE, I HAVE DISOBEYED ON OCCASION WHEN I BELIEVE THE THREAT IS GREAT ENOUGH.

THE FIRST TIME I BROKE MY WORD WAS FAR AWAY FROM HERE, IN ANOTHER SOLAR SYSTEM.

THERE, YOU COULD NOT FIND TWO WORLDS TO BE MORE OPPOSITE IN TERRAIN AND SOUL.

APOKOLIPS.

A PIT OF SLAVERY AND OPPRESSION, RULED BY FEAR AND FUELED BY DESPAIR.

AND NEW GENESIS.

A HAVEN OF CULTURE AND SCIENCE, THOUGH NOT A WORLD WITHOUT HIDDEN AND INSIDIOUS PROBLEMS OF ITS OWN.

EVEN NOW, MANY WOULD MISTAKE MY ALLEGIANCES TO BE WITH NEW GENESIS.

BUT MY ALLEGIANCES ARE TO NO ONE.

IT WOULD BE GOOD TO REMEMBER THAT.

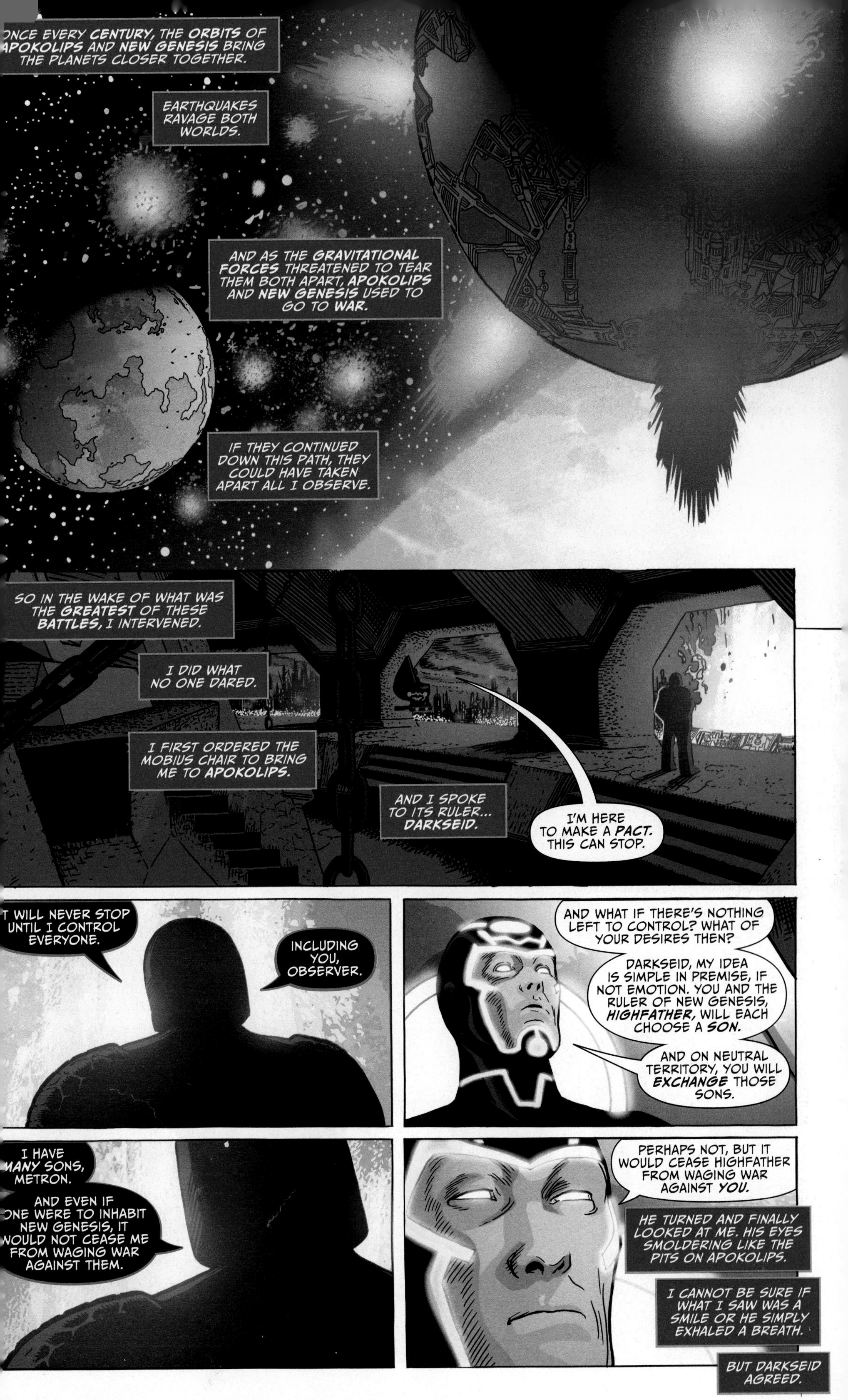
ONCE EVERY CENTURY, THE ORBITS OF APOKOLIPS AND NEW GENESIS BRING THE PLANETS CLOSER TOGETHER.
EARTHQUAKES RAVAGE BOTH WORLDS.
AND AS THE GRAVITATIONAL FORCES THREATENED TO TEAR THEM BOTH APART, APOKOLIPS AND NEW GENESIS USED TO GO TO WAR.
IF THEY CONTINUED DOWN THIS PATH, THEY COULD HAVE TAKEN APART ALL I OBSERVE.
SO IN THE WAKE OF WHAT WAS THE GREATEST OF THESE BATTLES, I INTERVENED.
I DID WHAT NO ONE DARED.
I FIRST ORDERED THE MOBIUS CHAIR TO BRING ME TO APOKOLIPS.
AND I SPOKE TO ITS RULER... DARKSEID.
I'M HERE TO MAKE A PACT. THIS CAN STOP.
IT WILL NEVER STOP UNTIL I CONTROL EVERYONE.
INCLUDING YOU, OBSERVER.
AND WHAT IF THERE'S NOTHING LEFT TO CONTROL? WHAT OF YOUR DESIRES THEN?
DARKSEID, MY IDEA IS SIMPLE IN PREMISE, IF NOT EMOTION. YOU AND THE RULER OF NEW GENESIS, HIGHFATHER, WILL EACH CHOOSE A SON.
AND ON NEUTRAL TERRITORY, YOU WILL EXCHANGE THOSE SONS.
I HAVE MANY SONS, METRON.
AND EVEN IF ONE WERE TO INHABIT NEW GENESIS, IT WOULD NOT CEASE ME FROM WAGING WAR AGAINST THEM.
PERHAPS NOT, BUT IT WOULD CEASE HIGHFATHER FROM WAGING WAR AGAINST YOU.
HE TURNED AND FINALLY LOOKED AT ME. HIS EYES SMOLDERING LIKE THE PITS ON APOKOLIPS.
I CANNOT BE SURE IF WHAT I SAW WAS A SMILE OR HE SIMPLY EXHALED A BREATH.
BUT DARKSEID AGREED.

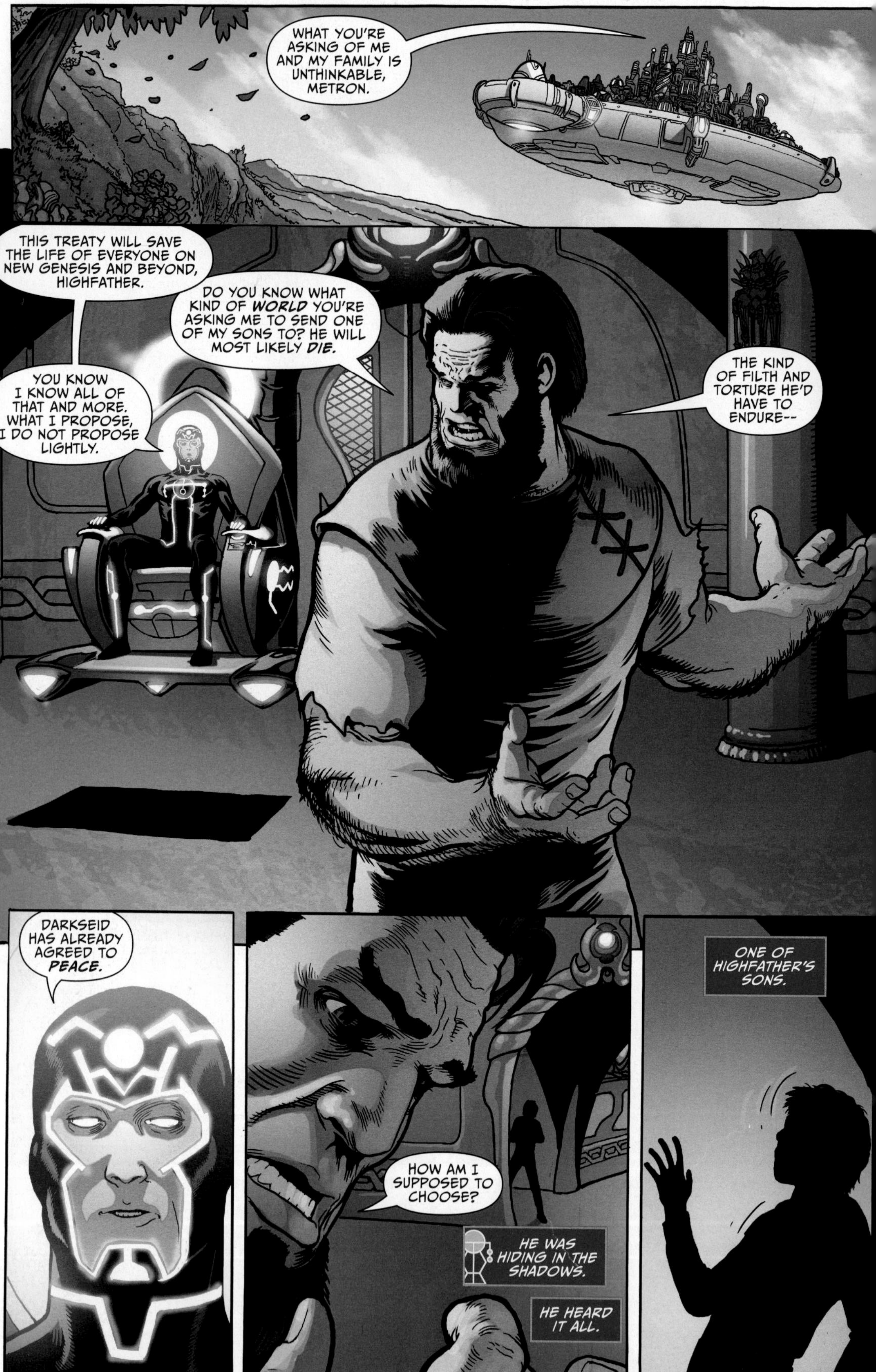
WHAT YOU'RE ASKING OF ME AND MY FAMILY IS UNTHINKABLE, METRON.
THIS TREATY WILL SAVE THE LIFE OF EVERYONE ON NEW GENESIS AND BEYOND, HIGHFATHER.
YOU KNOW I KNOW ALL OF THAT AND MORE. WHAT I PROPOSE, I DO NOT PROPOSE LIGHTLY.
DO YOU KNOW WHAT KIND OF WORLD YOU'RE ASKING ME TO SEND ONE OF MY SONS TO? HE WILL MOST LIKELY DIE.
THE KIND OF FILTH AND TORTURE HE'D HAVE TO ENDURE--
DARKSEID HAS ALREADY AGREED TO PEACE.
HOW AM I SUPPOSED TO CHOOSE?
HE WAS HIDING IN THE SHADOWS.
HE HEARD IT ALL.
ONE OF HIGHFATHER'S SONS.

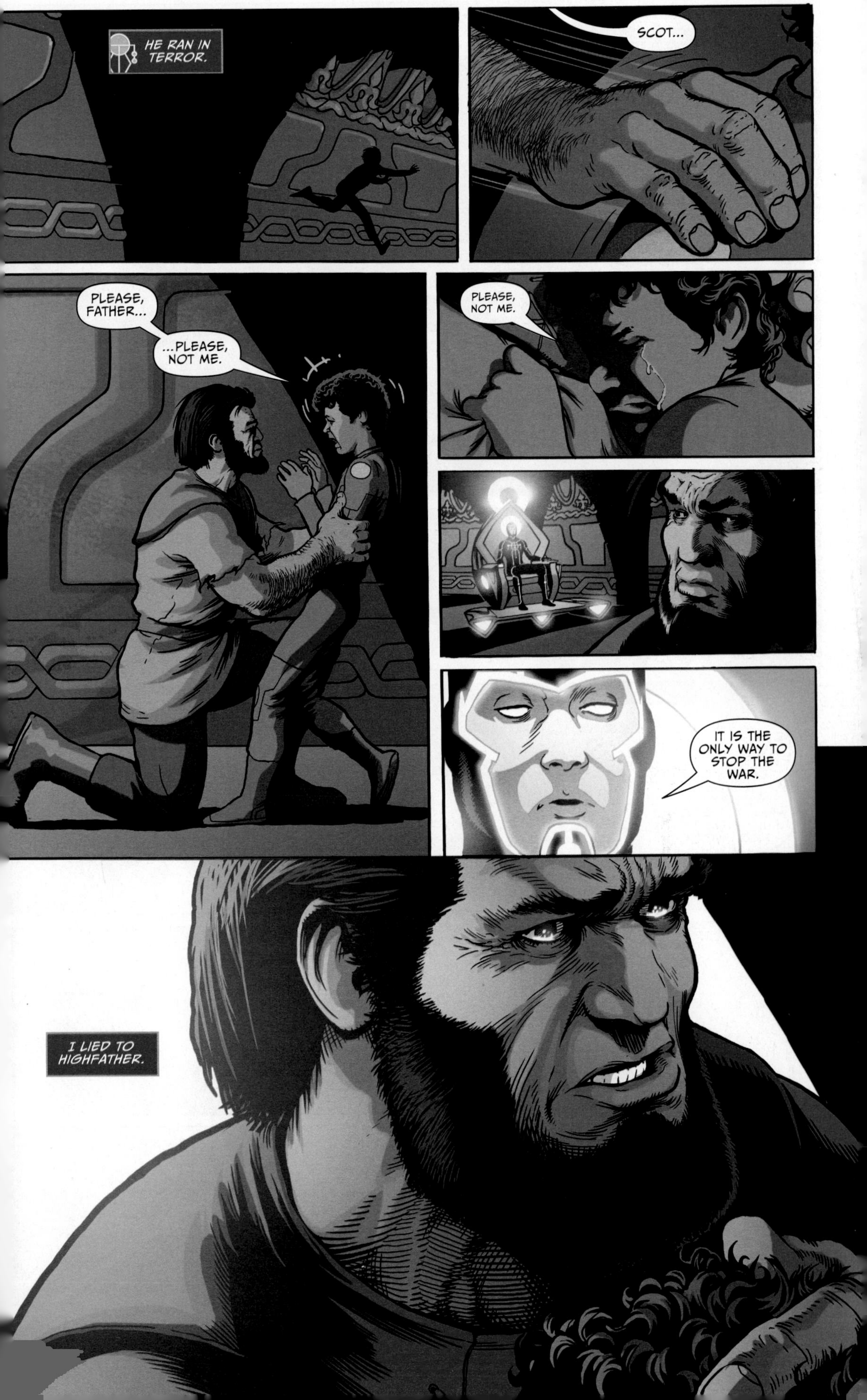
HE RAN IN TERROR.
SCOT...
PLEASE, FATHER...
...PLEASE, NOT ME.
PLEASE, NOT ME.
IT IS THE ONLY WAY TO STOP THE WAR.
I LIED TO HIGHFATHER.

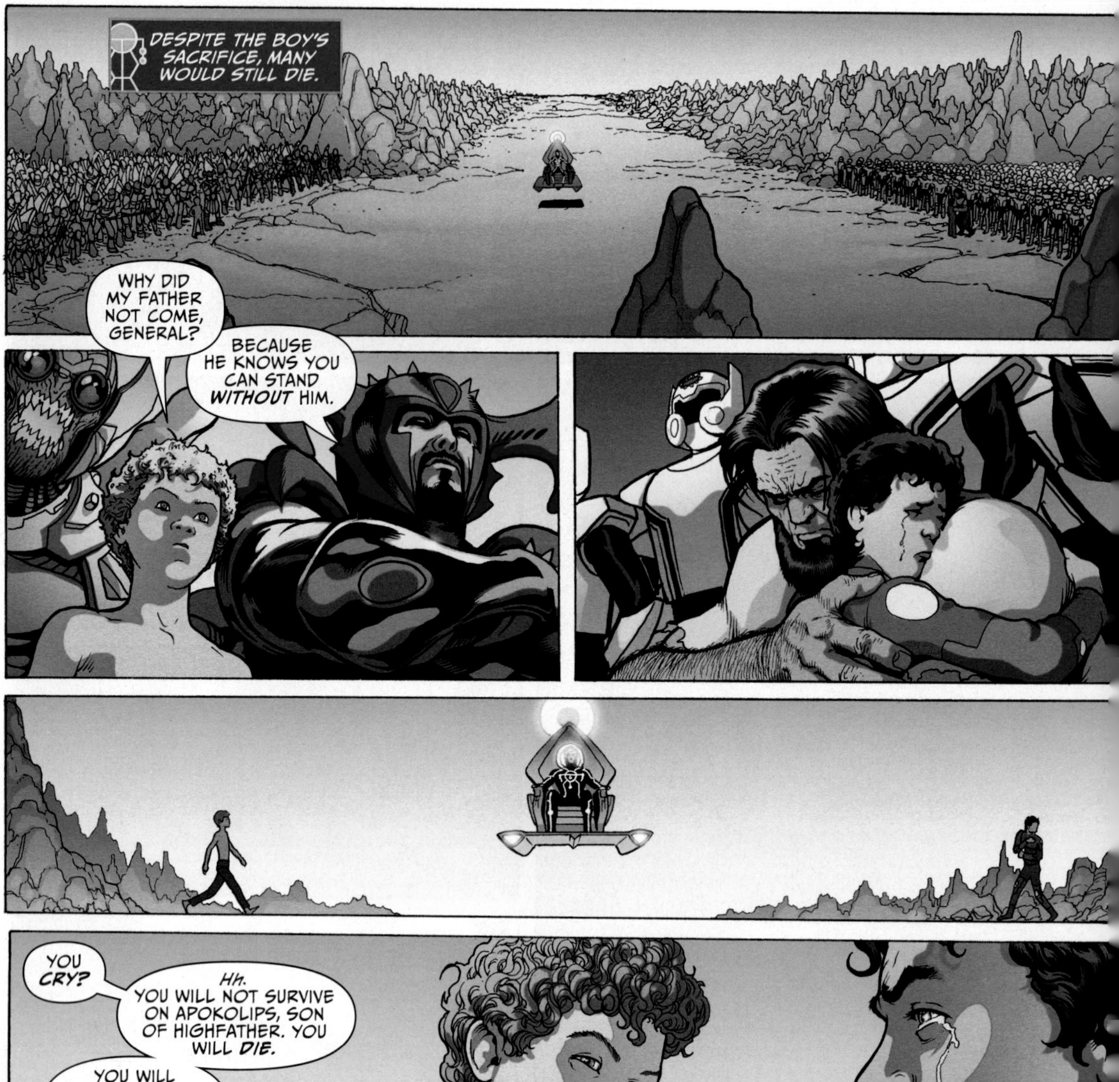
DESPITE THE BOY'S SACRIFICE, MANY WOULD STILL DIE.
WHY DID MY FATHER NOT COME, GENERAL?
BECAUSE HE KNOWS YOU CAN STAND WITHOUT HIM.
YOU CRY?
Hh. YOU WILL NOT SURVIVE ON APOKOLIPS, SON OF HIGHFATHER. YOU WILL DIE.
YOU WILL DIE CRYING WHILE I DESTROY NEW GENESIS FROM WITHIN.
I AM ORION. I AM THE SON OF DARKSEID.
AND UNLIKE YOU, I WILL NOT BE BROKEN.
WHILE THE YOUNGEST SON OF DARKSEID WAS A SAVAGE BEAST TO BE TAMED...

...THE SON OF HIGHFATHER WAS THROWN INTO THE SLAVE CAMPS. HE SUFFERED GREATLY.

BUT EXISTENCE WOULD CARRY ON, AND I COULD CONTINUE TO OBSERVE THE KNOWN AND UNKNOWN UNIVERSES.

A PACT WAS MADE.

AND WHETHER SCOT WOULD SURVIVE WAS IRRELEVANT TO ME.

AS LONG AS THE WAR WAS AVERTED, I COULD CONTINUE.

THEN, YEARS LATER, IT HAPPENED FOR THE FIRST TIME.

I WAS UNPREPARED...

...TO SEE THE END.

THE MYSTERIOUS BEING OTHERS CALLED THE ANTI-MONITOR HAD RISEN.

FOR REASONS UNKNOWN TO THEM... HE HAD THE POWER TO CONSUME ENTIRE UNIVERSES.

AAAARGHHHH!!

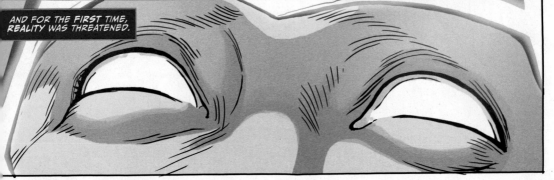

AND FOR THE FIRST TIME, REALITY WAS THREATENED.

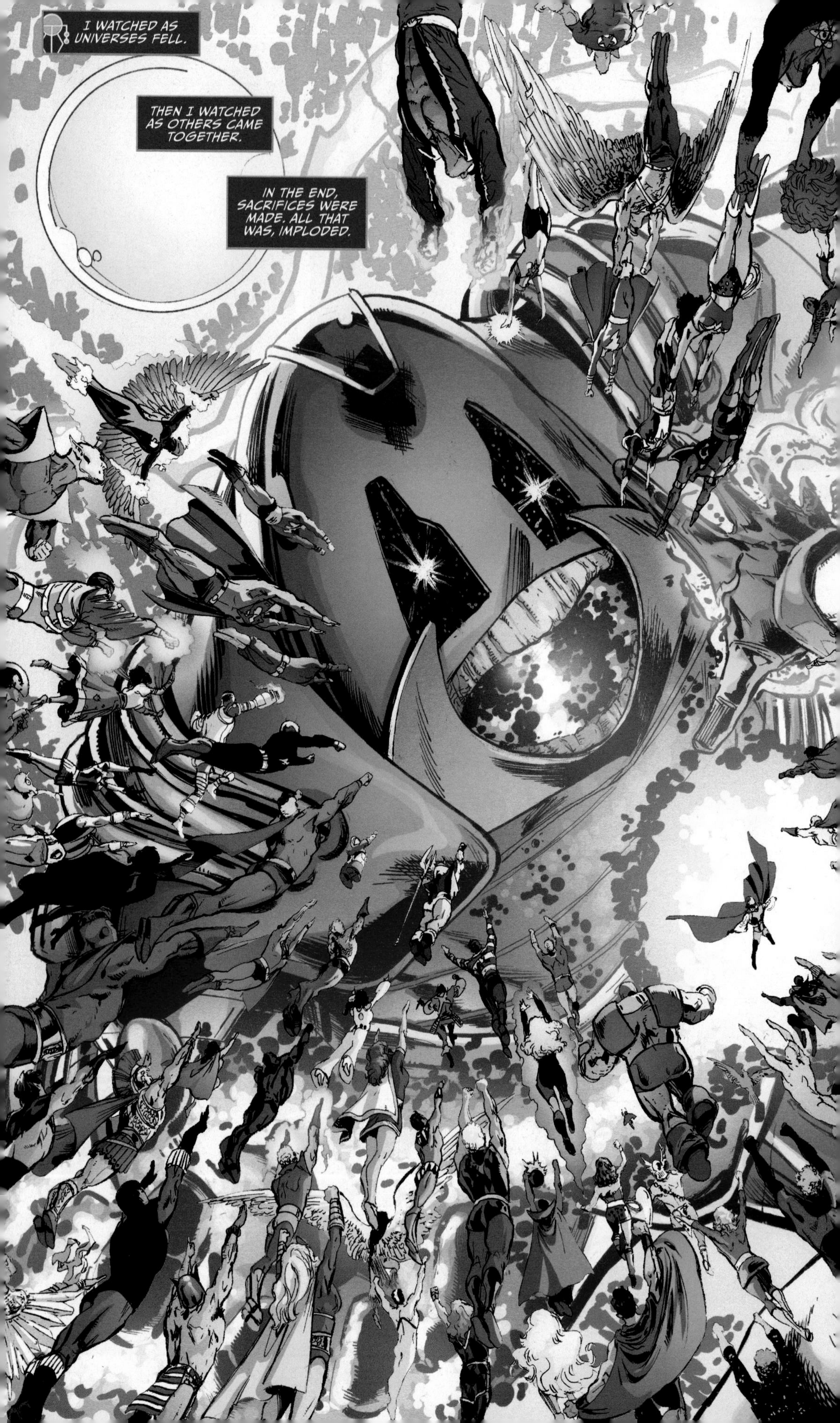
I WATCHED AS UNIVERSES FELL.
THEN I WATCHED AS OTHERS CAME TOGETHER.
IN THE END, SACRIFICES WERE MADE. ALL THAT WAS, IMPLODED.

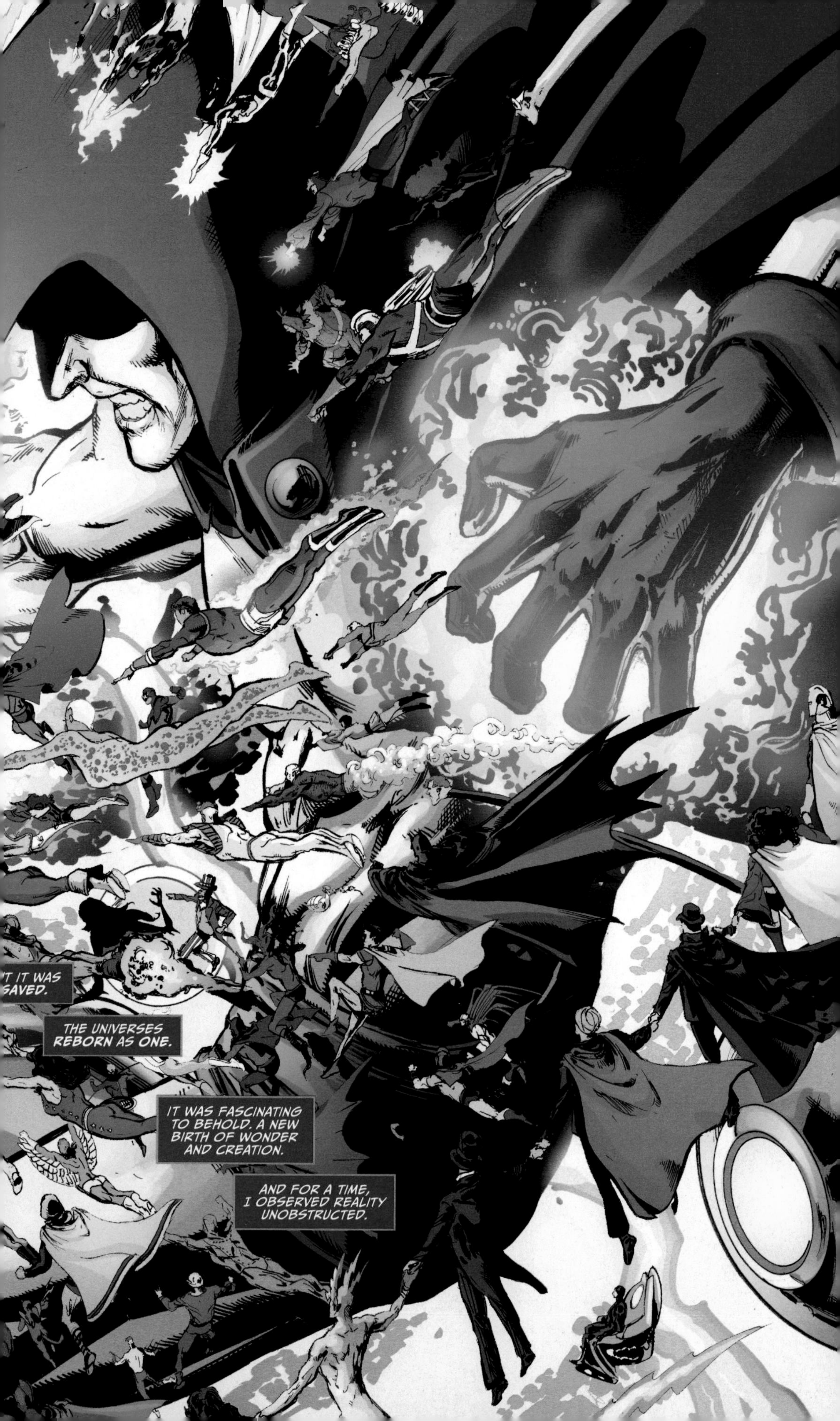

T IT WAS SAVED.
THE UNIVERSES REBORN AS ONE.
IT WAS FASCINATING TO BEHOLD. A NEW BIRTH OF WONDER AND CREATION.
AND FOR A TIME, I OBSERVED REALITY UNOBSTRUCTED.

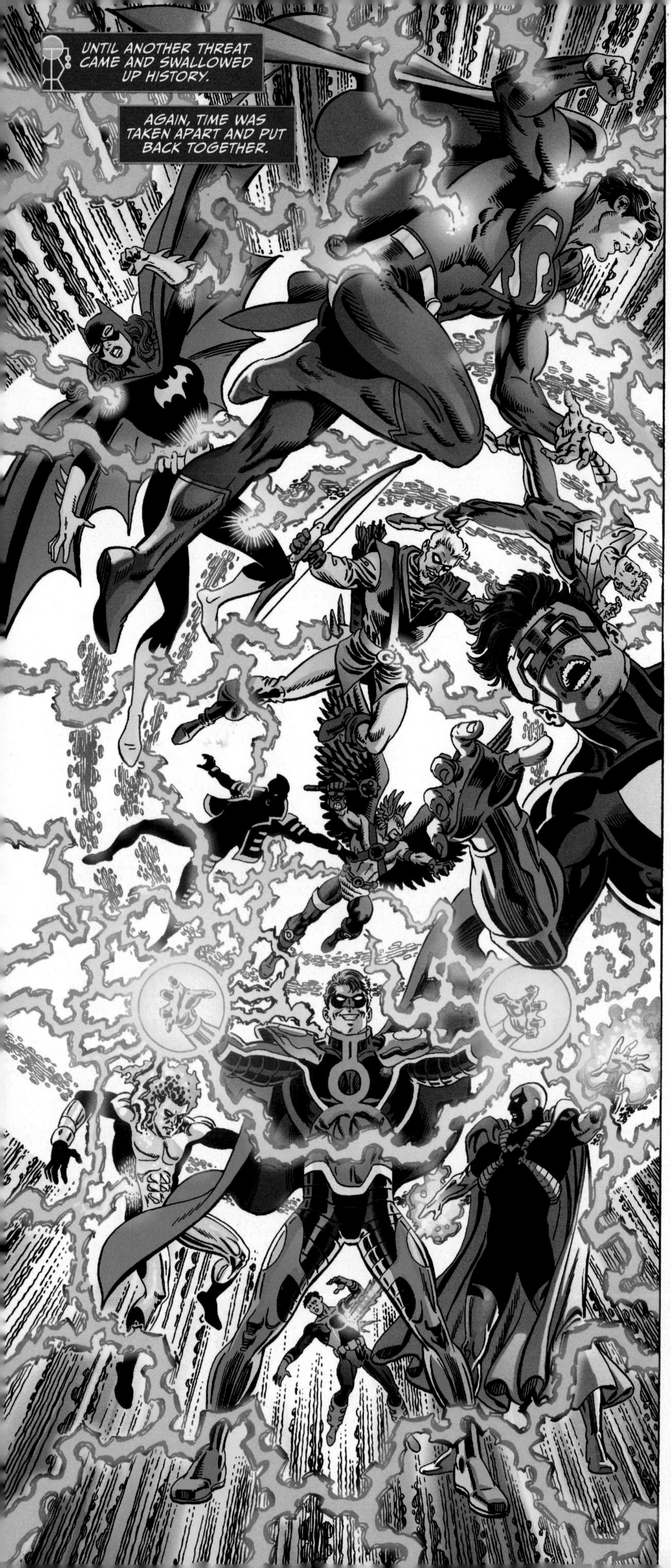
UNTIL ANOTHER THREAT CAME AND SWALLOWED UP HISTORY.
AGAIN, TIME WAS TAKEN APART AND PUT BACK TOGETHER.
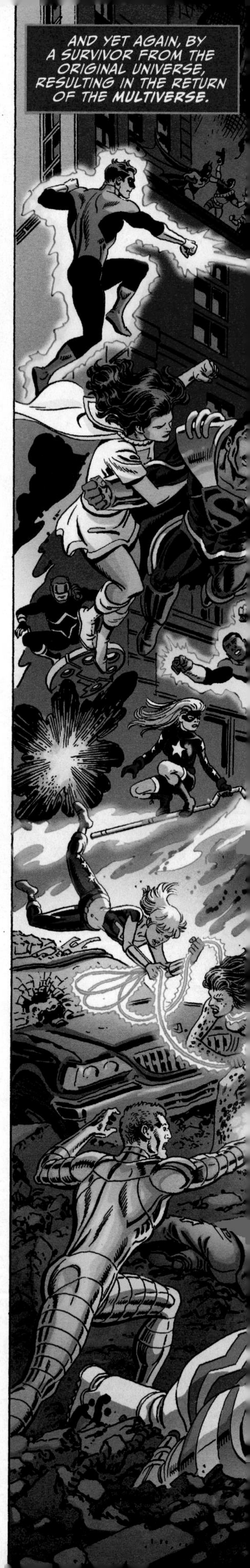
AND YET AGAIN, BY A SURVIVOR FROM THE ORIGINAL UNIVERSE, RESULTING IN THE RETURN OF THE MULTIVERSE.

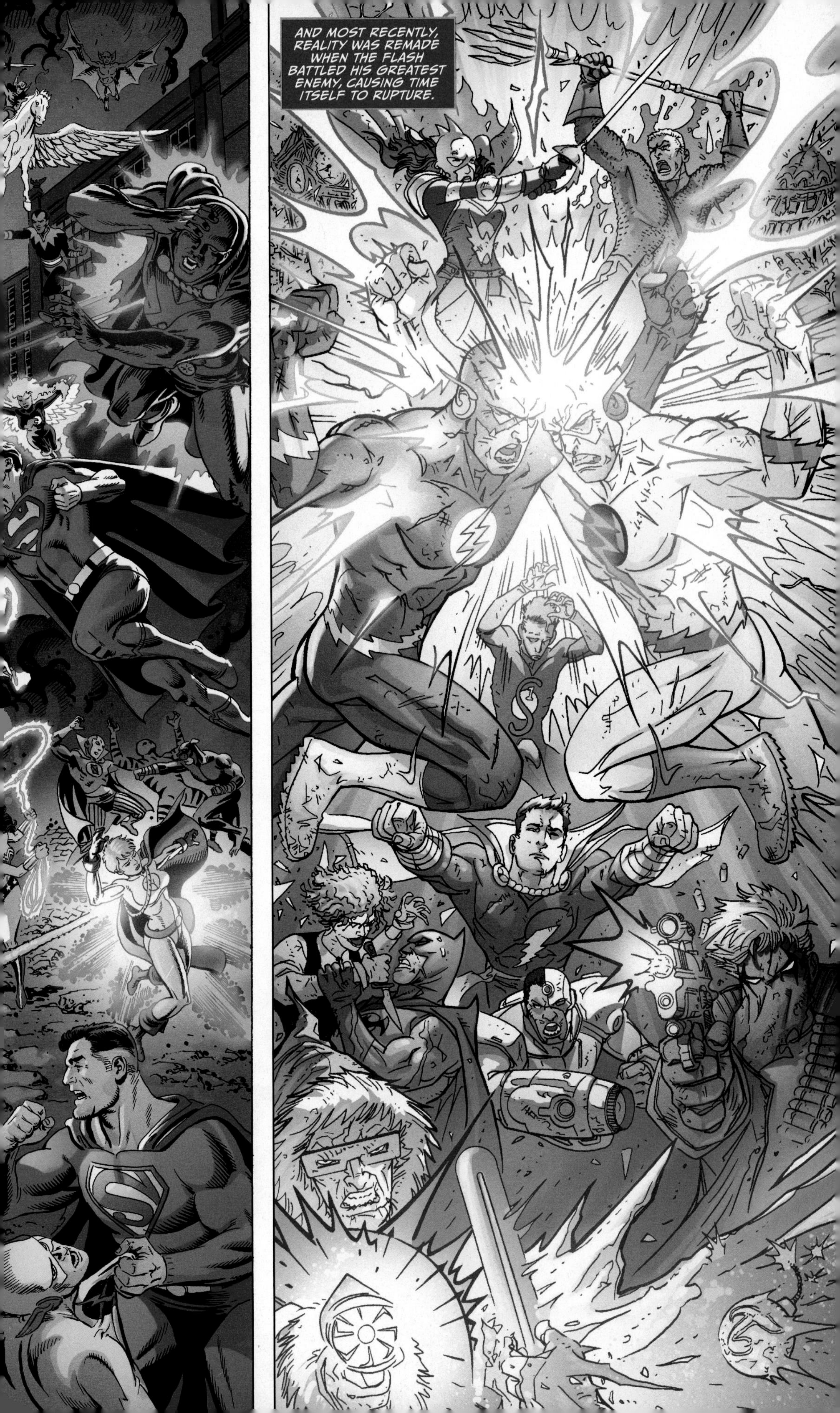
AND MOST RECENTLY, REALITY WAS REMADE WHEN THE FLASH BATTLED HIS GREATEST ENEMY, CAUSING TIME ITSELF TO RUPTURE.

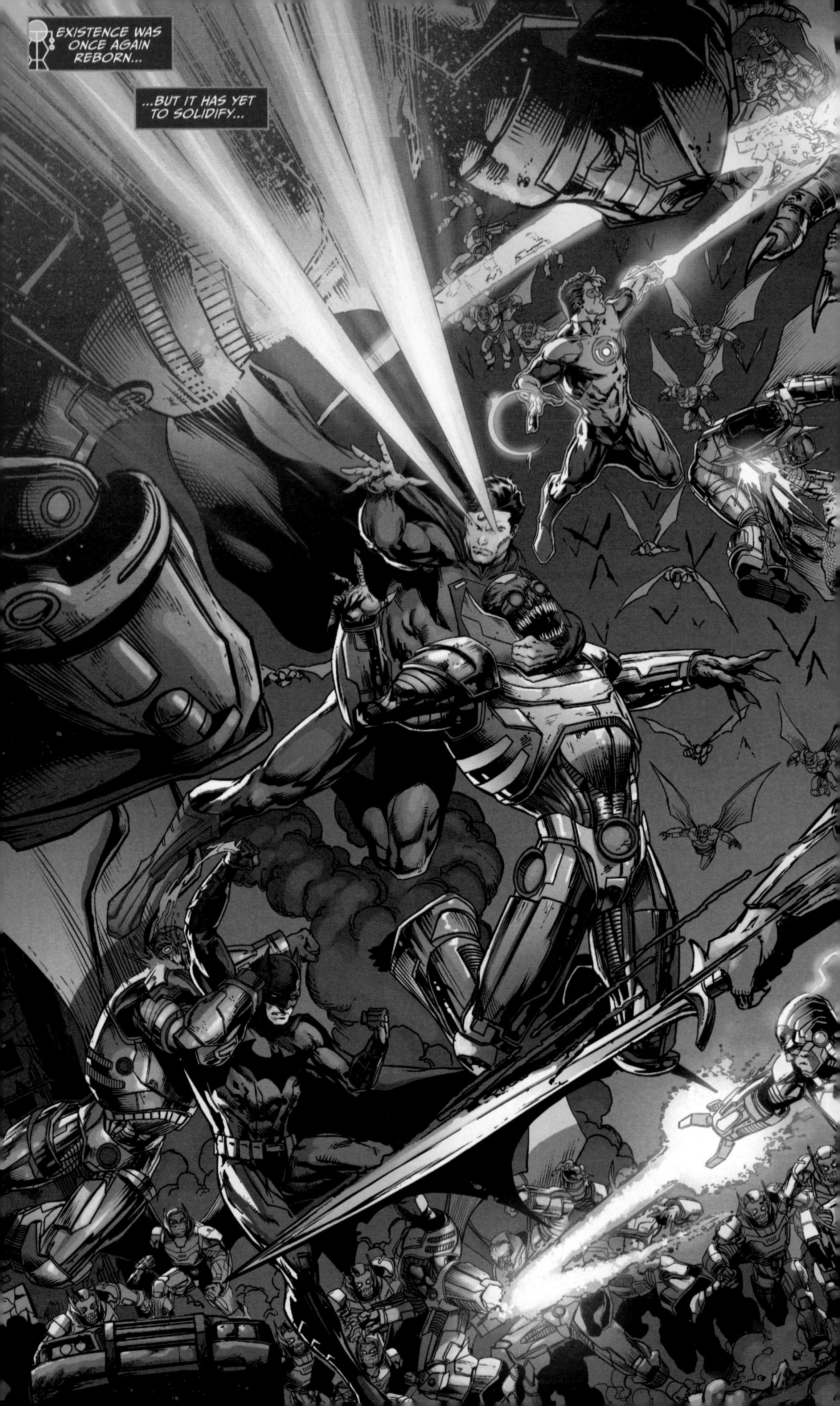
EXISTENCE WAS ONCE AGAIN REBORN...
...BUT IT HAS YET TO SOLIDIFY...

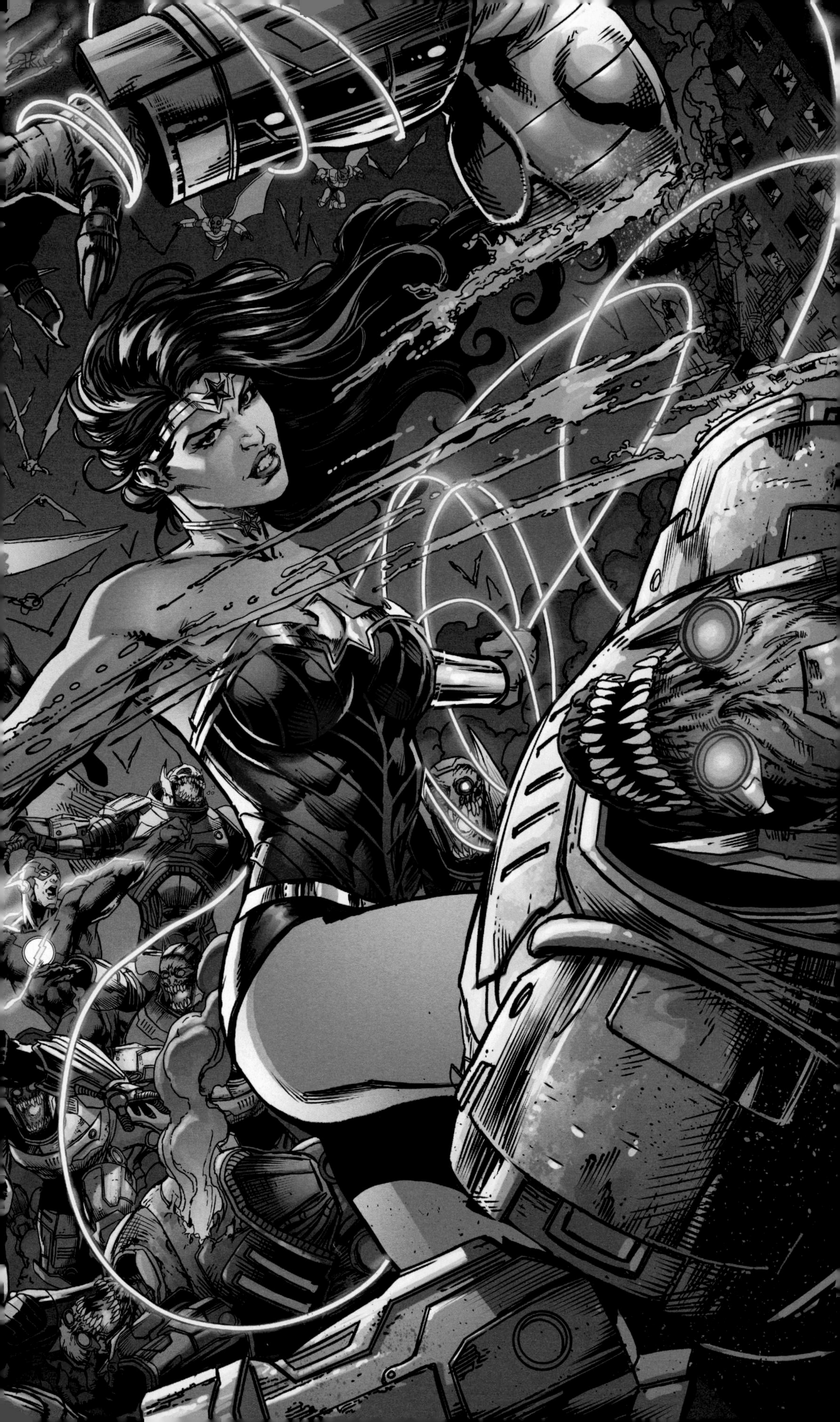

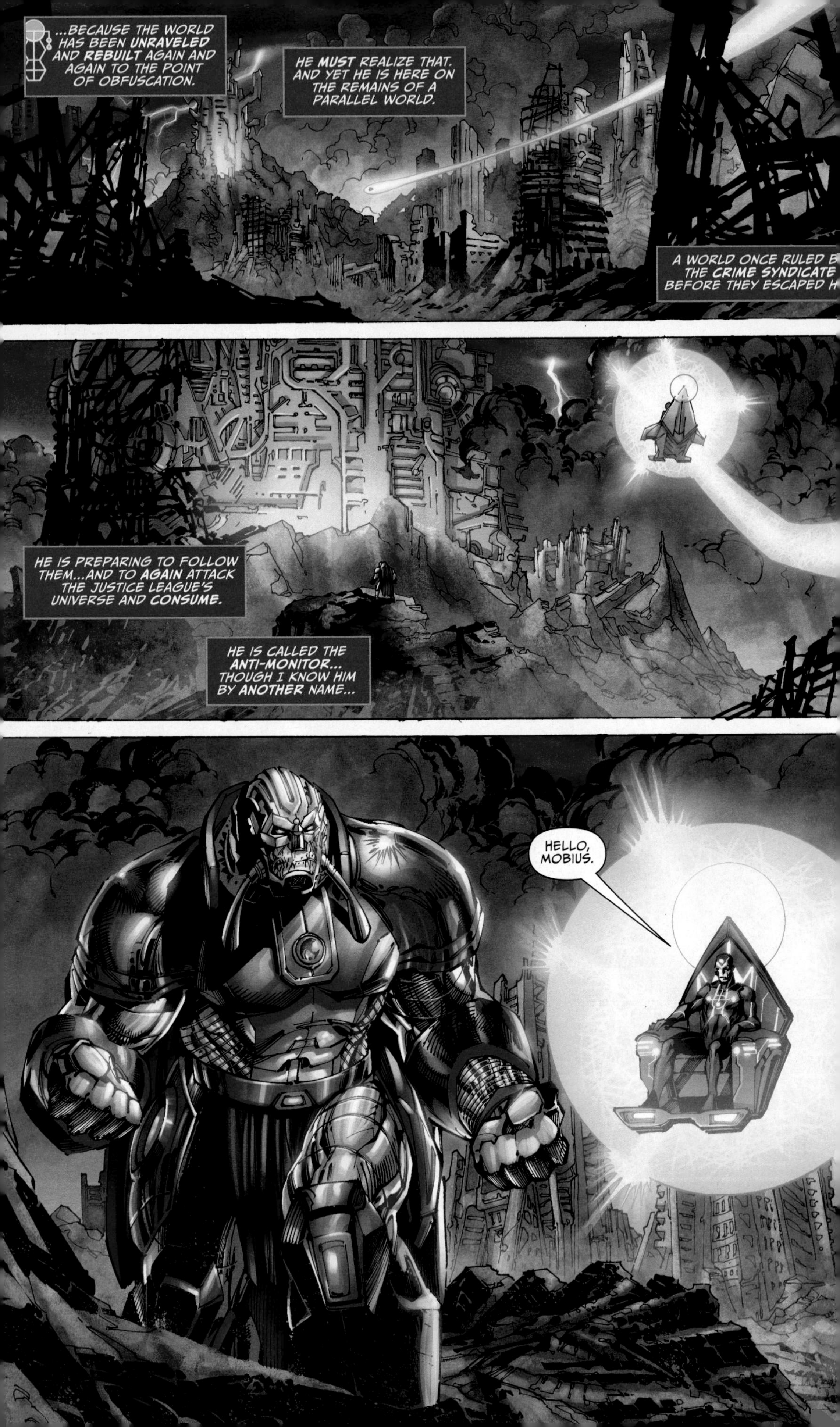
...BECAUSE THE WORLD HAS BEEN UNRAVELED AND REBUILT AGAIN AND AGAIN TO THE POINT OF OBFUSCATION.
HE MUST REALIZE THAT. AND YET HE IS HERE ON THE REMAINS OF A PARALLEL WORLD.
A WORLD ONCE RULED B
THE CRIME SYNDICATE
BEFORE THEY ESCAPED H
HE IS PREPARING TO FOLLOW THEM...AND TO AGAIN ATTACK THE JUSTICE LEAGUE'S UNIVERSE AND CONSUME.
HE IS CALLED THE ANTI-MONITOR... THOUGH I KNOW HIM BY ANOTHER NAME...
HELLO, MOBIUS.

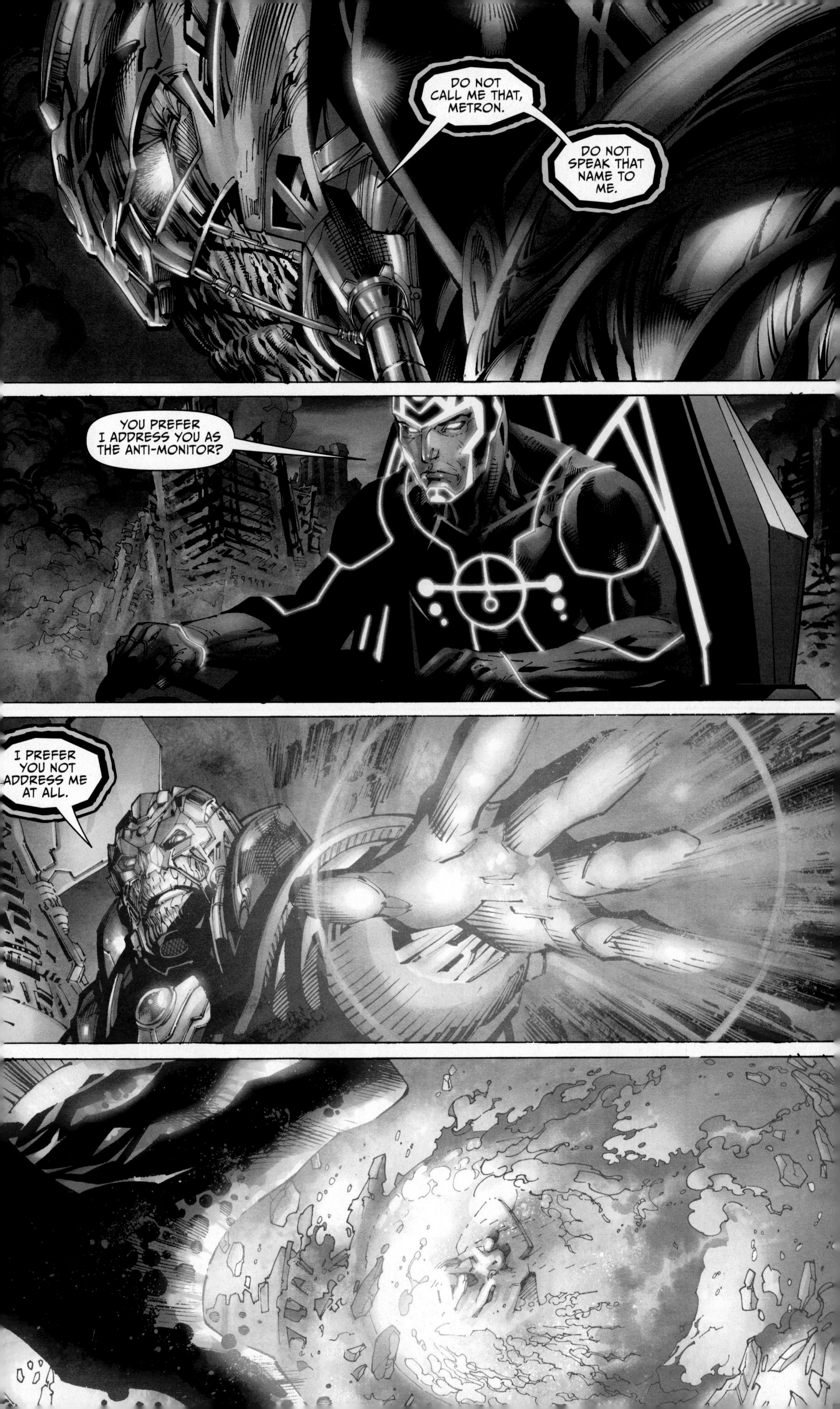
DO NOT CALL ME THAT, METRON.
DO NOT SPEAK THAT NAME TO ME.
YOU PREFER I ADDRESS YOU AS THE ANTI-MONITOR?
I PREFER YOU NOT ADDRESS ME AT ALL.

YOU KNOW AS LONG AS I SIT ON THIS CHAIR, YOUR ANTI-MATTER CANNOT AFFECT ME.

I SAT ON THAT CHAIR LONG BEFORE YOU.

I KNOW.

THEN WHY DO YOU TRY TO DESTROY IT EVERY TIME WE CONVERSE?

BECAUSE THAT IS WHAT I DO, METRON.

YOUR PENANCE?

MY CURSE. MY DESTINY. MY REASON. IT NO LONGER MATTERS. AS YOU ARE NOW *THE WITNESS*, I AM *THE DESTROYER*. IS THAT NOT WHAT YOU CLAIMED WHEN YOU TOOK THAT CHAIR?

YES, YOU DESTROY UNIVERSES. UNIVERSES THAT ARE THEN REBORN. YOU HAVE DONE THIS COUNTLESS TIMES, MOBIUS.

AND YOU PLAN TO AGAIN, DON'T YOU?

I'M HERE TO CONVINCE YOU OTHERWISE.

REALITY CAN SURVIVE AND *CRISIS*

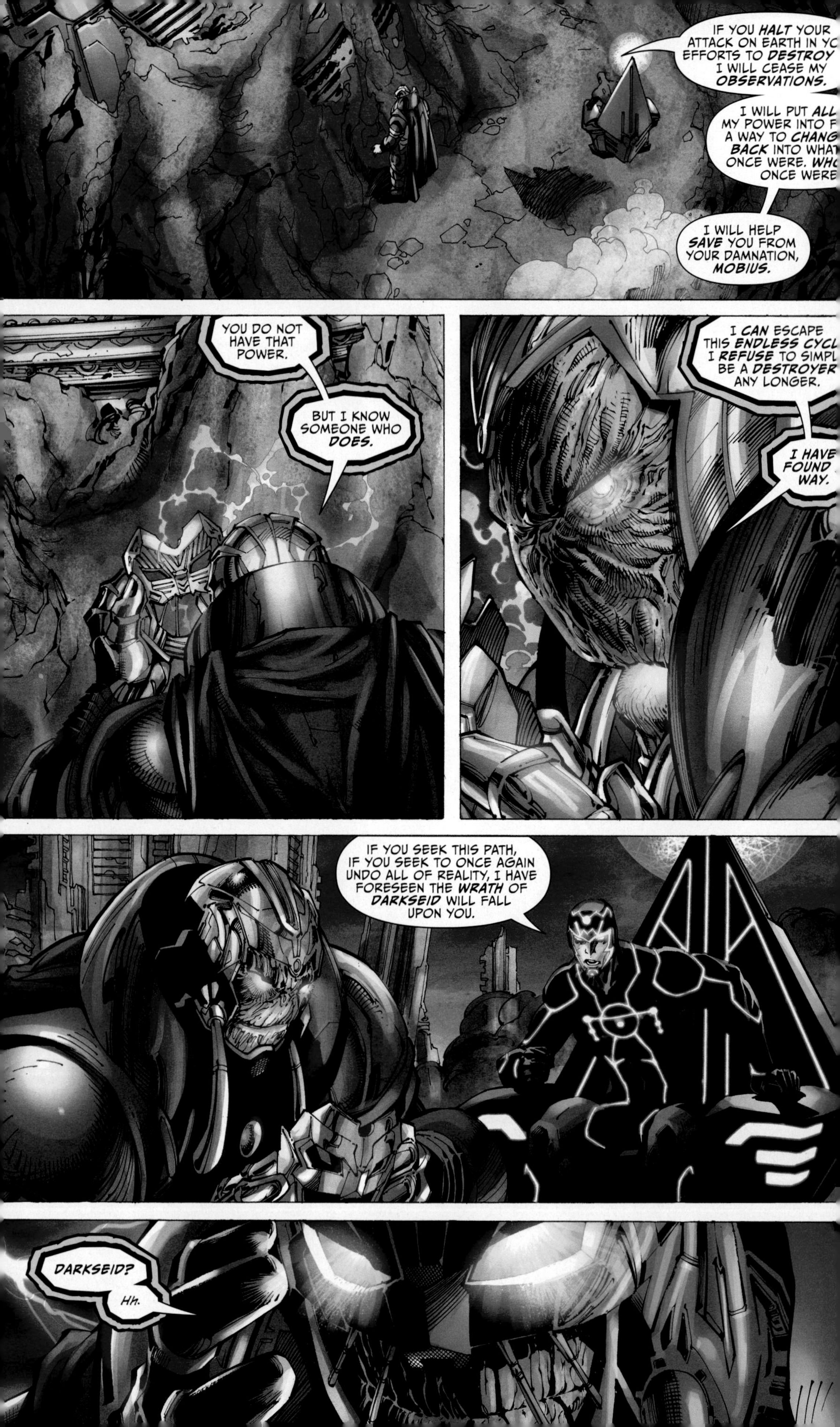
IF YOU **HALT** YOUR ATTACK ON EARTH IN YO EFFORTS TO **DESTROY** I WILL CEASE MY **OBSERVATIONS.**
I WILL PUT **ALL** MY POWER INTO F A WAY TO **CHANG** **BACK** INTO WHAT ONCE WERE. **WHO** ONCE WERE
I WILL HELP **SAVE** YOU FROM YOUR DAMNATION, **MOBIUS.**
YOU DO NOT HAVE THAT POWER.
BUT I KNOW SOMEONE WHO **DOES.**
I **CAN** ESCAPE THIS **ENDLESS CYCL** I **REFUSE** TO SIMPL BE A **DESTROYER** ANY LONGER.
I HAVE FOUND *WAY.*
IF YOU SEEK THIS PATH, IF YOU SEEK TO ONCE AGAIN UNDO ALL OF REALITY, I HAVE FORESEEN THE **WRATH** OF **DARKSEID** WILL FALL UPON YOU.
DARKSEID?
Hh.

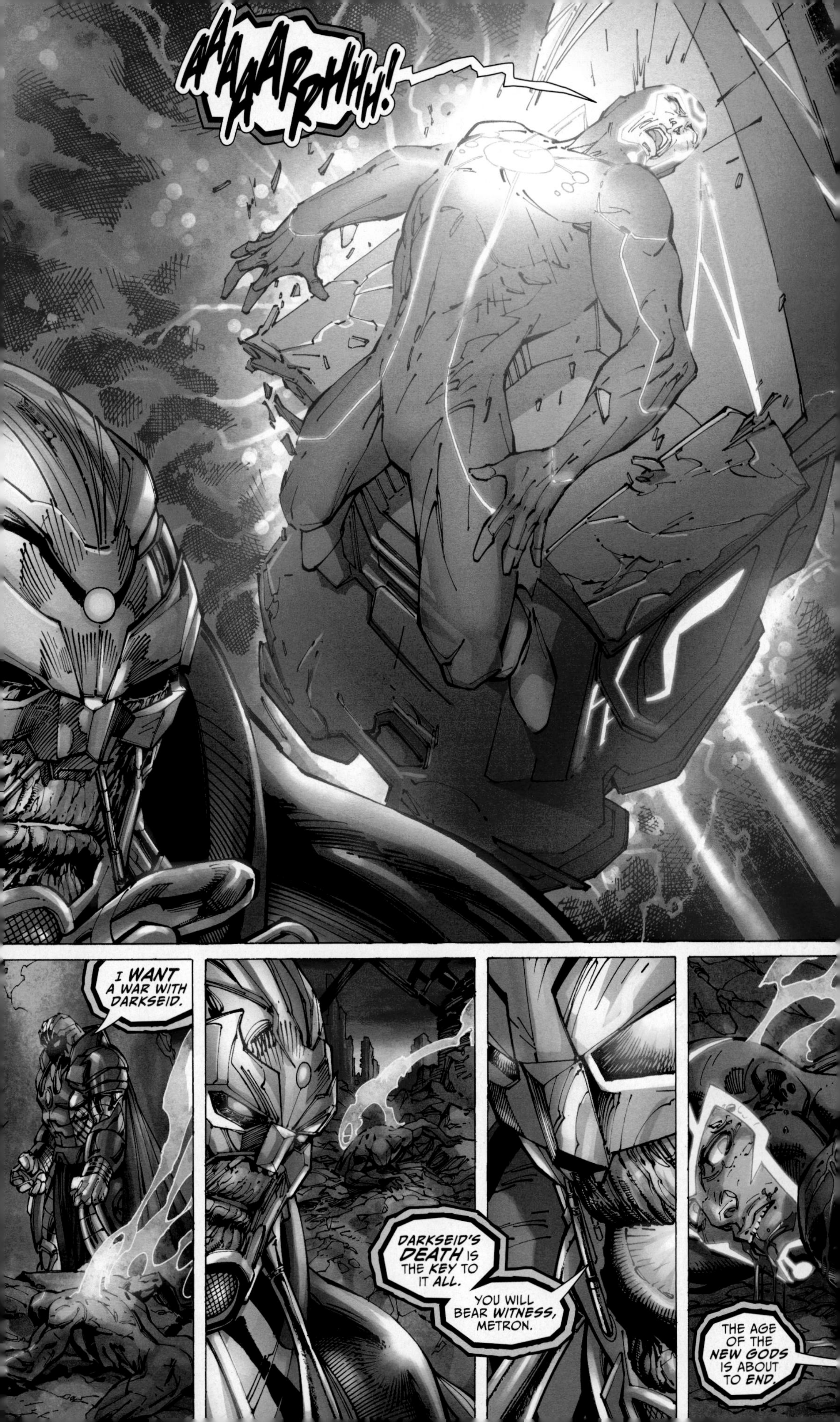
AAAAARRHHH!
I WANT A WAR WITH DARKSEID.
DARKSEID'S DEATH IS THE KEY TO IT ALL.
YOU WILL BEAR WITNESS, METRON.
THE AGE OF THE NEW GODS IS ABOUT TO END.

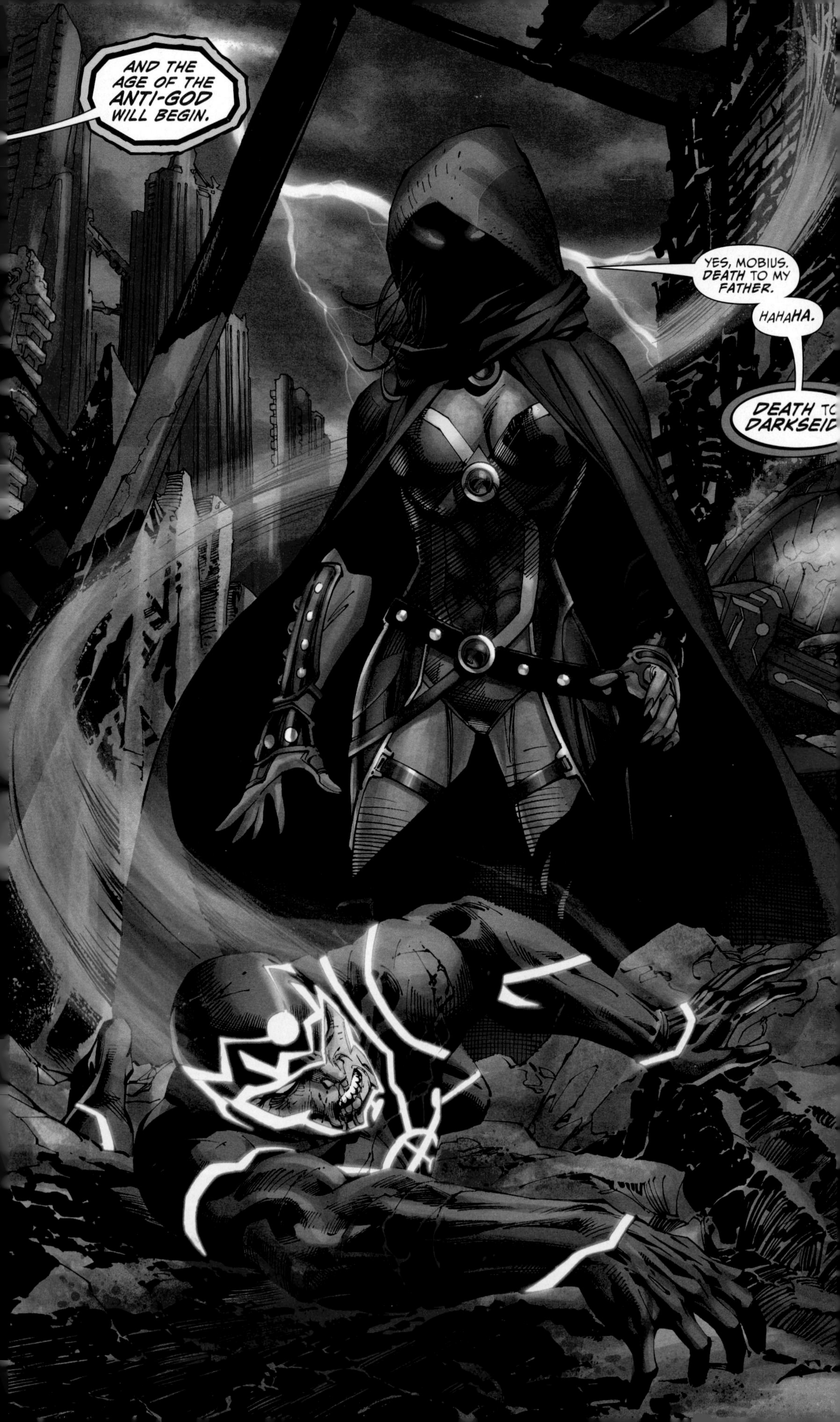
AND THE AGE OF THE ANTI-GOD WILL BEGIN.
YES, MOBIUS. DEATH TO MY FATHER.
HAHAHA.
DEATH TO DARKSEID

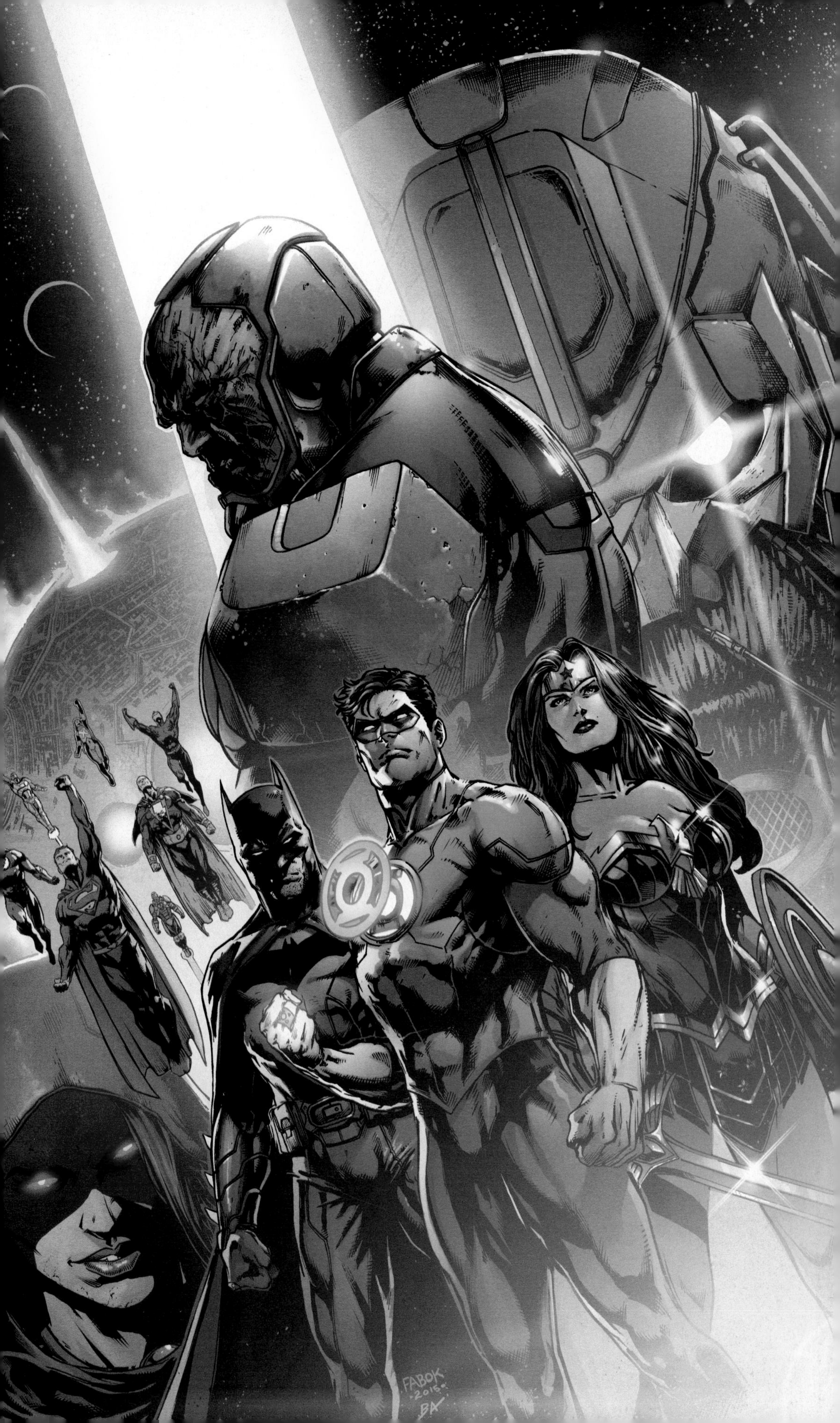
FABOK
2015
BA

DARKSEID WAR CHAPTER ONE: GOD VS. MAN

GEOFF JOHNS writer JASON FABOK artist BRAD ANDERSON colorist ROB LEIGH letterer cover by JASON FABOK and BRAD ANDERSON

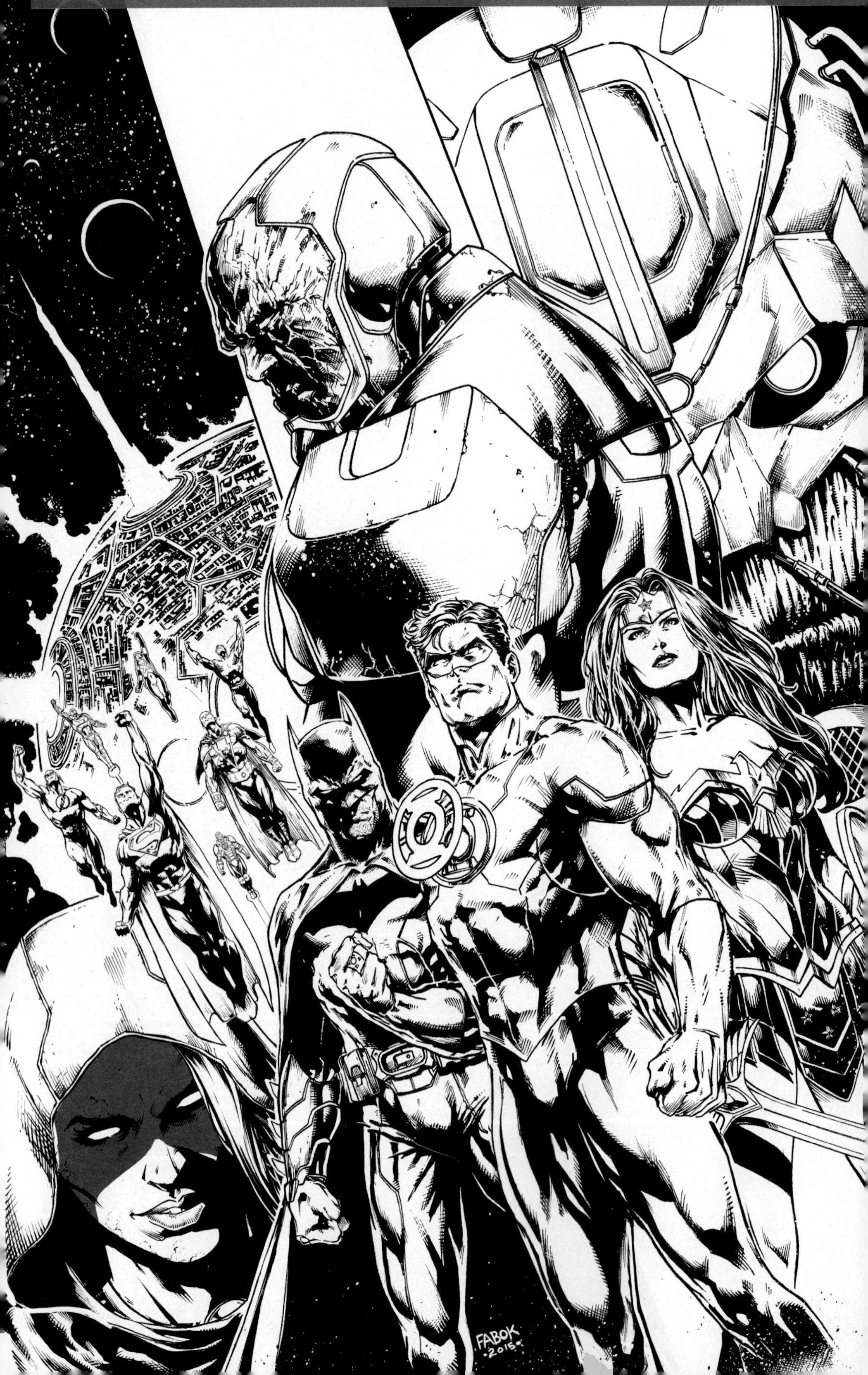
FABOK
2015

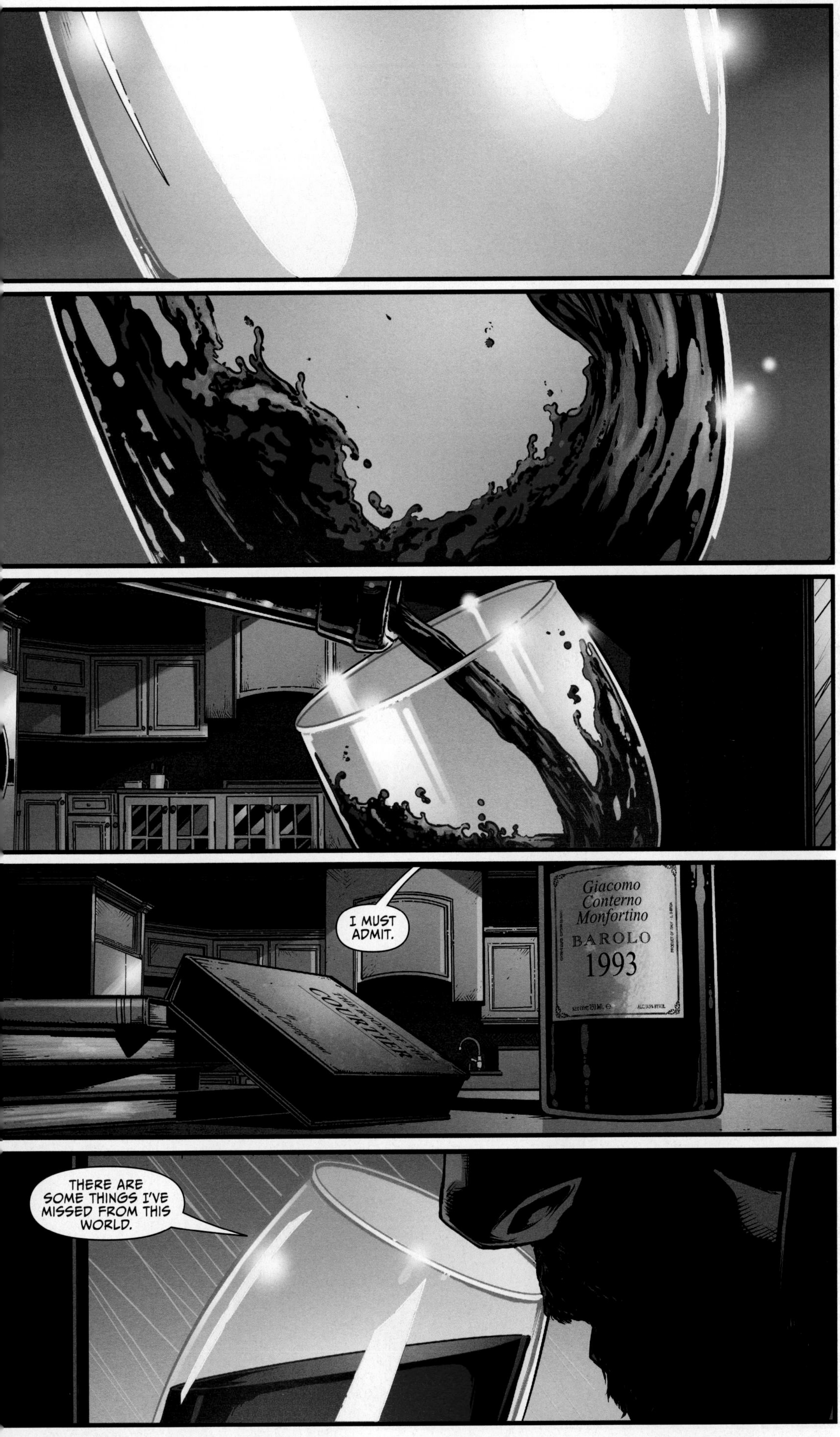
THE BOOK OF THE COURTIER
I MUST ADMIT.
Giacomo Conterno Monfortino
BAROLO
1993
THERE ARE SOME THINGS I'VE MISSED FROM THIS WORLD.

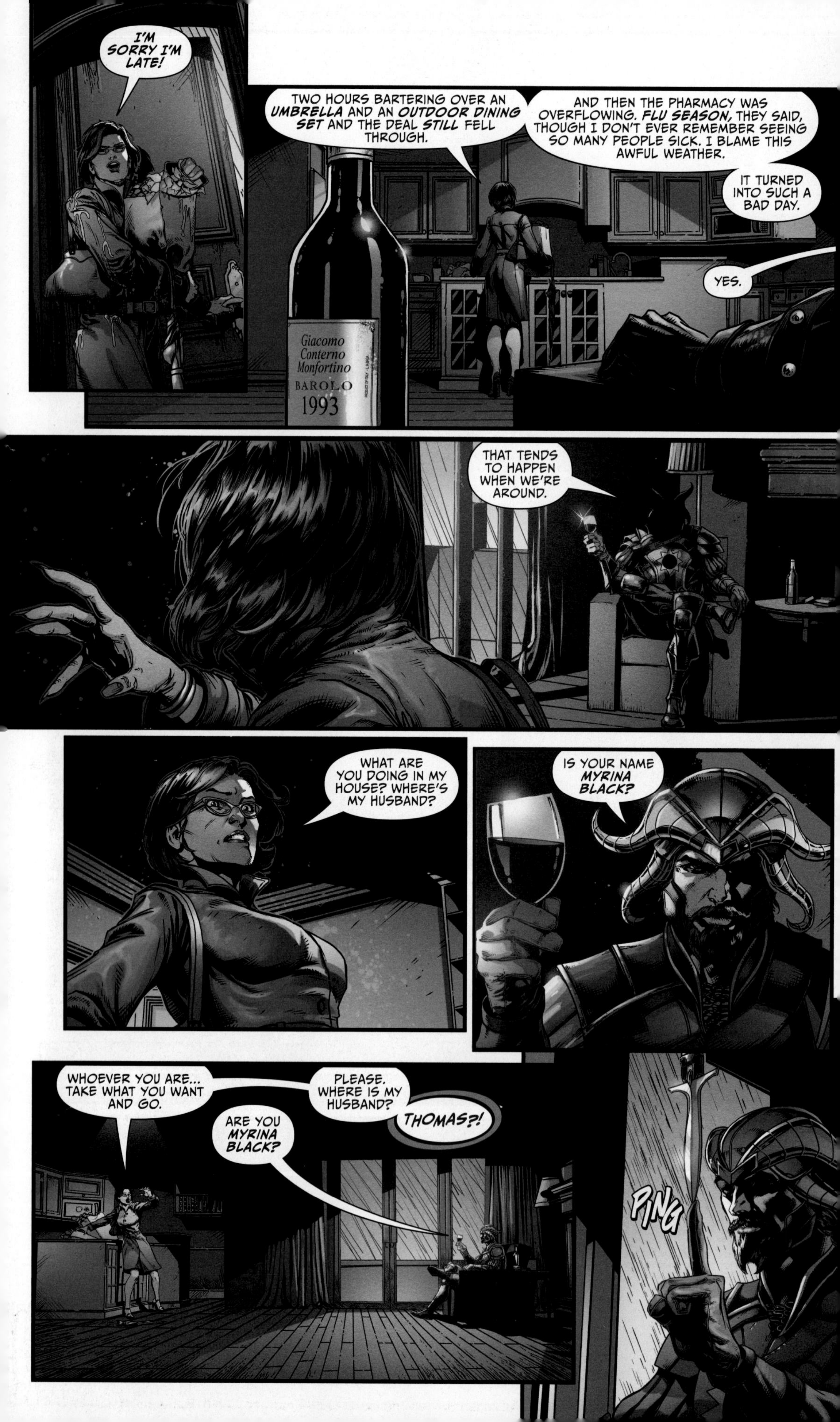
I'M SORRY I'M LATE!
TWO HOURS BARTERING OVER AN UMBRELLA AND AN OUTDOOR DINING SET AND THE DEAL STILL FELL THROUGH.
AND THEN THE PHARMACY WAS OVERFLOWING. FLU SEASON, THEY SAID, THOUGH I DON'T EVER REMEMBER SEEING SO MANY PEOPLE SICK. I BLAME THIS AWFUL WEATHER.
IT TURNED INTO SUCH A BAD DAY.
YES.
Giacomo Conterno Monfortino BAROLO 1993
THAT TENDS TO HAPPEN WHEN WE'RE AROUND.
WHAT ARE YOU DOING IN MY HOUSE? WHERE'S MY HUSBAND?
IS YOUR NAME MYRINA BLACK?
WHOEVER YOU ARE... TAKE WHAT YOU WANT AND GO.
PLEASE. WHERE IS MY HUSBAND?
THOMAS?!
ARE YOU MYRINA BLACK?
PING

THOMAS--!

IT'S NOT HER, KANTO.

SHE'S NOT THE ONE.

TRUTHFULLY, I KNEW THAT THE MOMENT SHE WALKED IN. *BUT* WE HAVE TO BE SURE, DON'T WE?

WOULD YOU *LIKE* A GLASS?

EVEN IF WE HAD NO MISSION AT HAND, I WOULDN'T LOWER MYSELF TO CONSUMING ANYTHING FROM THIS *WRETCHED* WORLD.

YOU HAVEN'T SPENT AS MUCH TIME HERE AS I HAVE, LASHINA. THIS IS ONE OF THE MORE COMPLEX ELIXIRS YOU'LL FIND ON THIS WORLD OR ANY OTHER.

AS I SAID, THERE ARE SOME THINGS ON EARTH WORTH ENJOYING.

WHILE WE STILL CAN, ANYWAY.

COME, MOTHER BOX.

PING

TAKE US TO THE NEXT STOP, WON'T YOU?

YES, KANTO. *FOR DARKSEID.*

OF COURSE. FOR DARKSEID.

BOOOOOM

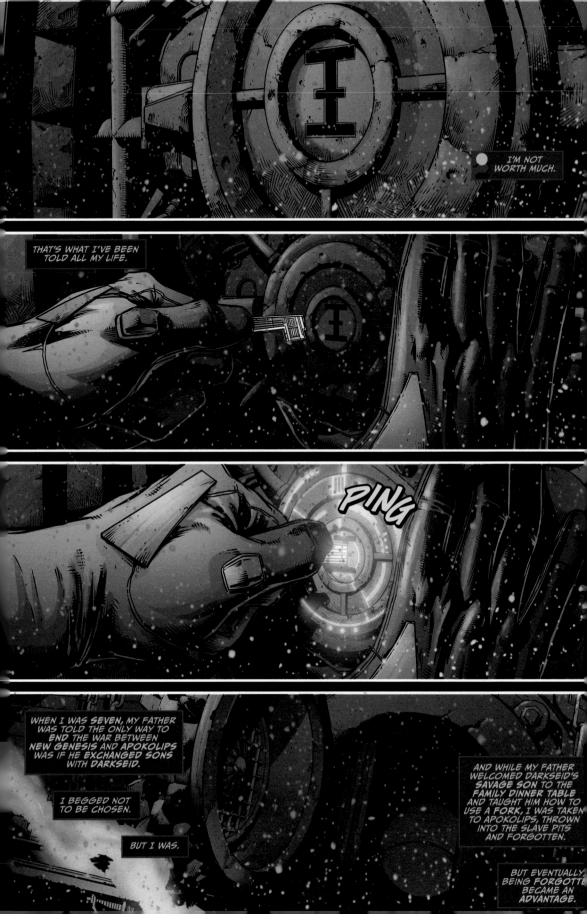

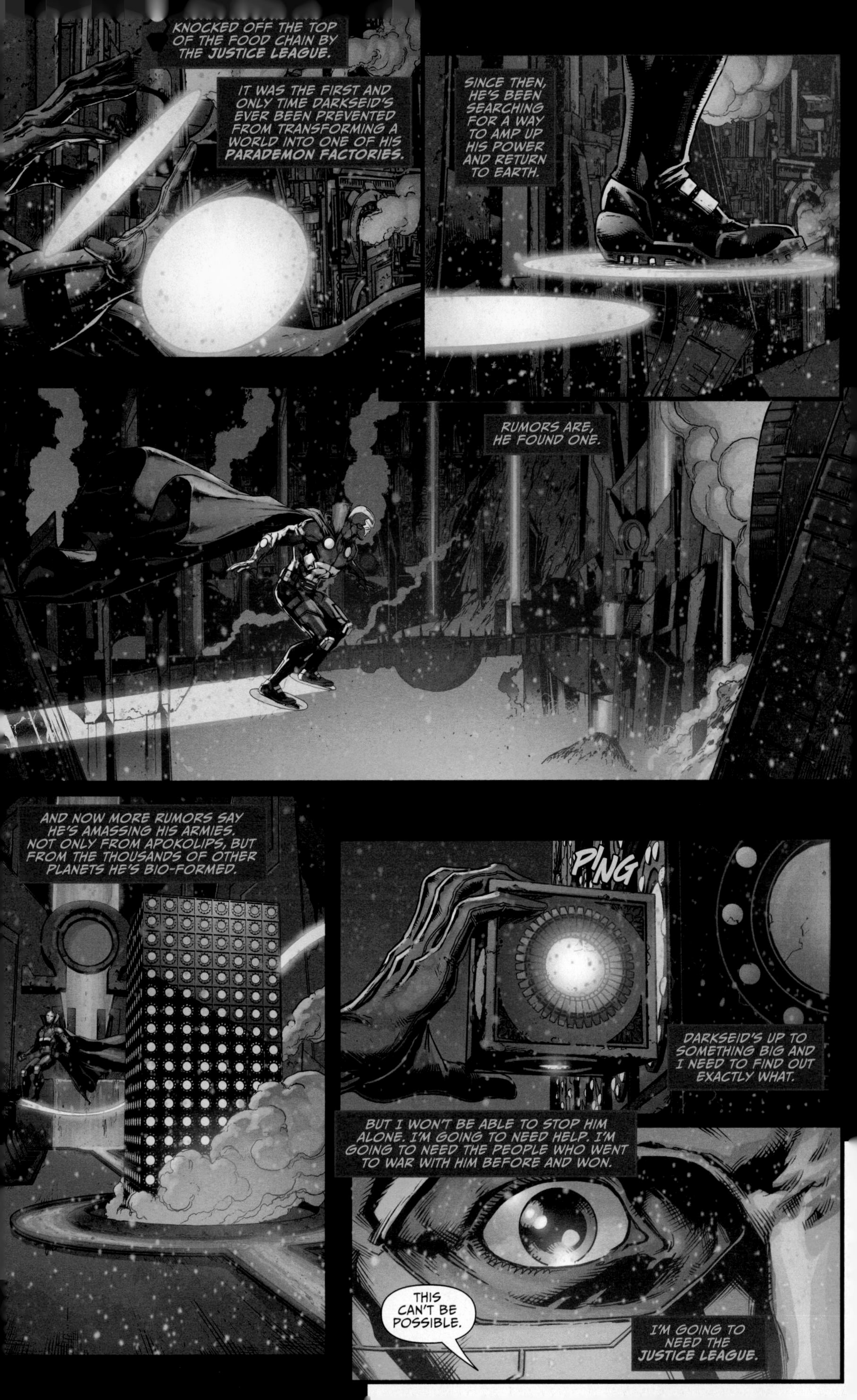
KNOCKED OFF THE TOP OF THE FOOD CHAIN BY THE JUSTICE LEAGUE.
IT WAS THE FIRST AND ONLY TIME DARKSEID'S EVER BEEN PREVENTED FROM TRANSFORMING A WORLD INTO ONE OF HIS PARADEMON FACTORIES.
SINCE THEN, HE'S BEEN SEARCHING FOR A WAY TO AMP UP HIS POWER AND RETURN TO EARTH.
RUMORS ARE, HE FOUND ONE.
AND NOW MORE RUMORS SAY HE'S AMASSING HIS ARMIES. NOT ONLY FROM APOKOLIPS, BUT FROM THE THOUSANDS OF OTHER PLANETS HE'S BIO-FORMED.
PING
DARKSEID'S UP TO SOMETHING BIG AND I NEED TO FIND OUT EXACTLY WHAT.
BUT I WON'T BE ABLE TO STOP HIM ALONE. I'M GOING TO NEED HELP. I'M GOING TO NEED THE PEOPLE WHO WENT TO WAR WITH HIM BEFORE AND WON.
THIS CAN'T BE POSSIBLE.
I'M GOING TO NEED THE JUSTICE LEAGUE.

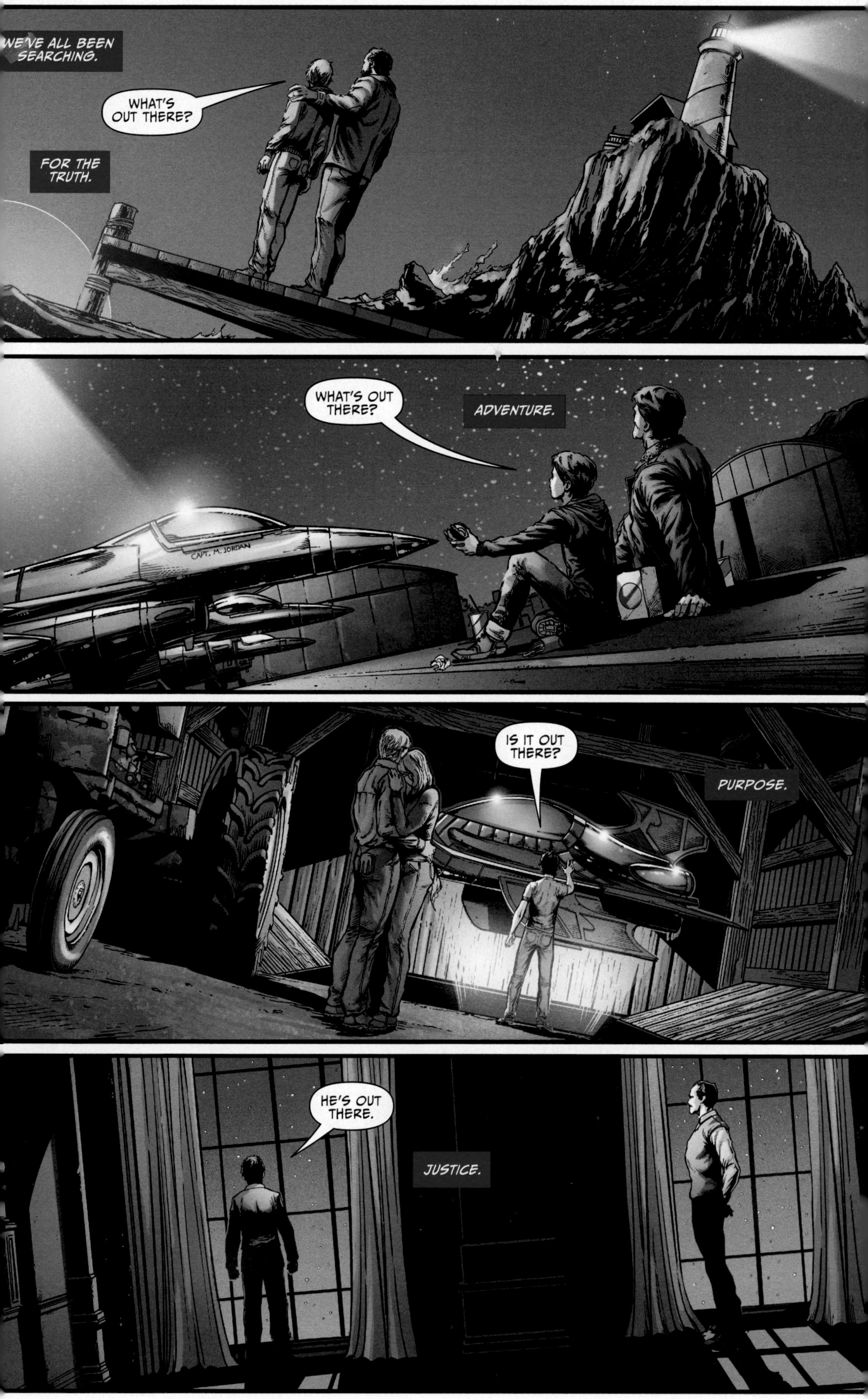
WE'VE ALL BEEN SEARCHING.
WHAT'S OUT THERE?
FOR THE TRUTH.
WHAT'S OUT THERE?
ADVENTURE.
CAPT. M. JORDAN
IS IT OUT THERE?
PURPOSE.
HE'S OUT THERE.
JUSTICE.

WE ALL WANT TO PROTECT THE WORLD WE SHARE. AND WE ALL WANT A PLACE IN IT. THAT'S WHY WE CAME TOGETHER.

NORMALLY, THE LEAGUE DOESN'T WORK CRIME SCENES, BUT THIS ONE'S DIFFERENT.

VICTOR'S BODY WAS REBUILT WITH UNKNOWN AND ALIEN TECHNOLOGY.

SOME OF IT FROM APOKOLIPS.

IF A BOOM TUBE OP ANYWHERE ON EART HE GETS A MIGRAIN

STEVE CLEARS THE AREA SO WE CAN GET TO WORK. HE'S TRIED TO LOOK OUT FOR ME SINCE THE DAY I LEFT THE ISLAND.

THANK YOU.

WHATEVER YOU NEED, DI. YOU KNOW THAT.

I STILL WONDER ABOUT US. THOUGH I'M NOT SURE HE DOES ANYMORE.

LOVE IS THE MOST POWERFUL FORCE IN THE WORLD. BUT IT CAN BE HARD. OR AT LEAST COMPLICATED.

THEY FOUND THE HUSBAND'S BODY IN THE UPSTAIRS HALLWAY.

HAL AND JESSICA CAN ISOLATE A SINGLE HAIR FOLLICLE OR SKIN CELL WITH THEIR RINGS.

THOUGH JESSICA'S CAN BE UNRELIABLE.

THERE'S SO MANY PEOPLE DOWNSTAIRS.

TREVO CLEAR THEM STA FOCUS POW RING

PROCESSING EVIDENCE, BRUCE AND BARRY PUT THEIR EGOS ASIDE. NOT THAT BARRY HAS ONE.

MILK'S CURDLED AND THE FRUIT'S STARTING TO ROT. LIKE IT'S BEEN SITTING OUT FOR A WEEK. BUT TIME OF DEATH WAS--

FORTY-THREE MINUTES AGO.

THE FLOWERS IN THE HOUSE ARE WILTING, TOO. WHY?

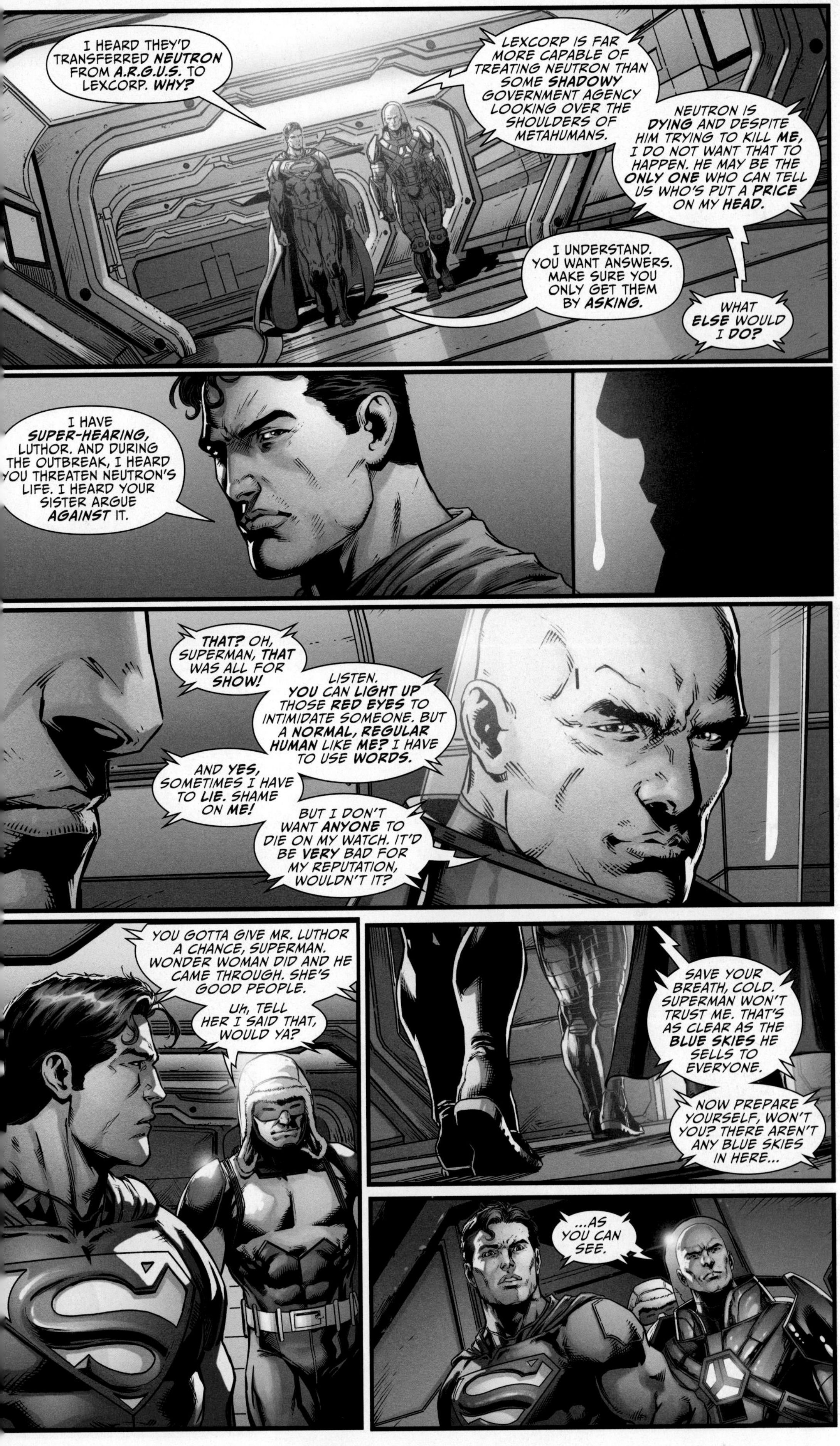
I HEARD THEY'D TRANSFERRED NEUTRON FROM A.R.G.U.S. TO LEXCORP. WHY?
LEXCORP IS FAR MORE CAPABLE OF TREATING NEUTRON THAN SOME SHADOWY GOVERNMENT AGENCY LOOKING OVER THE SHOULDERS OF METAHUMANS.
NEUTRON IS DYING AND DESPITE HIM TRYING TO KILL ME, I DO NOT WANT THAT TO HAPPEN. HE MAY BE THE ONLY ONE WHO CAN TELL US WHO'S PUT A PRICE ON MY HEAD.
I UNDERSTAND. YOU WANT ANSWERS. MAKE SURE YOU ONLY GET THEM BY ASKING.
WHAT ELSE WOULD I DO?
I HAVE SUPER-HEARING, LUTHOR. AND DURING THE OUTBREAK, I HEARD YOU THREATEN NEUTRON'S LIFE. I HEARD YOUR SISTER ARGUE AGAINST IT.
THAT? OH, SUPERMAN, THAT WAS ALL FOR SHOW!
LISTEN. YOU CAN LIGHT UP THOSE RED EYES TO INTIMIDATE SOMEONE. BUT A NORMAL, REGULAR HUMAN LIKE ME? I HAVE TO USE WORDS.
AND YES, SOMETIMES I HAVE TO LIE. SHAME ON ME!
BUT I DON'T WANT ANYONE TO DIE ON MY WATCH. IT'D BE VERY BAD FOR MY REPUTATION, WOULDN'T IT?
YOU GOTTA GIVE MR. LUTHOR A CHANCE, SUPERMAN. WONDER WOMAN DID AND HE CAME THROUGH. SHE'S GOOD PEOPLE.
Uh, TELL HER I SAID THAT, WOULD YA?
SAVE YOUR BREATH, COLD. SUPERMAN WON'T TRUST ME. THAT'S AS CLEAR AS THE BLUE SKIES HE SELLS TO EVERYONE.
NOW PREPARE YOURSELF, WON'T YOU? THERE AREN'T ANY BLUE SKIES IN HERE...
...AS YOU CAN SEE.

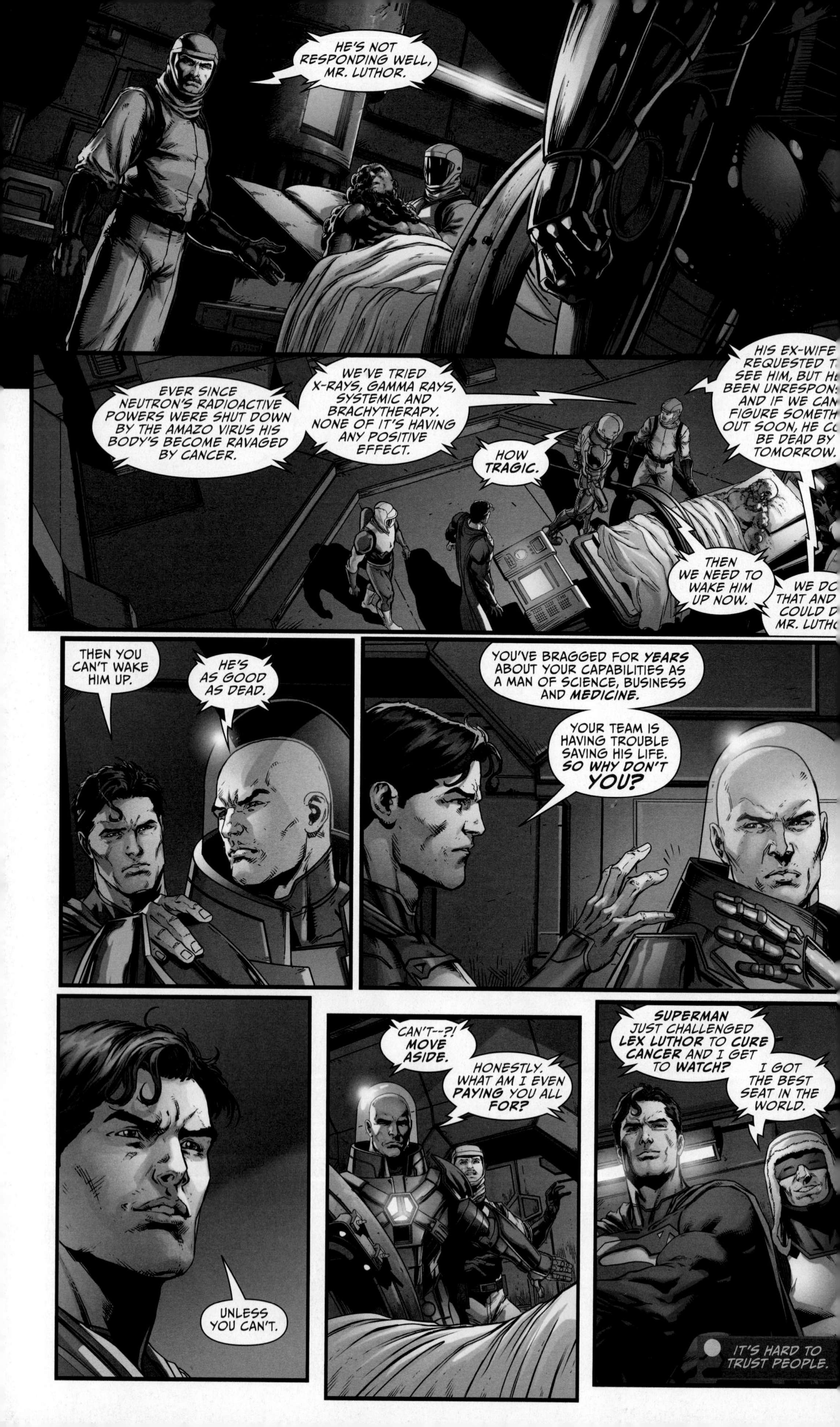
HE'S NOT RESPONDING WELL, MR. LUTHOR.
EVER SINCE NEUTRON'S RADIOACTIVE POWERS WERE SHUT DOWN BY THE AMAZO VIRUS HIS BODY'S BECOME RAVAGED BY CANCER.
WE'VE TRIED X-RAYS, GAMMA RAYS, SYSTEMIC AND BRACHYTHERAPY. NONE OF IT'S HAVING ANY POSITIVE EFFECT.
HOW TRAGIC.
HIS EX-WIFE REQUESTED T SEE HIM, BUT H BEEN UNRESPON AND IF WE CAN FIGURE SOMETH OUT SOON, HE CO BE DEAD BY TOMORROW.
THEN WE NEED TO WAKE HIM UP NOW.
WE DO THAT AND COULD D MR. LUTHO
THEN YOU CAN'T WAKE HIM UP.
HE'S AS GOOD AS DEAD.
YOU'VE BRAGGED FOR YEARS ABOUT YOUR CAPABILITIES AS A MAN OF SCIENCE, BUSINESS AND MEDICINE.
YOUR TEAM IS HAVING TROUBLE SAVING HIS LIFE. SO WHY DON'T YOU?
UNLESS YOU CAN'T.
CAN'T--?! MOVE ASIDE.
HONESTLY. WHAT AM I EVEN PAYING YOU ALL FOR?
SUPERMAN JUST CHALLENGED LEX LUTHOR TO CURE CANCER AND I GET TO WATCH?
I GOT THE BEST SEAT IN THE WORLD.
IT'S HARD TO TRUST PEOPLE.

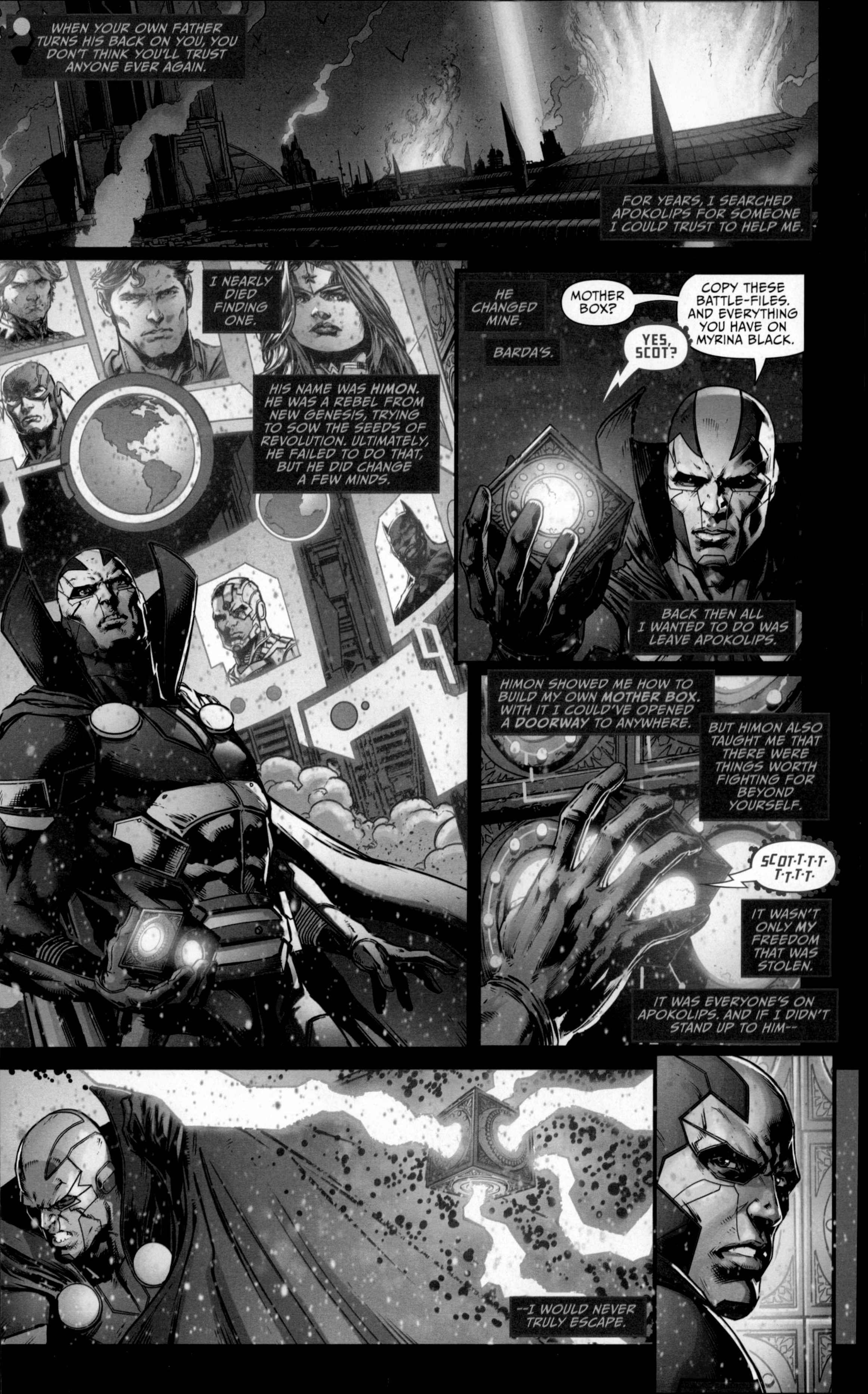
WHEN YOUR OWN FATHER TURNS HIS BACK ON YOU, YOU DON'T THINK YOU'LL TRUST ANYONE EVER AGAIN.
FOR YEARS, I SEARCHED APOKOLIPS FOR SOMEONE I COULD TRUST TO HELP ME.
I NEARLY DIED FINDING ONE.
HIS NAME WAS HIMON. HE WAS A REBEL FROM NEW GENESIS, TRYING TO SOW THE SEEDS OF REVOLUTION. ULTIMATELY, HE FAILED TO DO THAT, BUT HE DID CHANGE A FEW MINDS.
HE CHANGED MINE.
BARDA'S.
MOTHER BOX?
YES, SCOT?
COPY THESE BATTLE-FILES. AND EVERYTHING YOU HAVE ON MYRINA BLACK.
BACK THEN ALL I WANTED TO DO WAS LEAVE APOKOLIPS.
HIMON SHOWED ME HOW TO BUILD MY OWN MOTHER BOX. WITH IT I COULD'VE OPENED A DOORWAY TO ANYWHERE.
BUT HIMON ALSO TAUGHT ME THAT THERE WERE THINGS WORTH FIGHTING FOR BEYOND YOURSELF.
SCOT-T-T-T-T-T-T-T-
IT WASN'T ONLY MY FREEDOM THAT WAS STOLEN.
IT WAS EVERYONE'S ON APOKOLIPS. AND IF I DIDN'T STAND UP TO HIM--
--I WOULD NEVER TRULY ESCAPE.

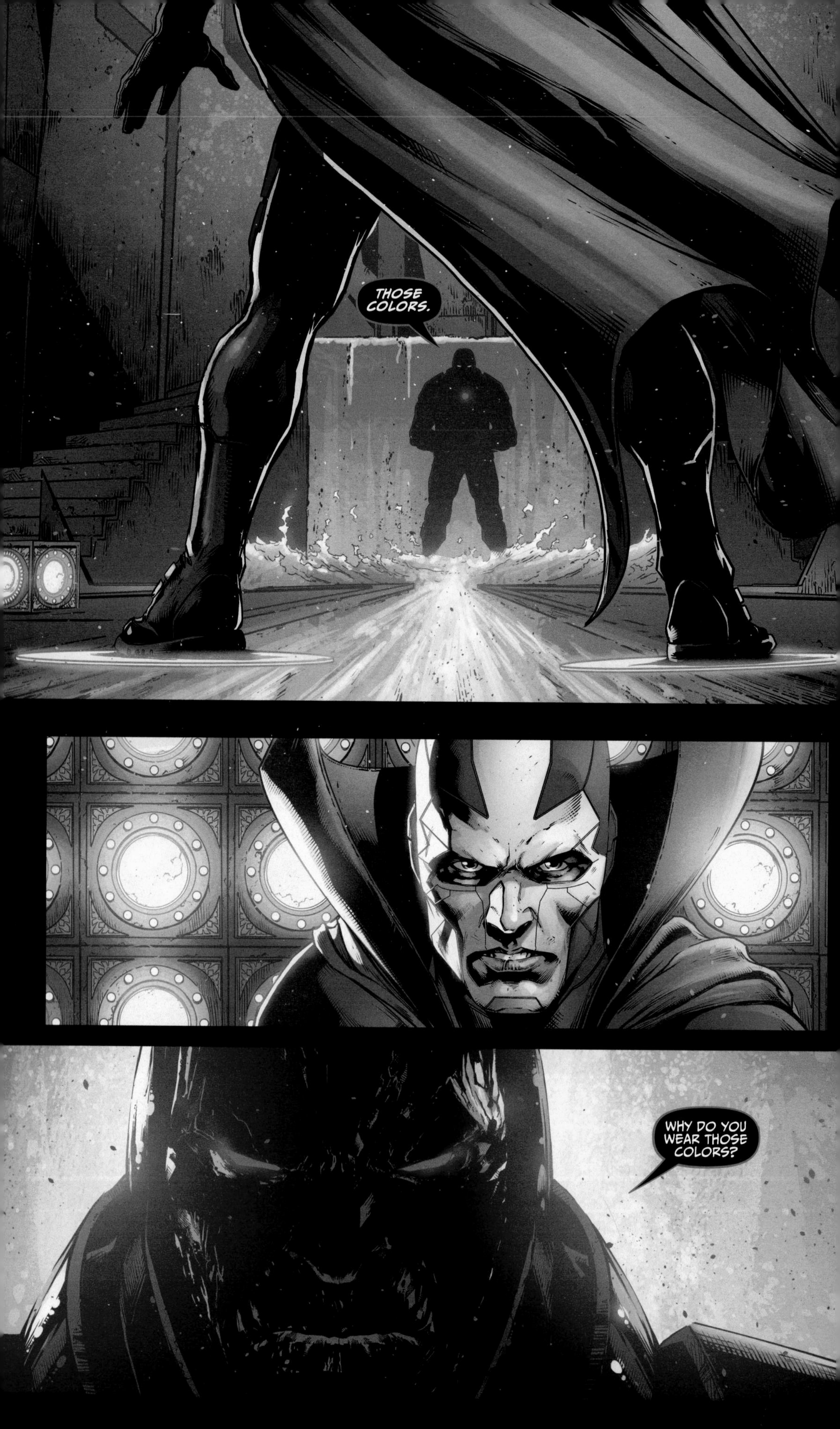

THOSE COLORS.
WHY DO YOU WEAR THOSE COLORS?

WHAT?

WHY DO YOU WEAR THOSE COLORS?

IF YOU THINK I'LL GO DOWN WITHOUT A FIGHT--

DO YOU WEAR THEM BECAUSE THEY COME FROM NEW GENESIS?

THE WORLD THAT PRETENDS TO EMBODY FAIRNESS AND TOLERANCE? THE WORLD YOU DESPISE FOR SENDING YOU HERE? THE WORLD YOU REFUSE TO RETURN TO? IS IT BECAUSE THERE ARE COLORS LIKE THOSE THERE? IS THAT WHY YOU WEAR THEM?

I CHOOSE TO WEAR THEM!

YOU CHOOSE?

YOU THINK BECAUSE YOU SURVIVED MY CAMPS, BECAUSE YOU ESCAPED YOUR CELLS, BECAUSE YOU RUN "FREE" THAT YOU ARE?

THAT IS NOT YOUR NAME. YOU ARE NOT FREE, SLAVE.

YOU NEVER HAVE BEEN.

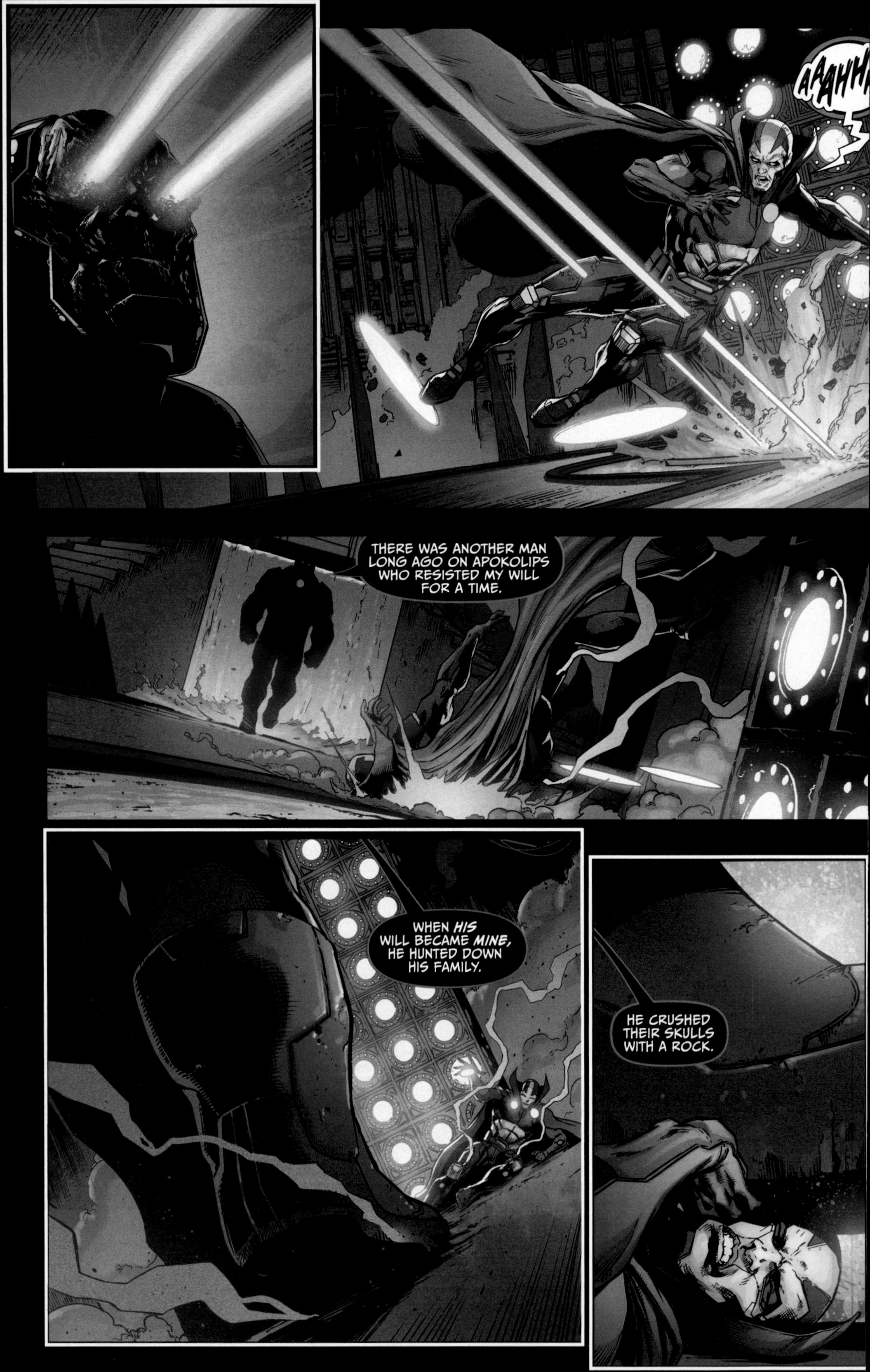
AAAHHH
THERE WAS ANOTHER MAN LONG AGO ON APOKOLIPS WHO RESISTED MY WILL FOR A TIME.
WHEN HIS WILL BECAME MINE, HE HUNTED DOWN HIS FAMILY.
HE CRUSHED THEIR SKULLS WITH A ROCK.

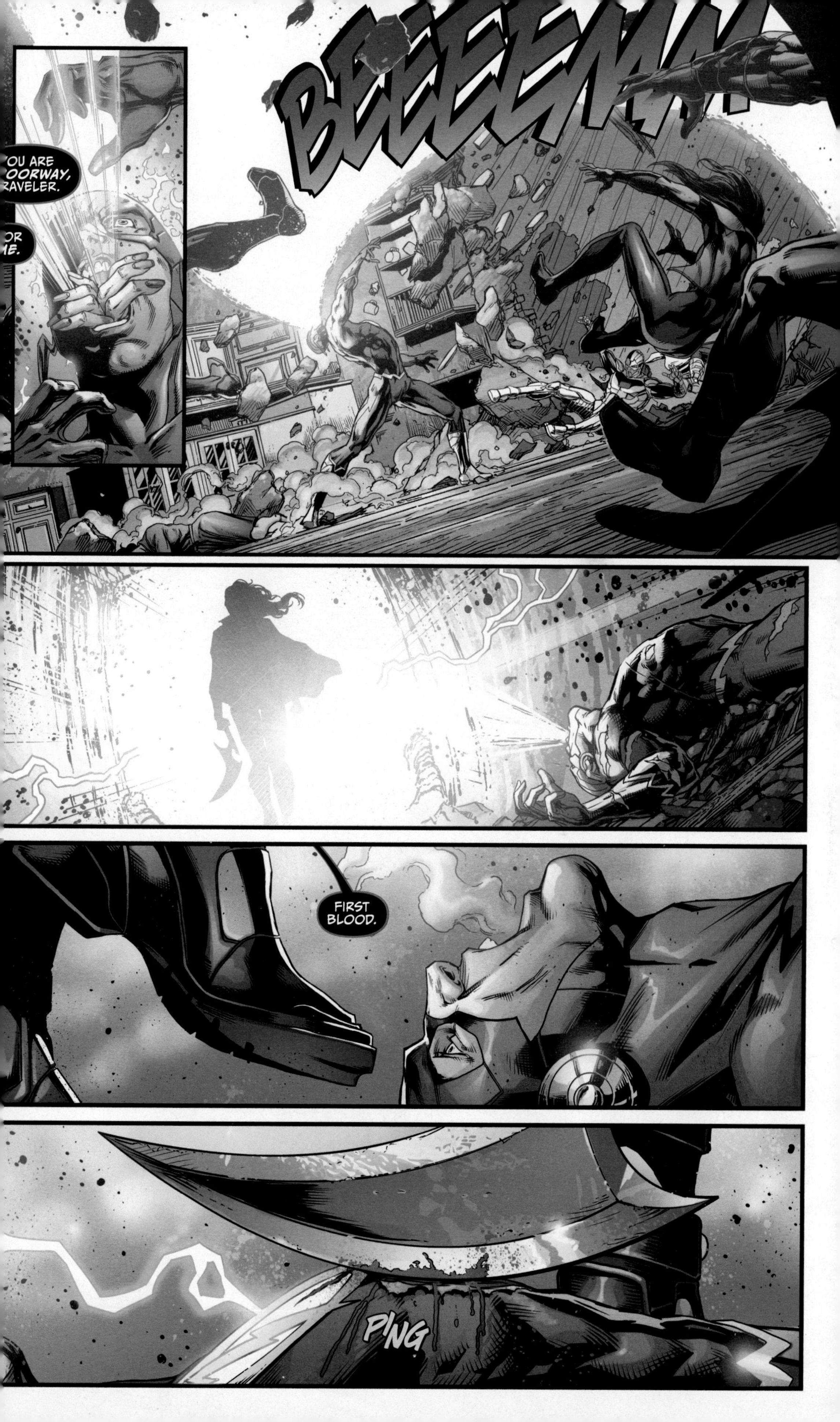

BEEEEMM!
OU ARE
OORWAY,
RAVELER.
OR
ME.
FIRST
BLOOD.
PING

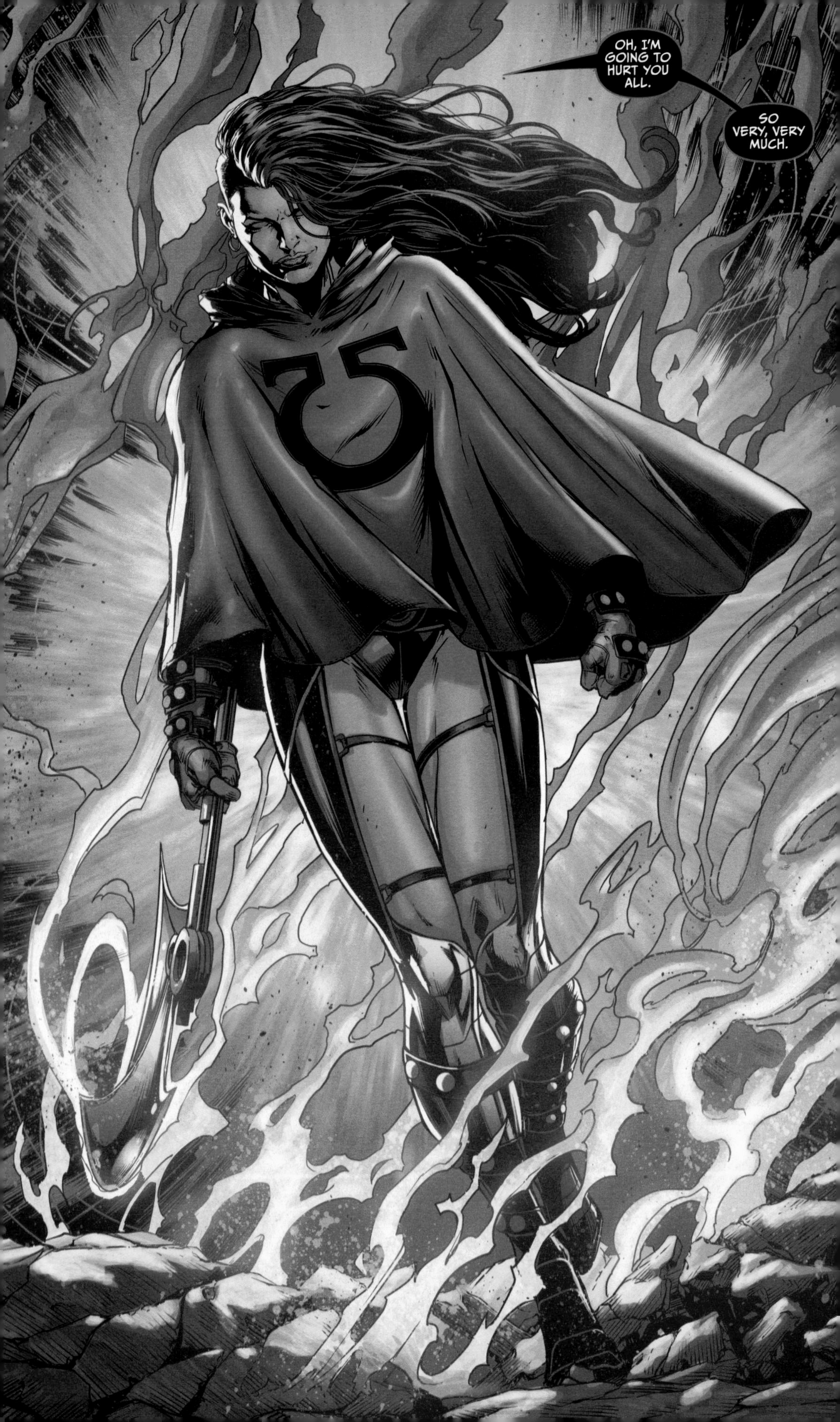

OH, I'M GOING TO HURT YOU ALL.
SO VERY, VERY MUCH.

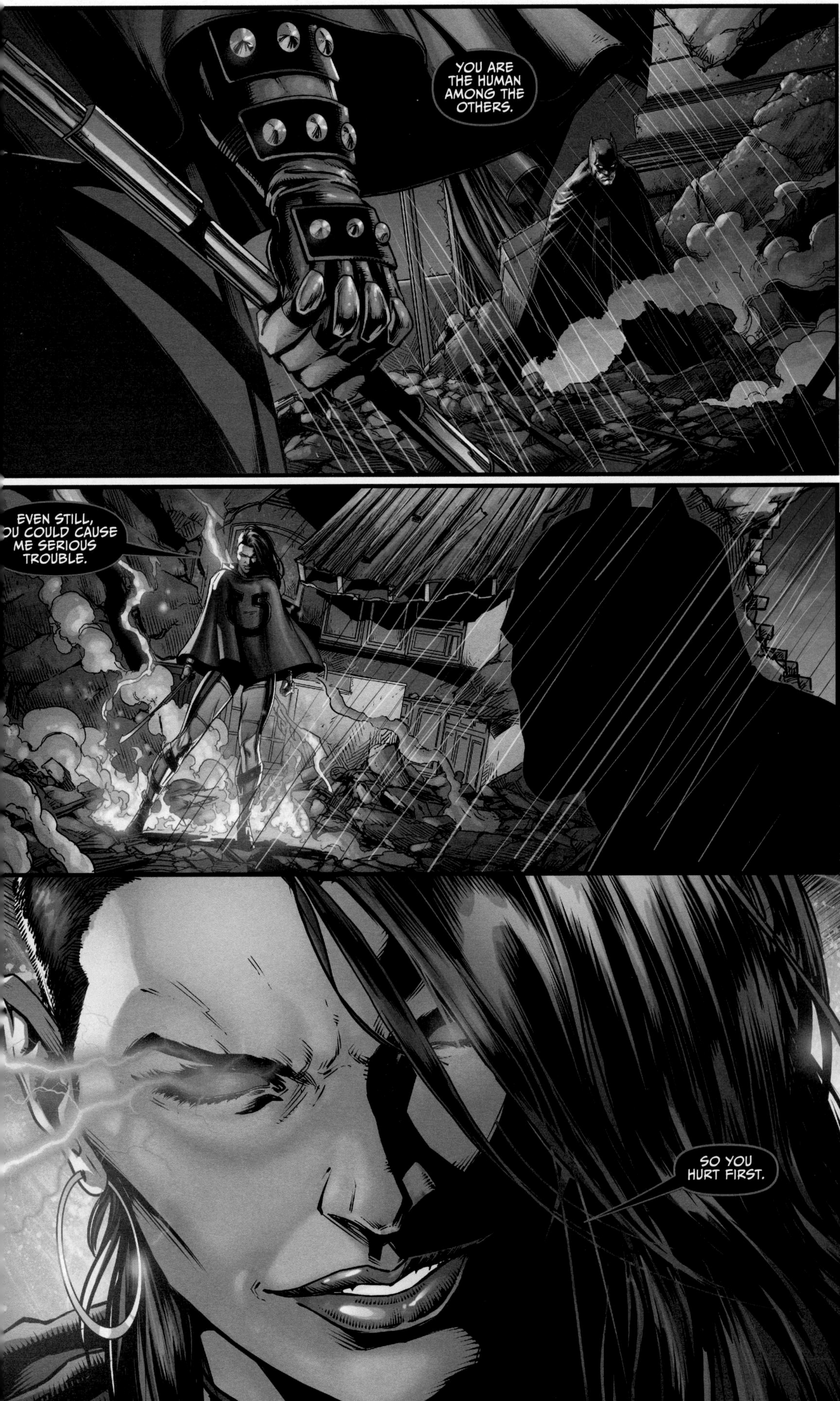
YOU ARE THE HUMAN AMONG THE OTHERS.
EVEN STILL, OU COULD CAUSE ME SERIOUS TROUBLE.
SO YOU HURT FIRST.

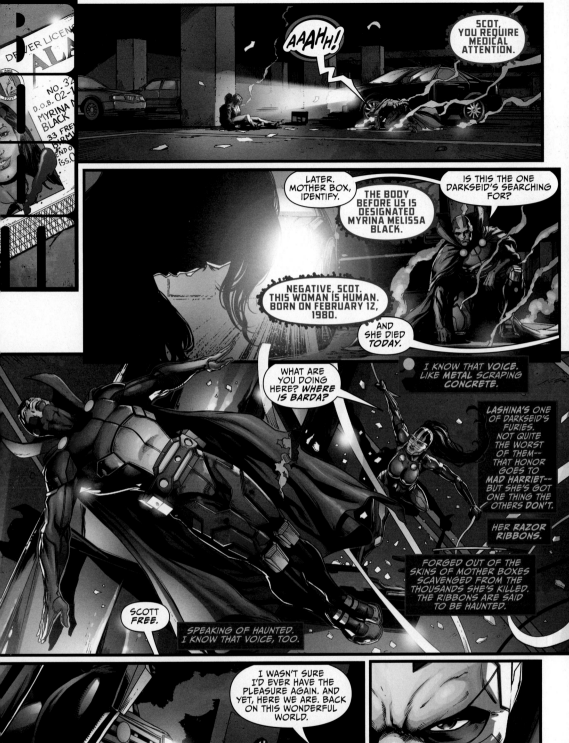

AAAHH!

SCOT, YOU REQUIRE MEDICAL ATTENTION.

LATER. MOTHER BOX, IDENTIFY.

THE BODY BEFORE US IS DESIGNATED MYRINA MELISSA BLACK.

IS THIS THE ONE DARKSEID'S SEARCHING FOR?

NEGATIVE, SCOT. THIS WOMAN IS HUMAN. BORN ON FEBRUARY 12, 1980.

AND SHE DIED TODAY.

WHAT ARE YOU DOING HERE? WHERE IS BARDA?

I KNOW THAT VOICE. LIKE METAL SCRAPING CONCRETE.

LASHINA'S ONE OF DARKSEID'S FURIES. NOT QUITE THE WORST OF THEM-- THAT HONOR GOES TO MAD HARRIET-- BUT SHE'S GOT ONE THING THE OTHERS DON'T.

HER RAZOR RIBBONS.

FORGED OUT OF THE SKINS OF MOTHER BOXES SCAVENGED FROM THE THOUSANDS SHE'S KILLED. THE RIBBONS ARE SAID TO BE HAUNTED.

SCOTT FREE.

SPEAKING OF HAUNTED. I KNOW THAT VOICE, TOO.

I WASN'T SURE I'D EVER HAVE THE PLEASURE AGAIN. AND YET, HERE WE ARE. BACK ON THIS WONDERFUL WORLD.

KANTO. DARKSEID'S FAVORITE ASSASSIN. THE LAST TIME I SAW HIM HE KILLED HIMON.

HE'LL KILL ME IF I GIVE HIM THE CHANCE.

BUT I NEED TO SURVIVE.

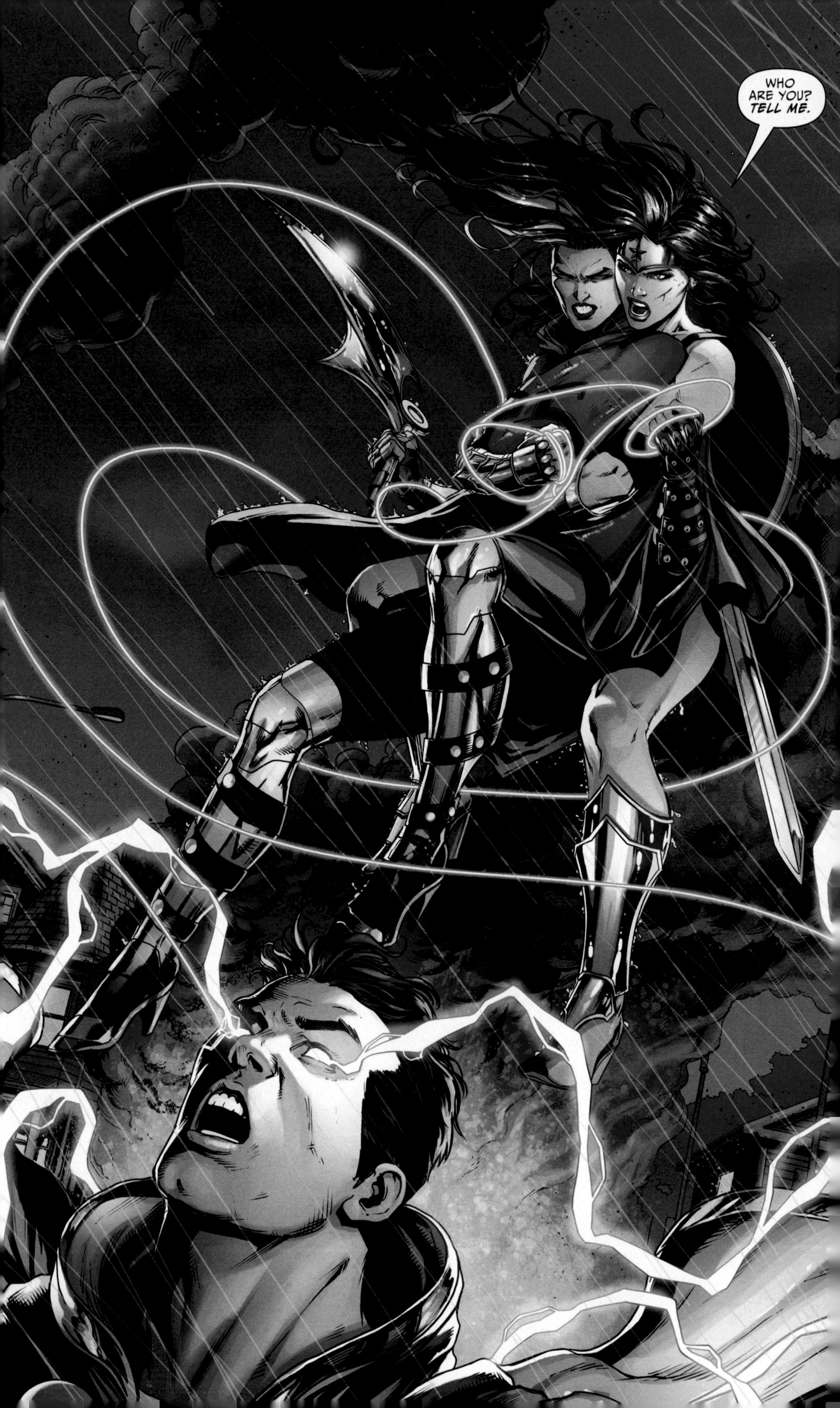
WHO ARE YOU? TELL ME.

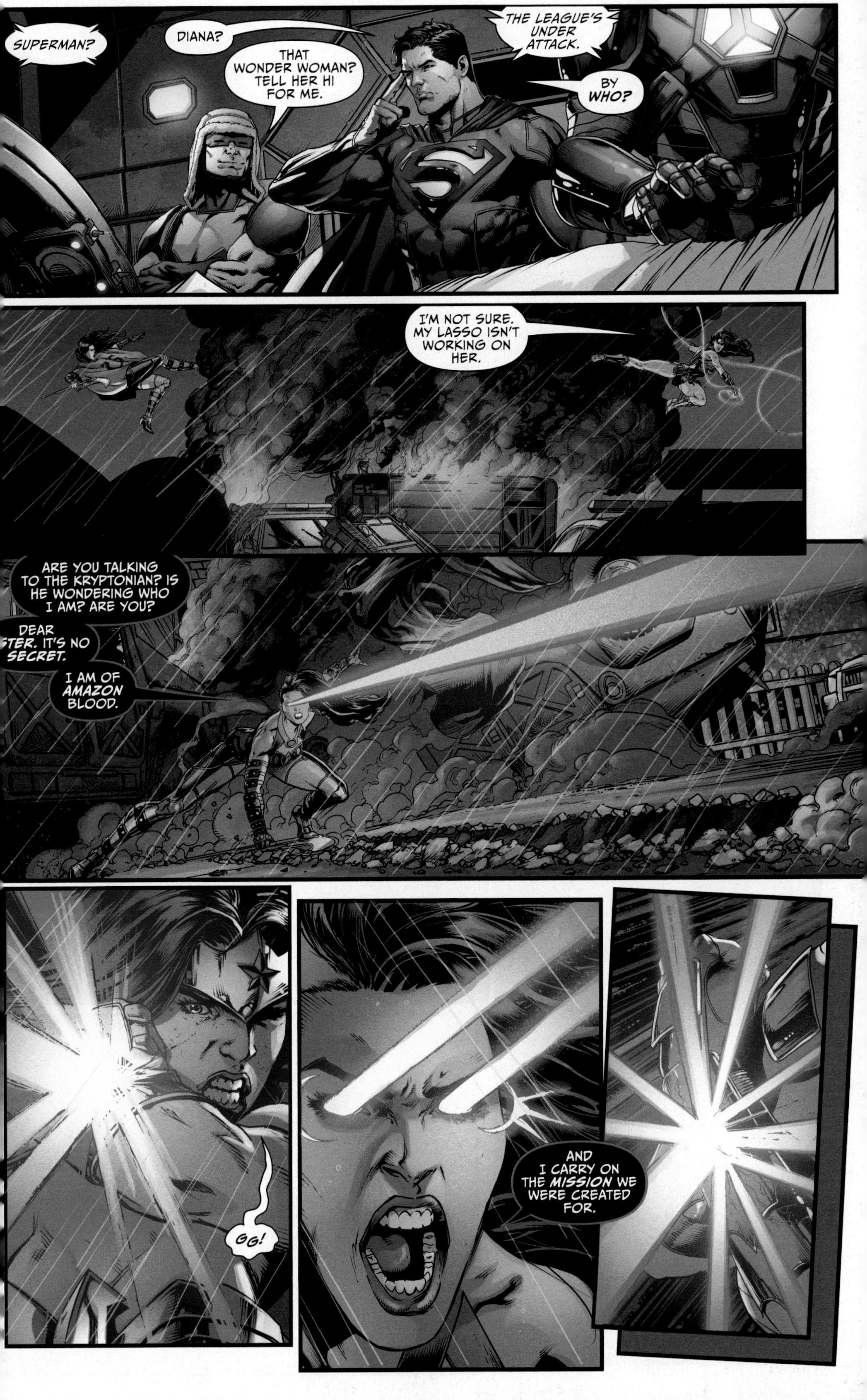
SUPERMAN?
DIANA?
THAT WONDER WOMAN? TELL HER HI FOR ME.
THE LEAGUE'S UNDER ATTACK.
BY WHO?
I'M NOT SURE. MY LASSO ISN'T WORKING ON HER.
ARE YOU TALKING TO THE KRYPTONIAN? IS HE WONDERING WHO I AM? ARE YOU?
DEAR
TER. IT'S NO SECRET.
I AM OF AMAZON BLOOD.
GG!
AND I CARRY ON THE MISSION WE WERE CREATED FOR.

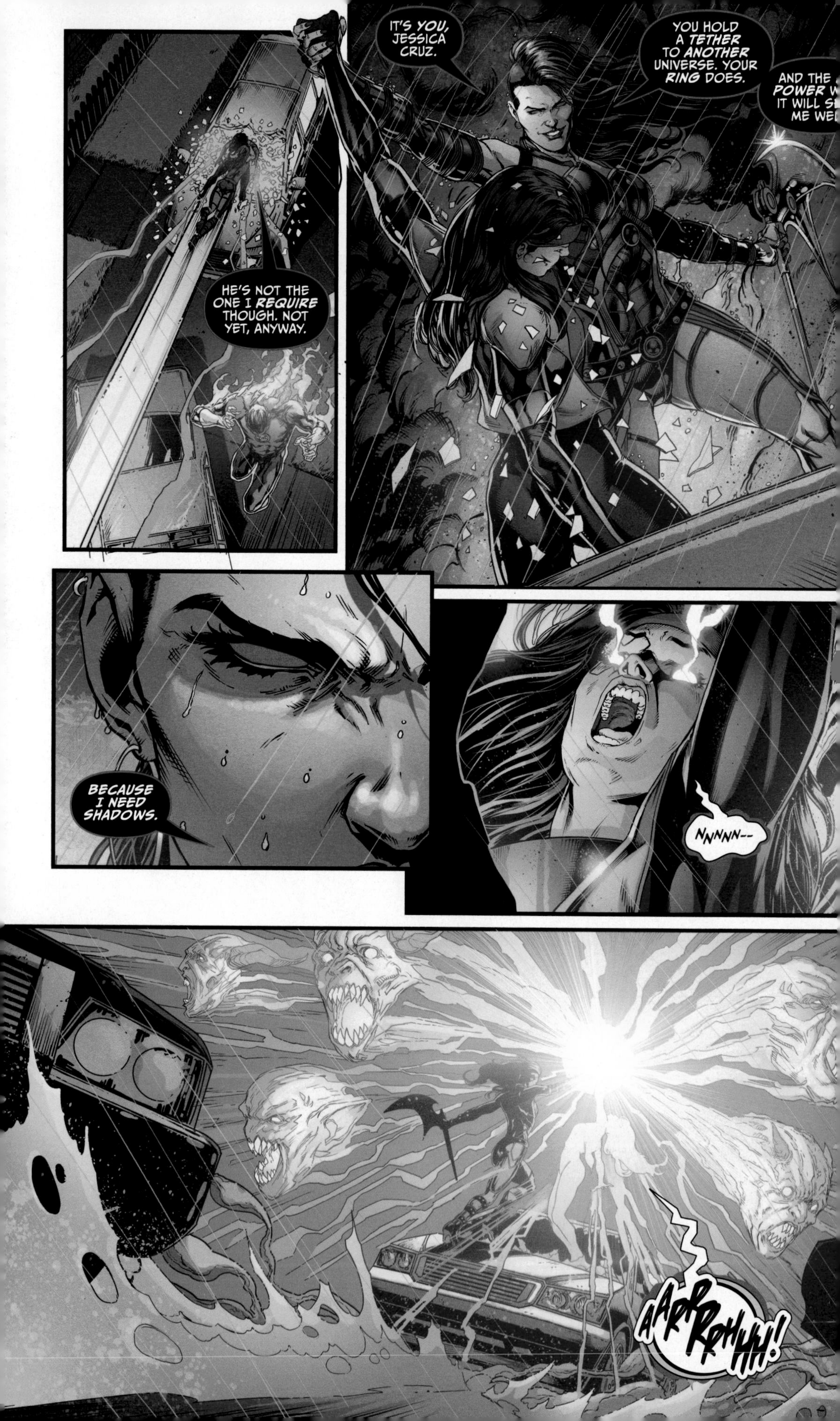
HE'S NOT THE ONE I REQUIRE THOUGH. NOT YET, ANYWAY.
IT'S YOU, JESSICA CRUZ.
YOU HOLD A TETHER TO ANOTHER UNIVERSE. YOUR RING DOES.
AND THE POWER W IT WILL S ME WE
BECAUSE I NEED SHADOWS.
NNNNN--
AARRRHHHH!

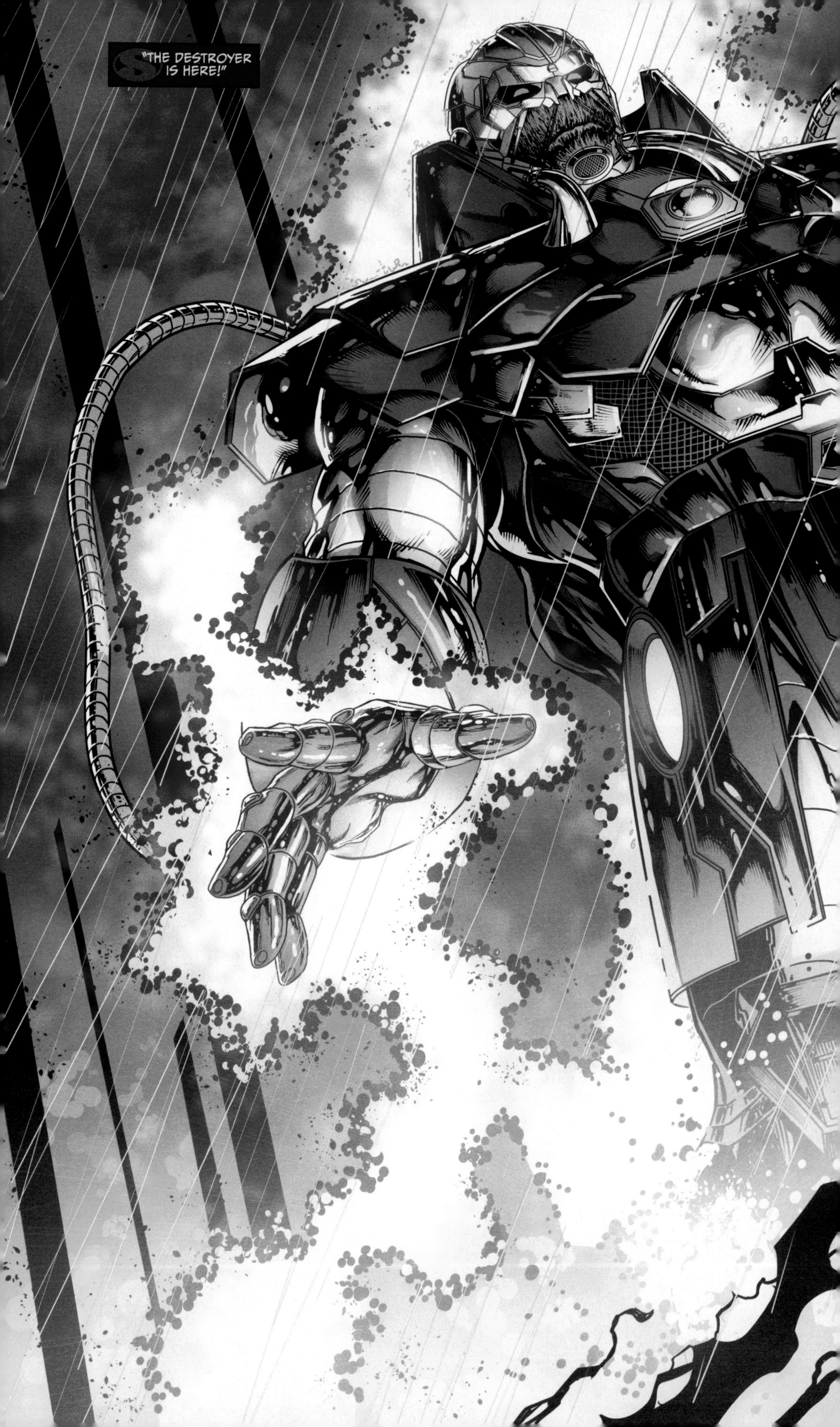
"THE DESTROYER IS HERE!"

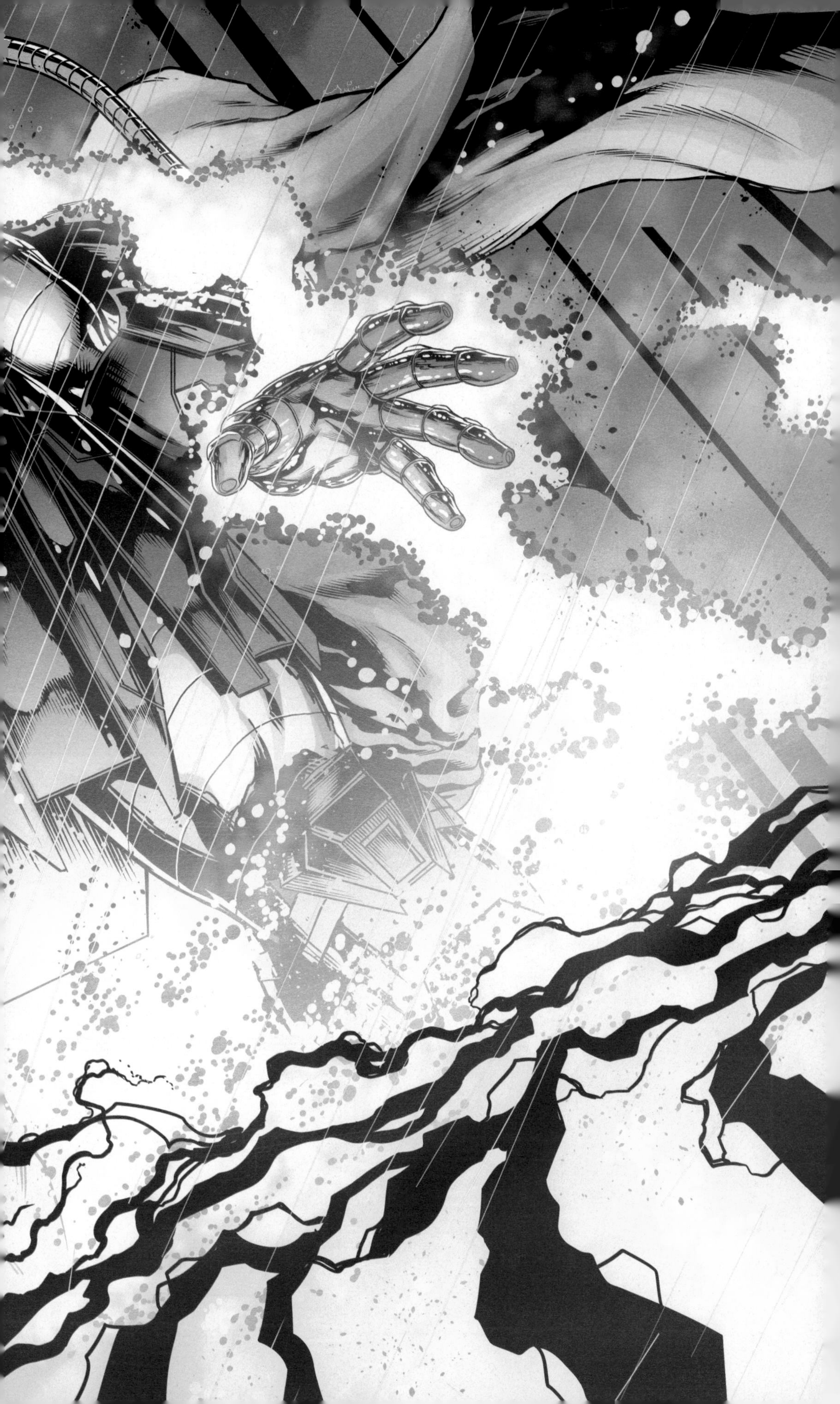

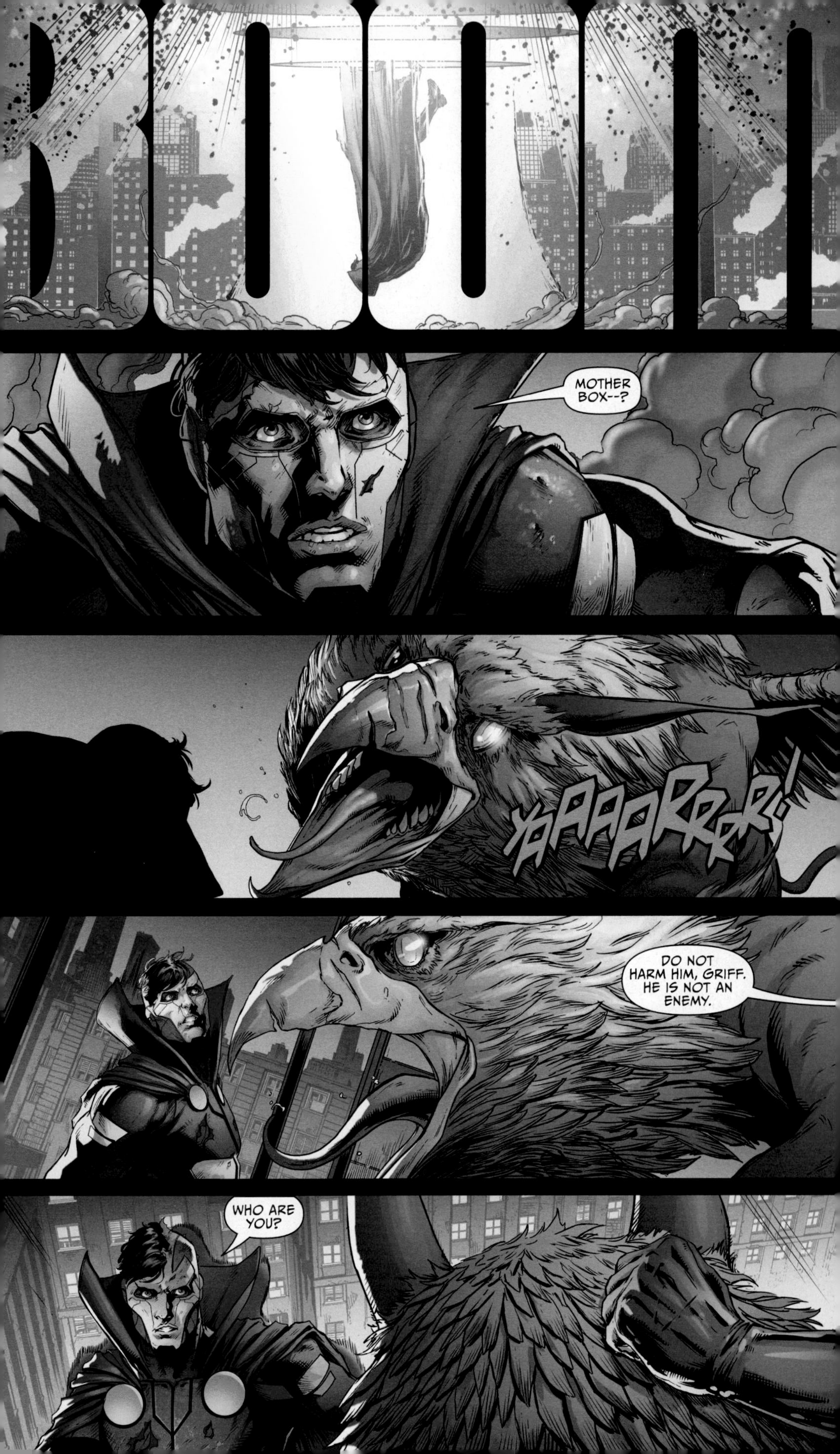
BOOOM!
MOTHER BOX--?
YAAAARRRR!
DO NOT HARM HIM, GRIFF. HE IS NOT AN ENEMY.
WHO ARE YOU?

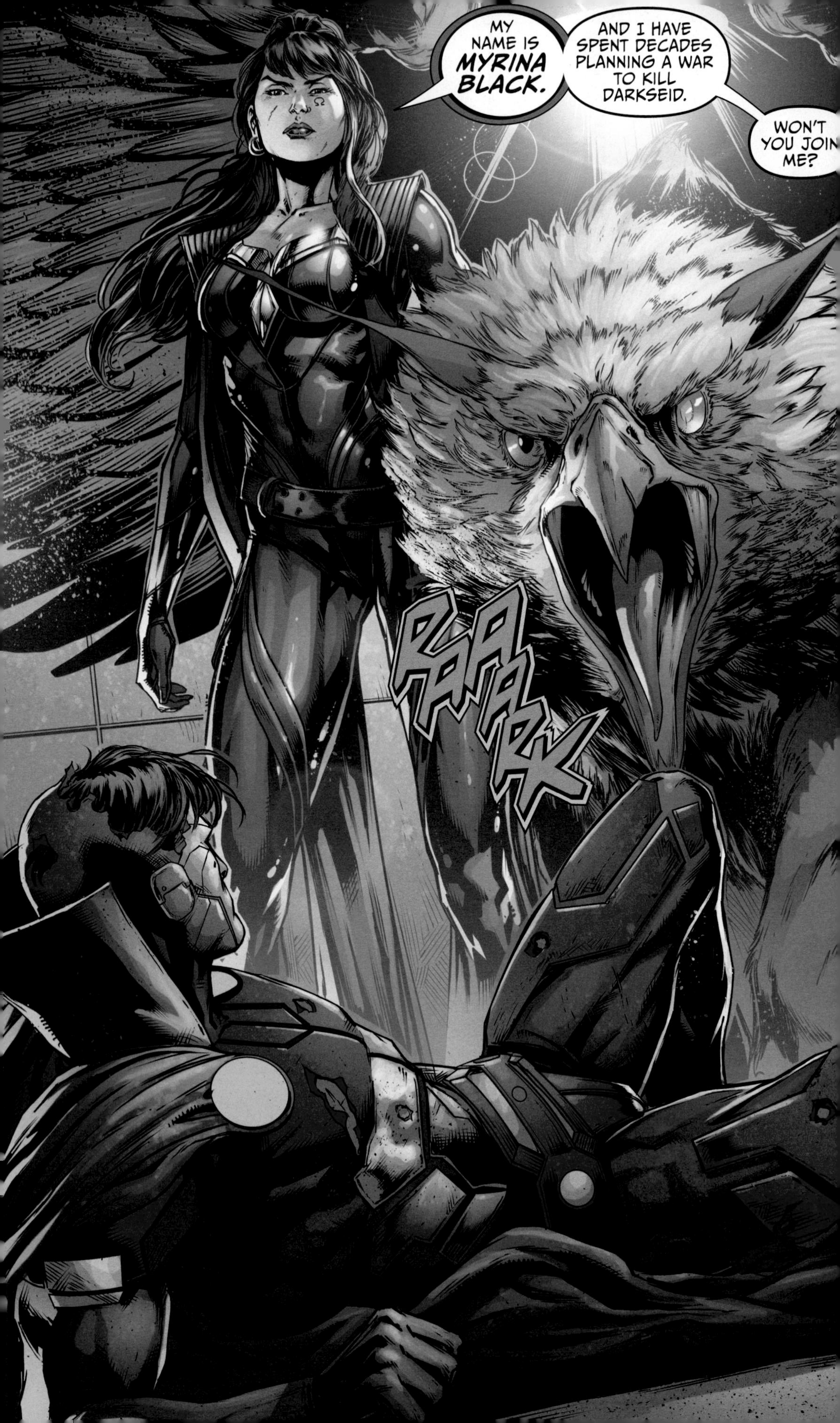
MY NAME IS *MYRINA BLACK.*
AND I HAVE SPENT DECADES PLANNING A WAR TO KILL DARKSEID.
WON'T YOU JOIN ME?
RAAARK

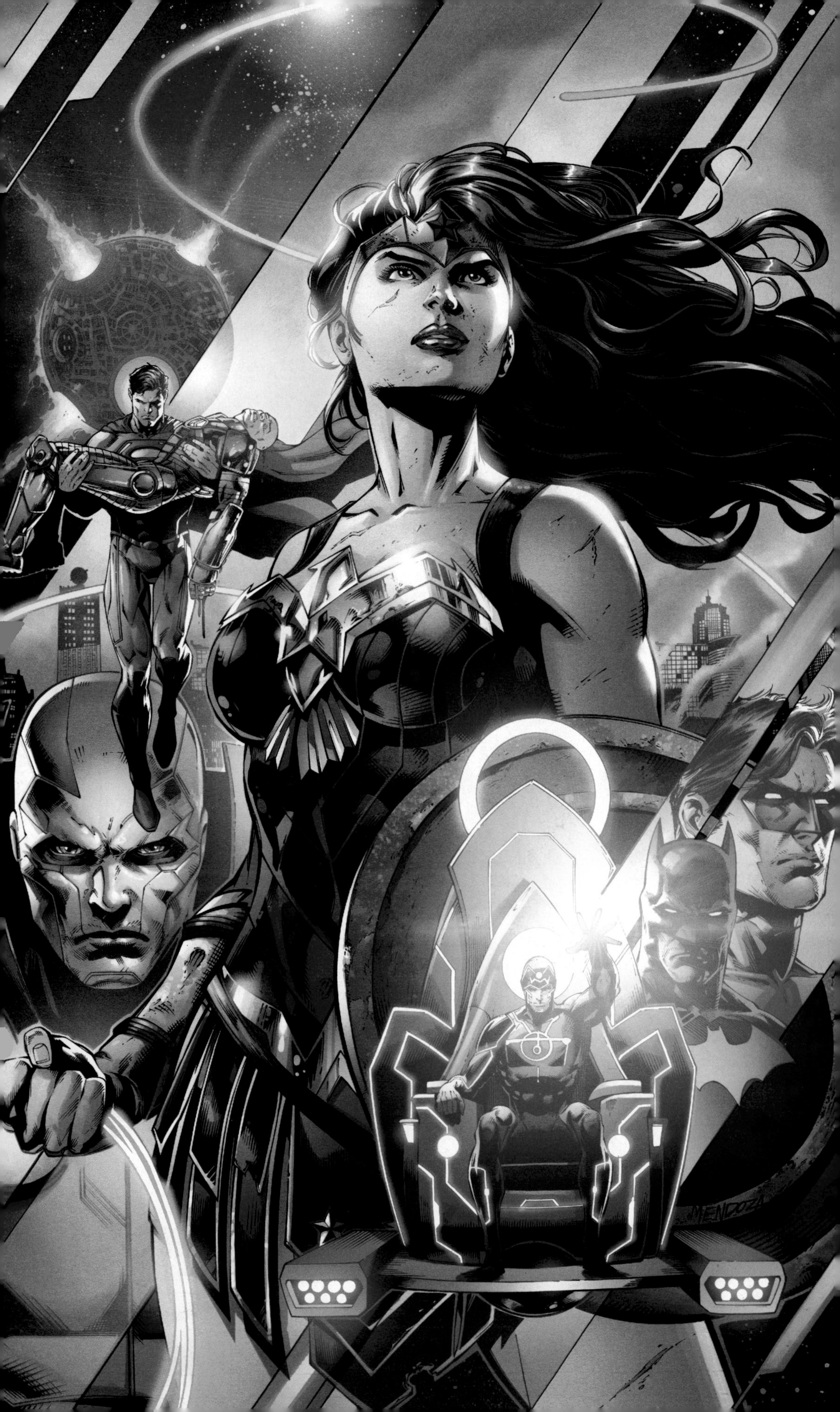

DARKSEID WAR CHAPTER TWO: THE NEW GOD

GEOFF JOHNS writer **JASON FABOK** artist **BRAD ANDERSON** colorist **ROB LEIGH** letterer cover by **JASON FABOK, JAIME MENDOZA** and **BRAD ANDERSON**

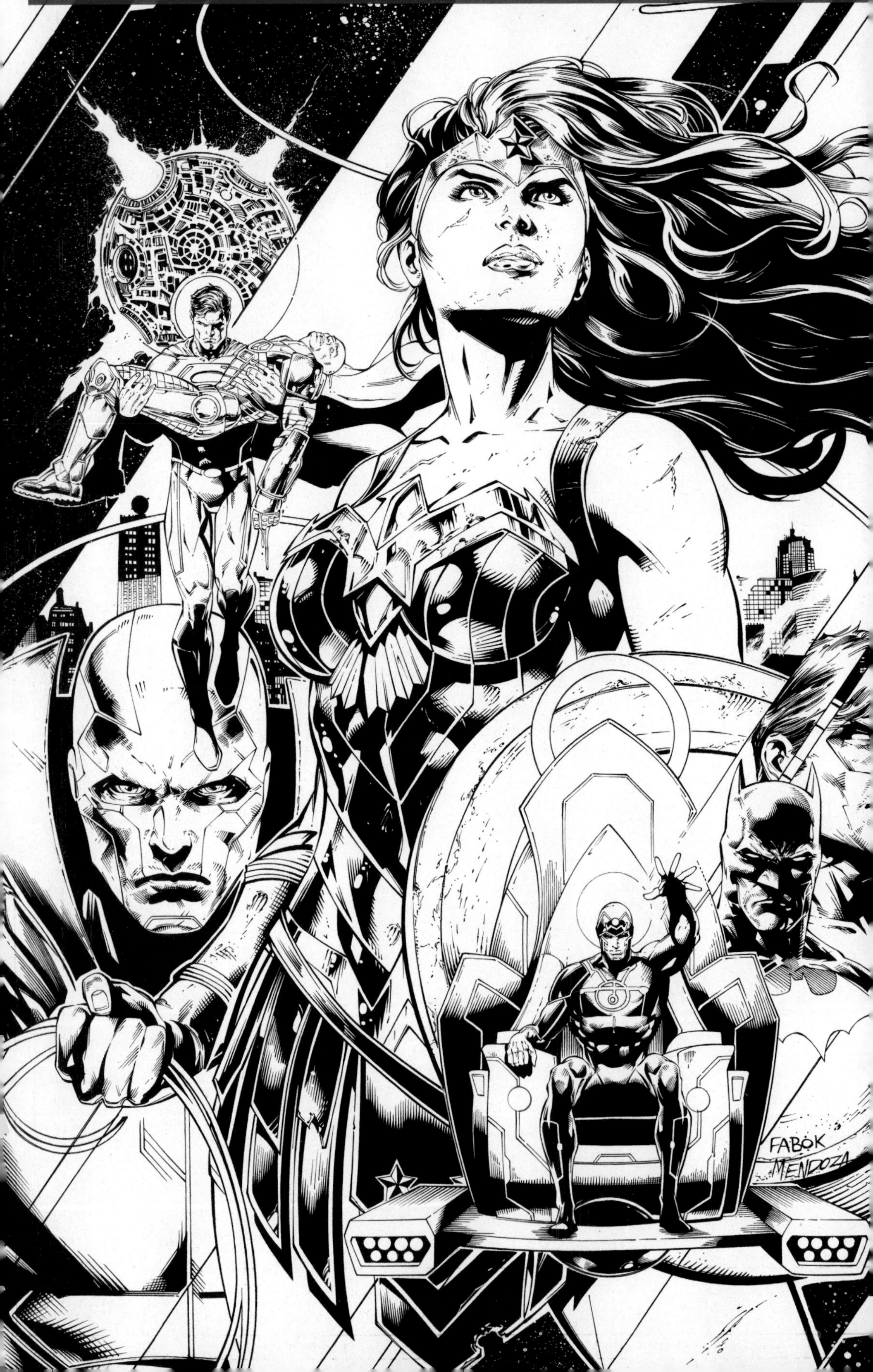
FABOK
MENDOZA

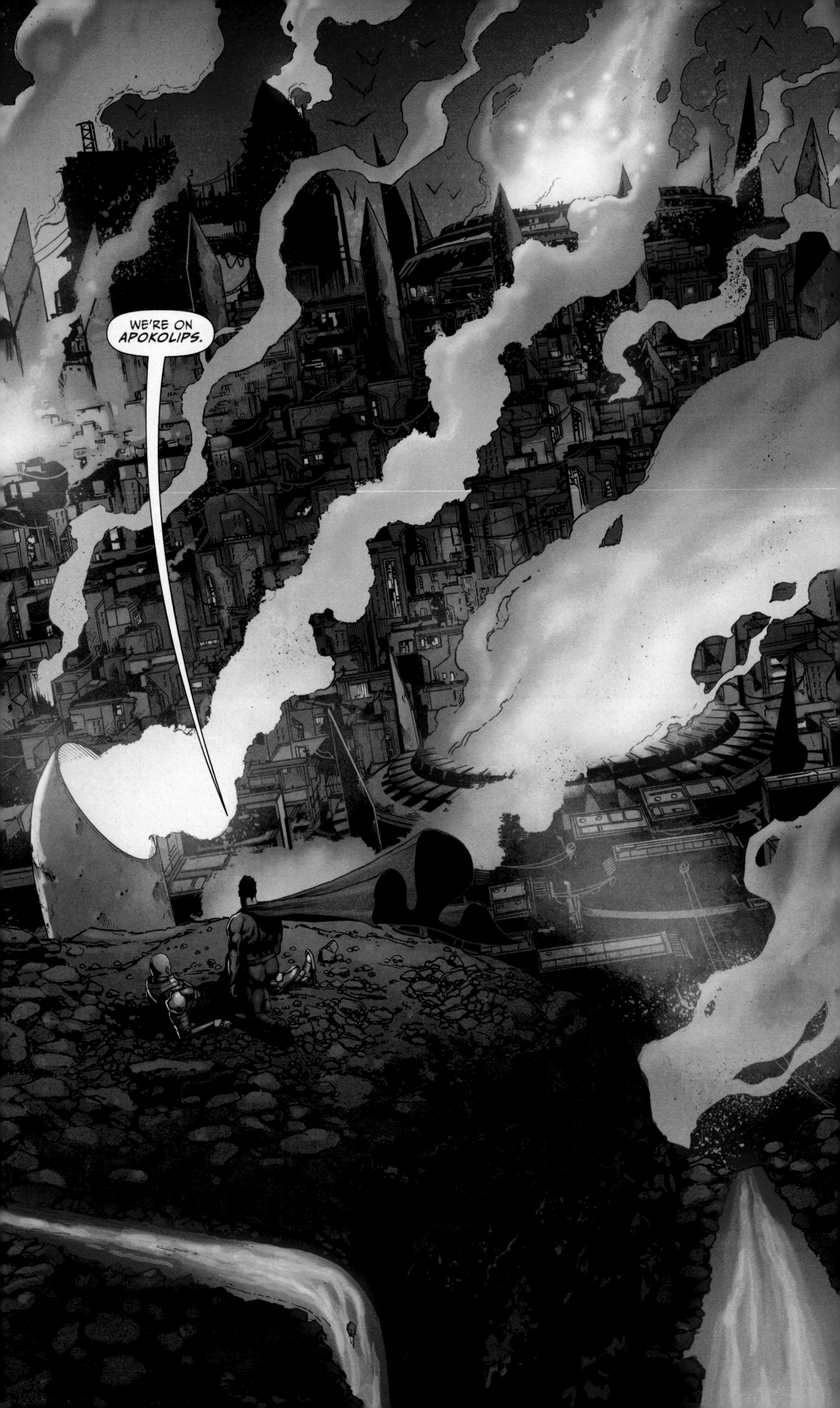
WE'RE ON APOKOLIPS.

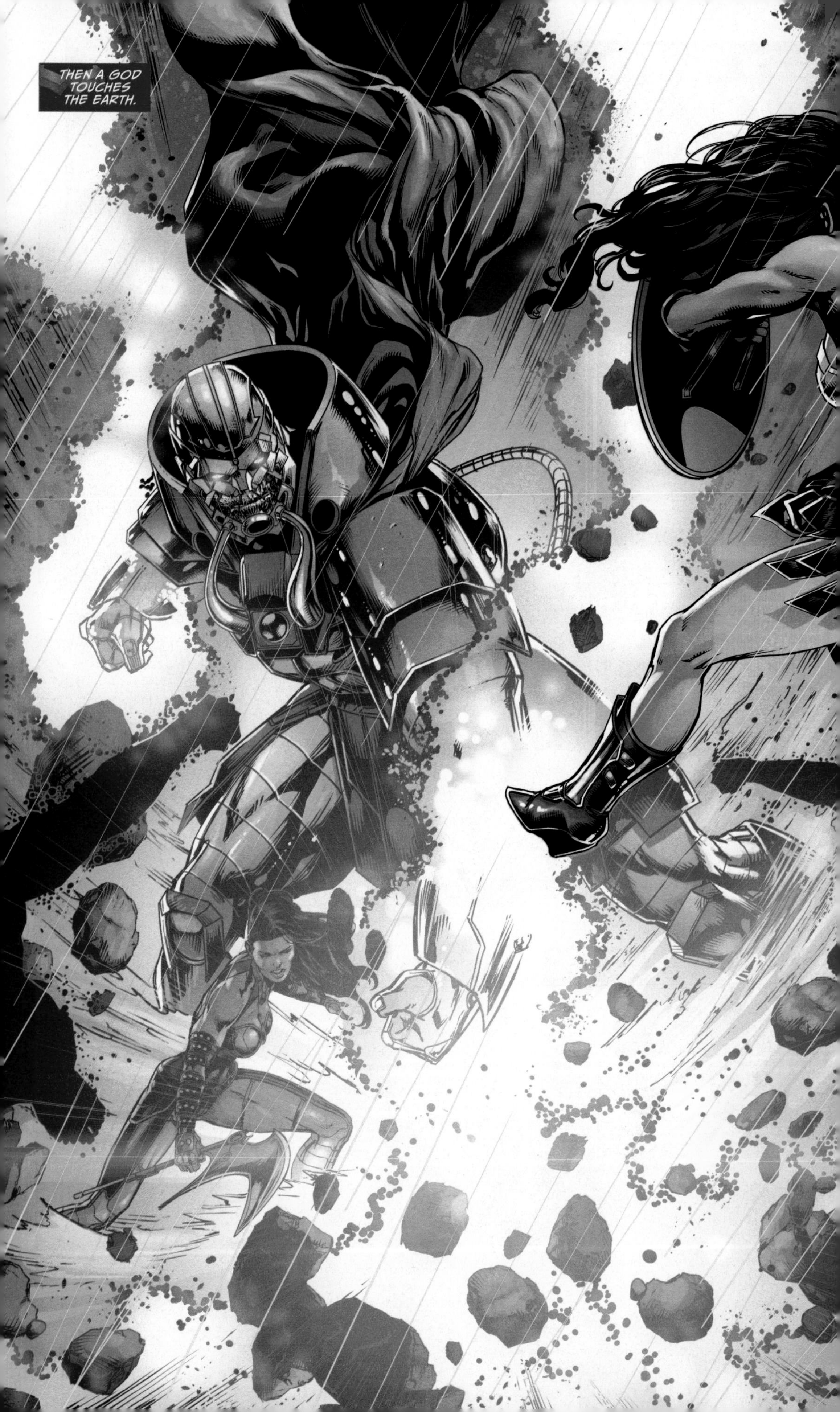
THEN A GOD TOUCHES THE EARTH.

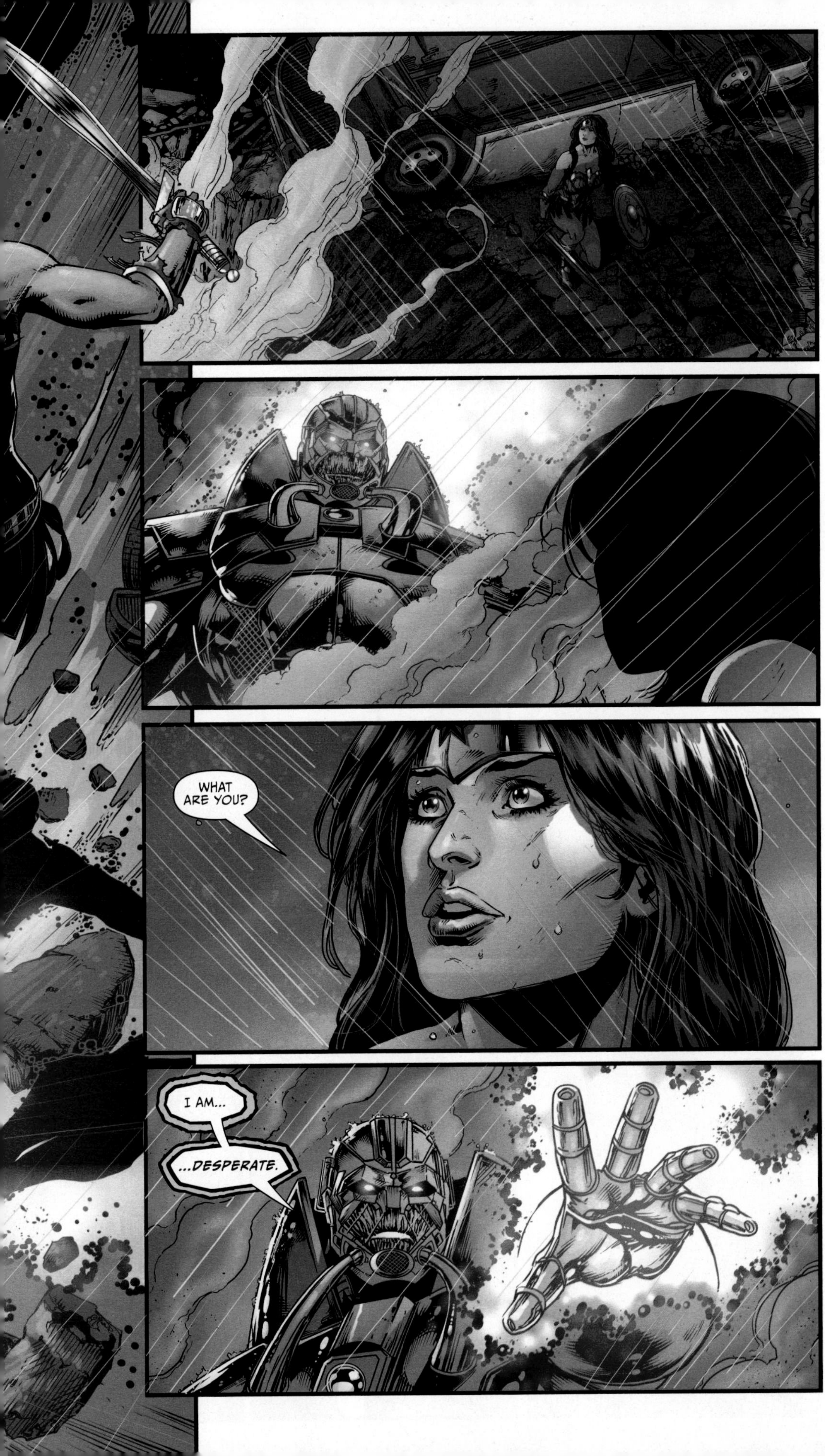
WHAT ARE YOU?
I AM...
...DESPERATE.

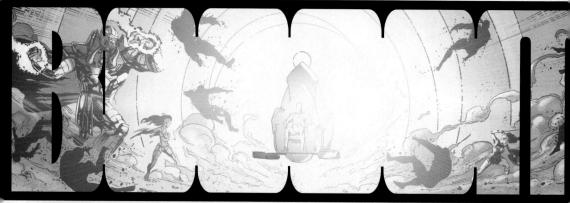

METRON! HOW DELIGHTFUL.

I AM STILL WATCHING YOU, GRAIL.

WHY? DO YOU FIND ME *PRETTY?*

I FIND YOU DANGERO[US] BUT ULTIMATEL[Y] PRECARIOU[S].

YOU PLAY THIS GAME WELL, BUT SO DO I.

METRON BELIEVES HE CAN *HIDE* THE LEAGUE FROM ME, BUT I WILL *FIND* THEM.

I WILL *HAVE* MY TROPHIES.

FIRST, YOU WILL BRING YOUR *FATHER* TO ME.

OH, *DARKSEID* IS COMING. YOU *WILL* GET YOUR WISH, MOBIUS. YOU WILL GET YOUR *BRAND-NEW DAY.* YOUR *NEW LIFE.*

YOU WILL GET YOUR *WAR.*

MOTHER PROMISED ME...

HOW DO I GET THE ANSWERS TO MY QUESTIONS?

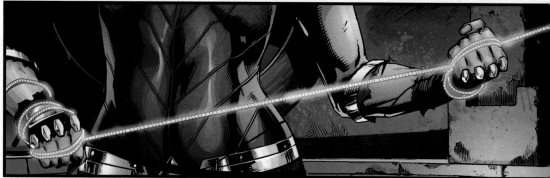

T-TAKE...

TAKE THE CHAIR FROM ME.

UNDERSTOOD.

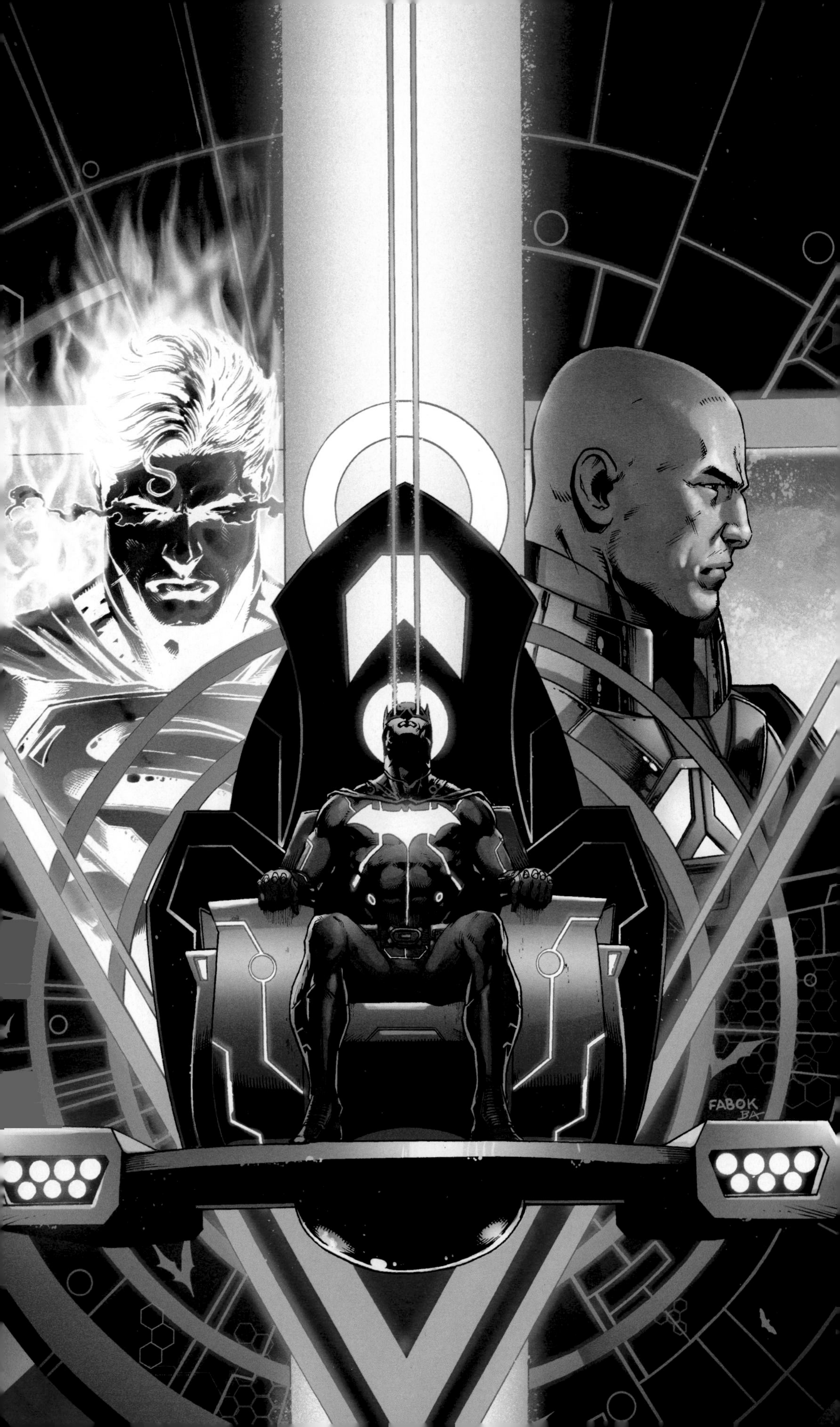
FABOK
BA

DARKSEID WAR CHAPTER THREE: TAKEN

GEOFF JOHNS writer JASON FABOK artist BRAD ANDERSON colorist ROB LEIGH letterer cover by JASON FABOK and BRAD ANDERSON

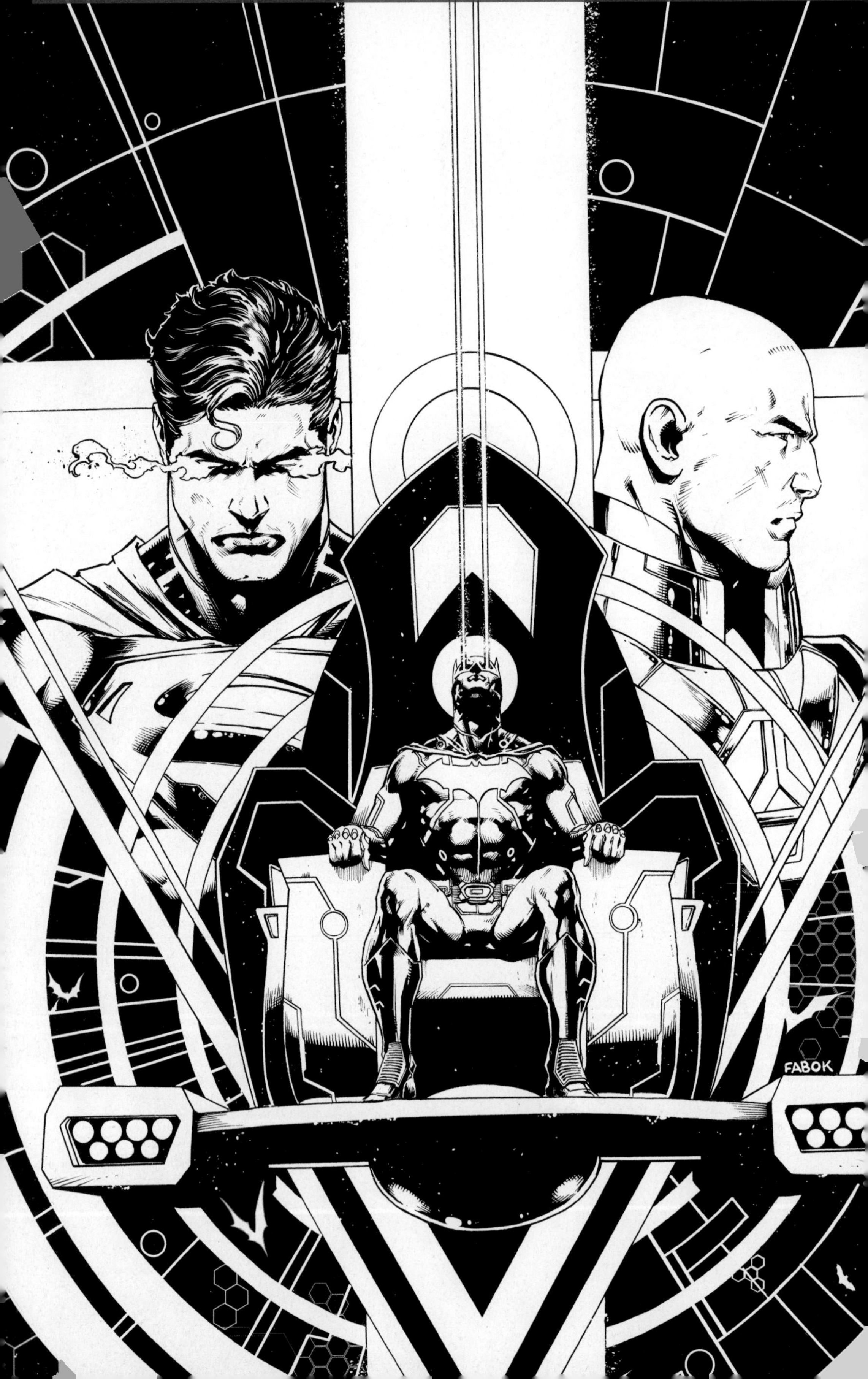
FABOK

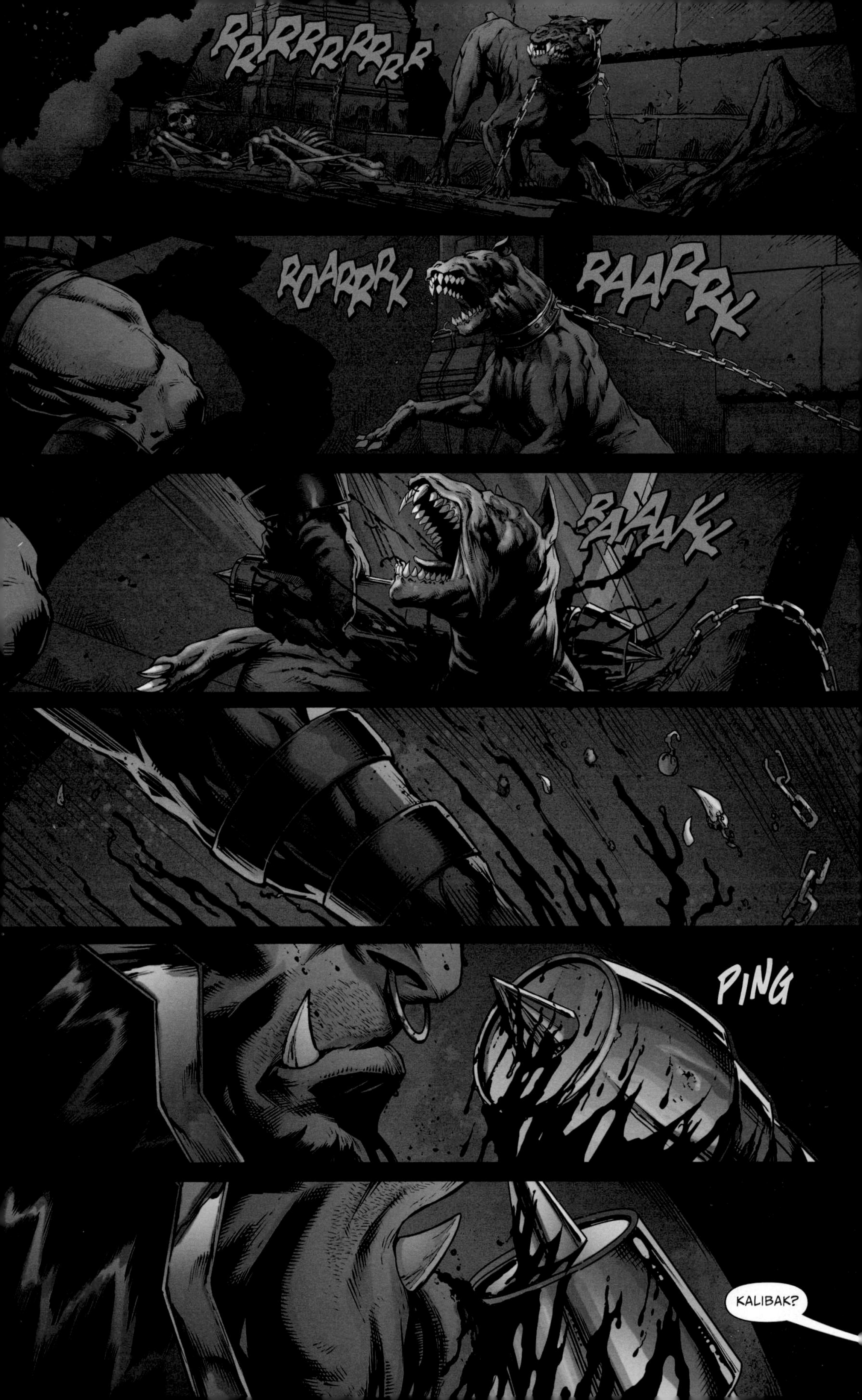
RRRRRRRRRR
ROARRRK
RAARRK
PING
KALIBAK?

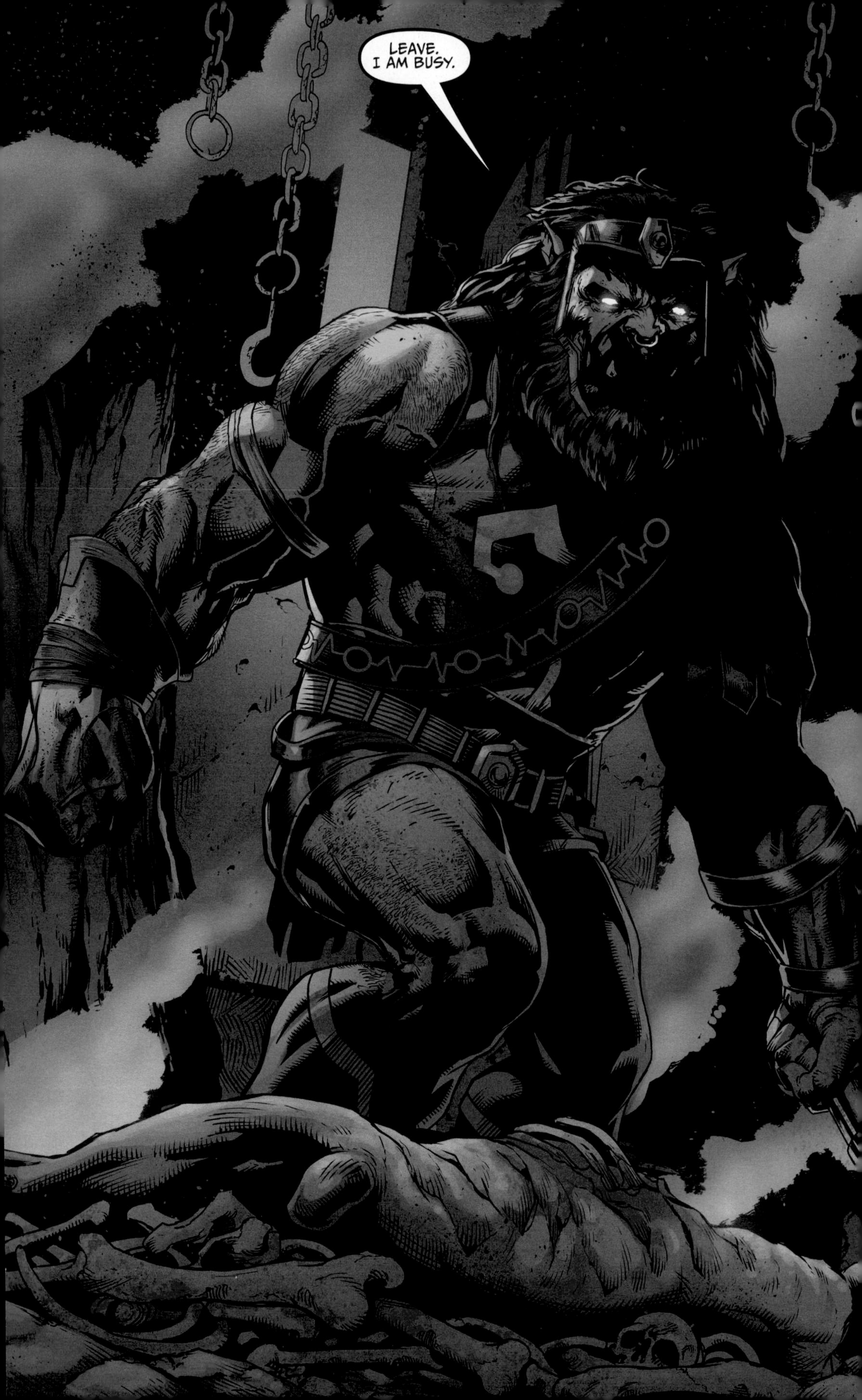
LEAVE. I AM BUSY.

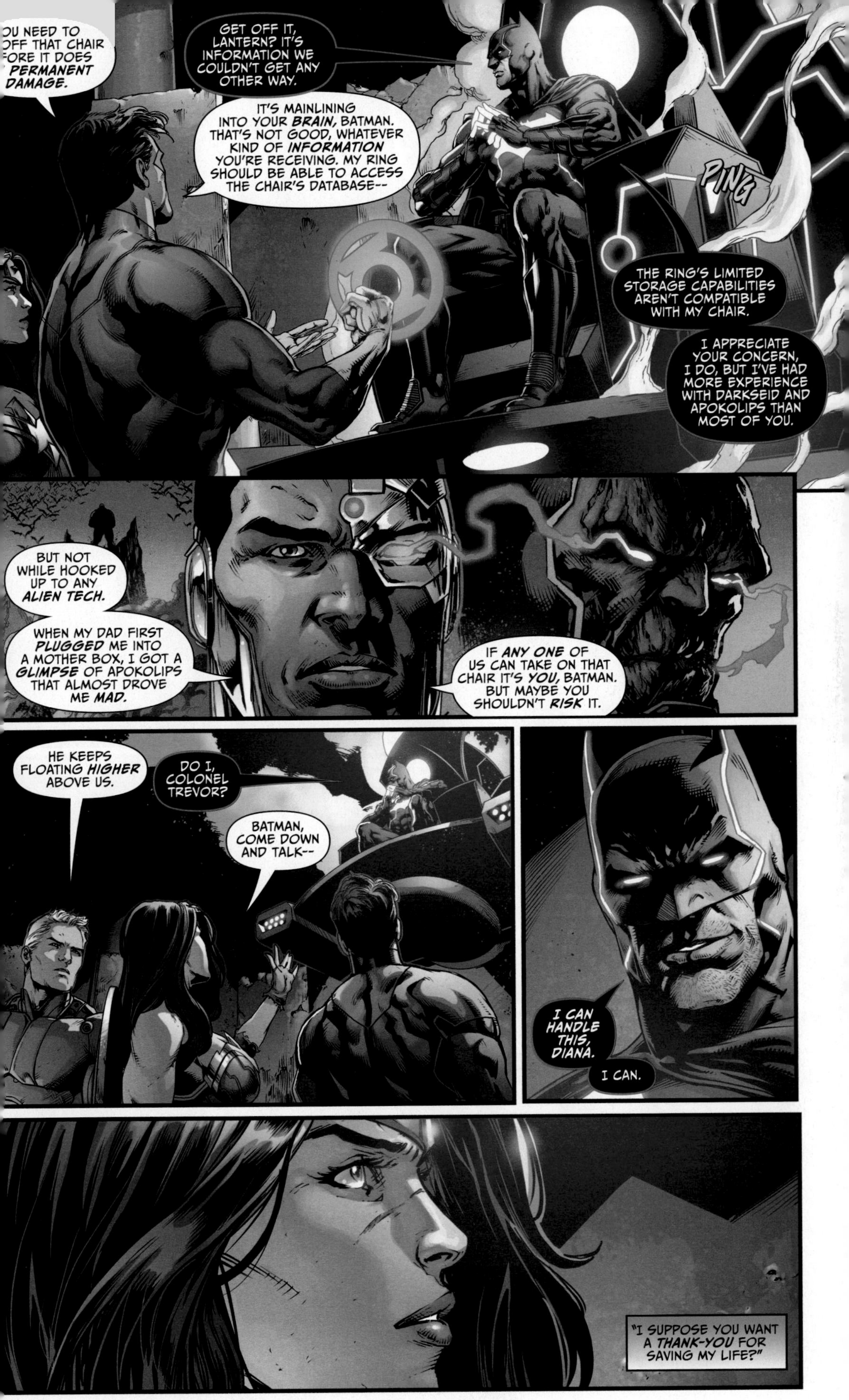
OU NEED TO
OFF THAT CHAIR
FORE IT DOES
PERMANENT
DAMAGE.
GET OFF IT, LANTERN? IT'S INFORMATION WE COULDN'T GET ANY OTHER WAY.
IT'S MAINLINING INTO YOUR BRAIN, BATMAN. THAT'S NOT GOOD, WHATEVER KIND OF INFORMATION YOU'RE RECEIVING. MY RING SHOULD BE ABLE TO ACCESS THE CHAIR'S DATABASE--
PING
THE RING'S LIMITED STORAGE CAPABILITIES AREN'T COMPATIBLE WITH MY CHAIR.
I APPRECIATE YOUR CONCERN, I DO, BUT I'VE HAD MORE EXPERIENCE WITH DARKSEID AND APOKOLIPS THAN MOST OF YOU.
BUT NOT WHILE HOOKED UP TO ANY ALIEN TECH.
WHEN MY DAD FIRST PLUGGED ME INTO A MOTHER BOX, I GOT A GLIMPSE OF APOKOLIPS THAT ALMOST DROVE ME MAD.
IF ANY ONE OF US CAN TAKE ON THAT CHAIR IT'S YOU, BATMAN. BUT MAYBE YOU SHOULDN'T RISK IT.
HE KEEPS FLOATING HIGHER ABOVE US.
DO I, COLONEL TREVOR?
BATMAN, COME DOWN AND TALK--
I CAN HANDLE THIS, DIANA.
I CAN.
"I SUPPOSE YOU WANT A THANK-YOU FOR SAVING MY LIFE?"

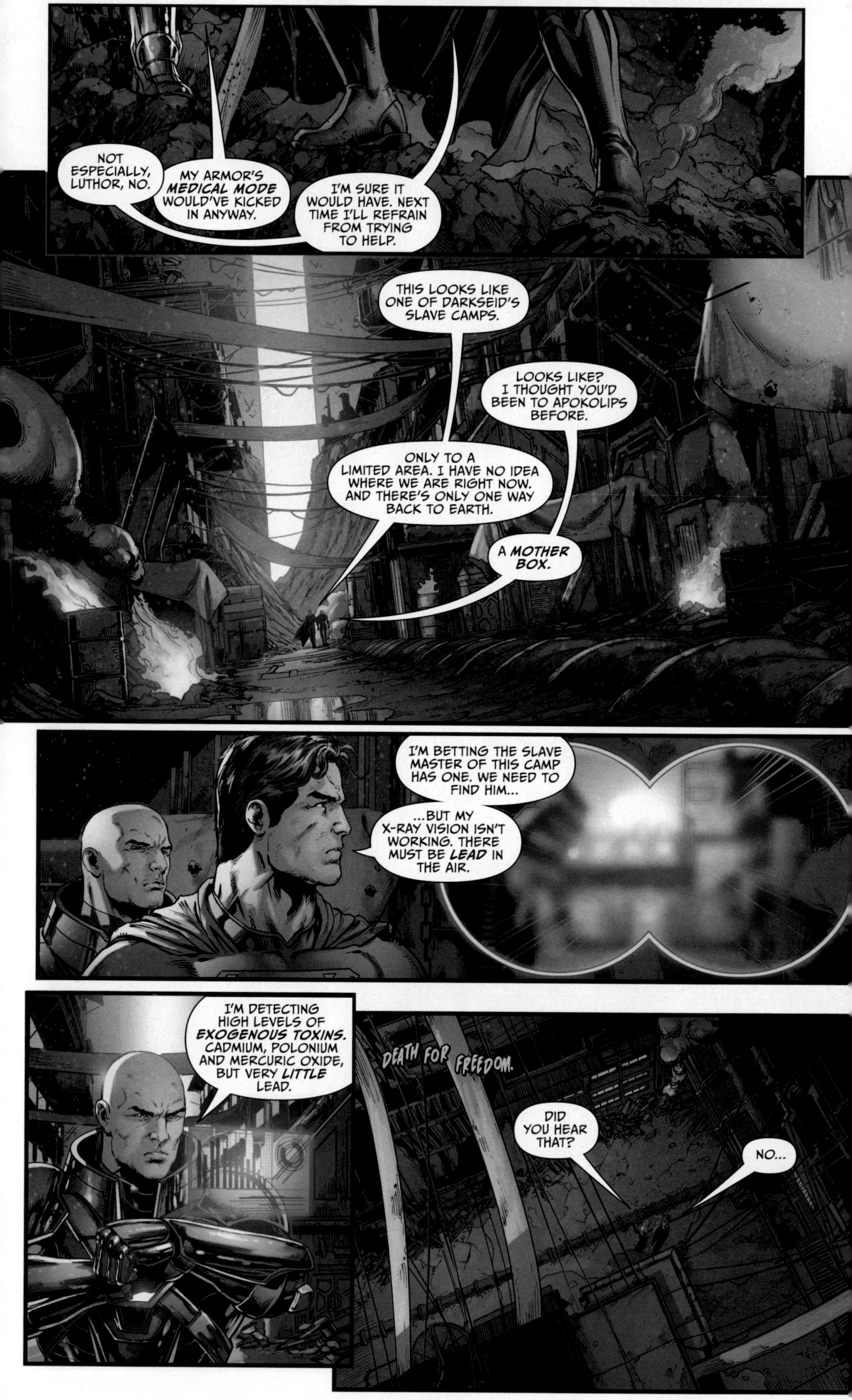
NOT ESPECIALLY, LUTHOR, NO.
MY ARMOR'S MEDICAL MODE WOULD'VE KICKED IN ANYWAY.
I'M SURE IT WOULD HAVE. NEXT TIME I'LL REFRAIN FROM TRYING TO HELP.
THIS LOOKS LIKE ONE OF DARKSEID'S SLAVE CAMPS.
LOOKS LIKE? I THOUGHT YOU'D BEEN TO APOKOLIPS BEFORE.
ONLY TO A LIMITED AREA. I HAVE NO IDEA WHERE WE ARE RIGHT NOW. AND THERE'S ONLY ONE WAY BACK TO EARTH.
A MOTHER BOX.
I'M BETTING THE SLAVE MASTER OF THIS CAMP HAS ONE. WE NEED TO FIND HIM...
...BUT MY X-RAY VISION ISN'T WORKING. THERE MUST BE LEAD IN THE AIR.
I'M DETECTING HIGH LEVELS OF EXOGENOUS TOXINS. CADMIUM, POLONIUM AND MERCURIC OXIDE, BUT VERY LITTLE LEAD.
DEATH FOR FREEDOM.
DID YOU HEAR THAT?
NO...

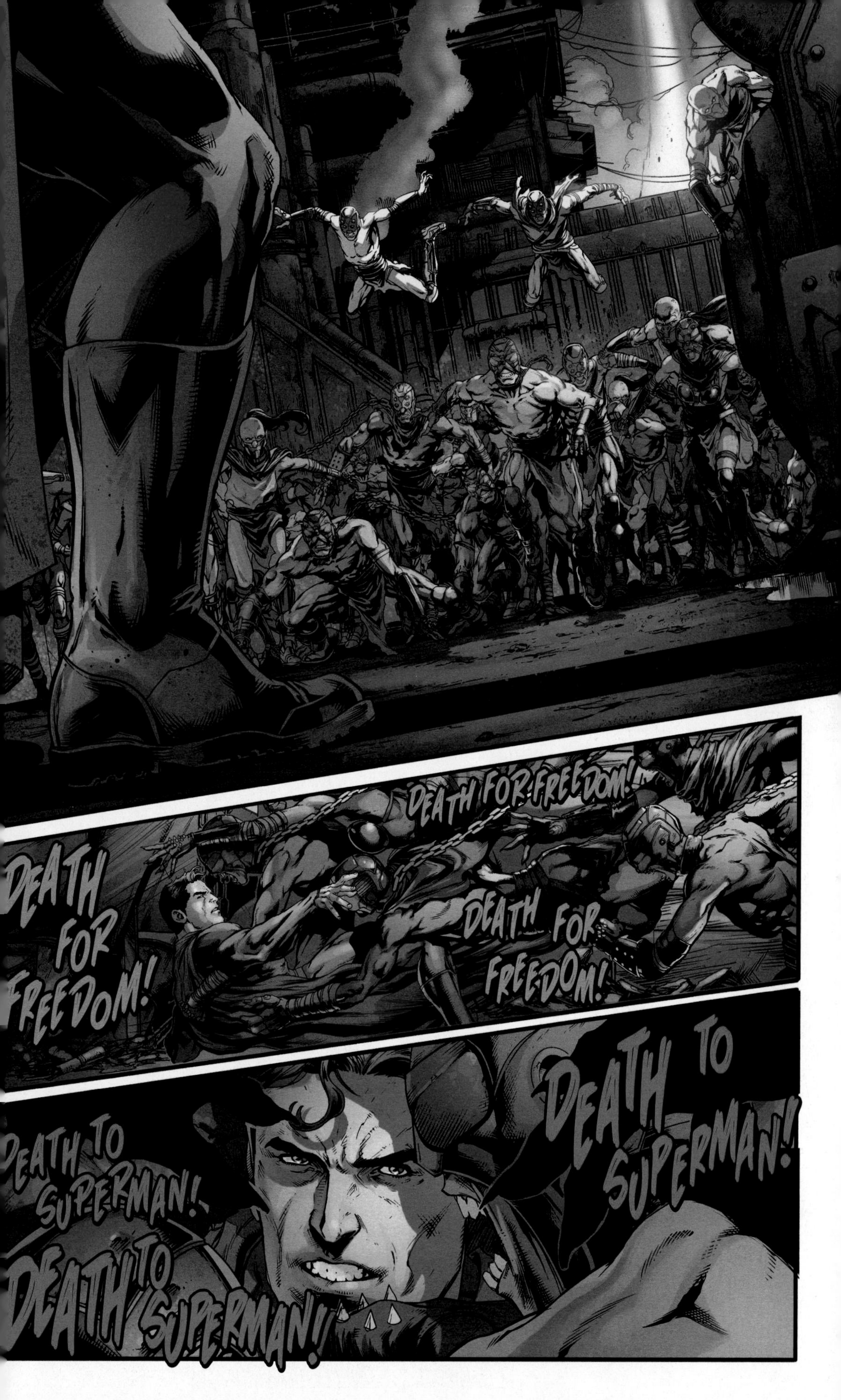
DEATH FOR FREEDOM!
DEATH FOR FREEDOM!
DEATH FOR FREEDOM!
DEATH TO SUPERMAN!
DEATH TO SUPERMAN!
DEATH TO SUPERMAN!

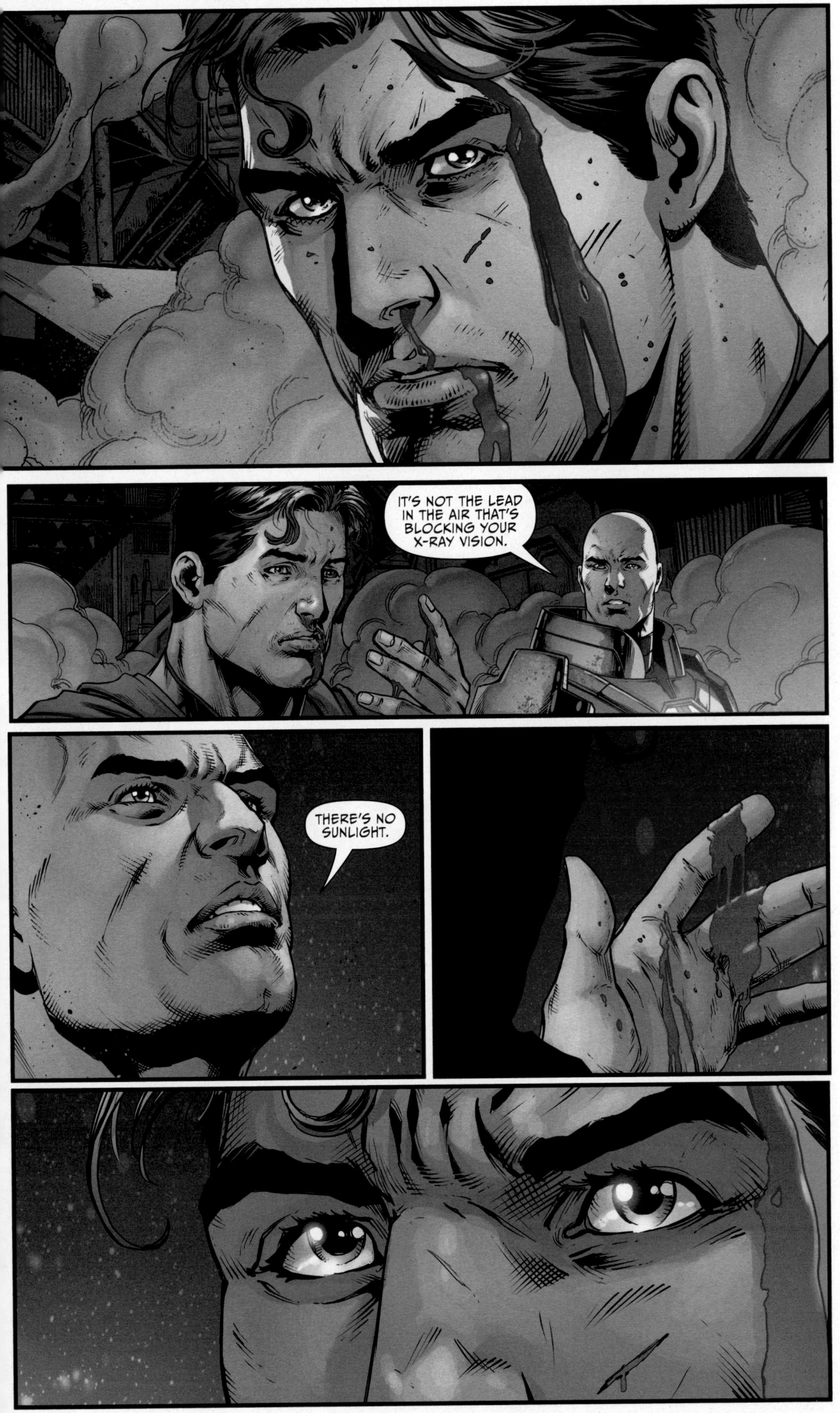
IT'S NOT THE LEAD IN THE AIR THAT'S BLOCKING YOUR X-RAY VISION.
THERE'S NO SUNLIGHT.

UH, WHAT ABOUT THIS DUDE?

HE STAYS HERE. SAFER FOR ALL OF US.

PING

CYBORG, I'M SYNCING MY MOTHER BOX JUMP COORDINATES WITH YOU.

PING PING

GOT 'EM.

HEY, GOOD LUCK, BATM--

BOOM BOOM

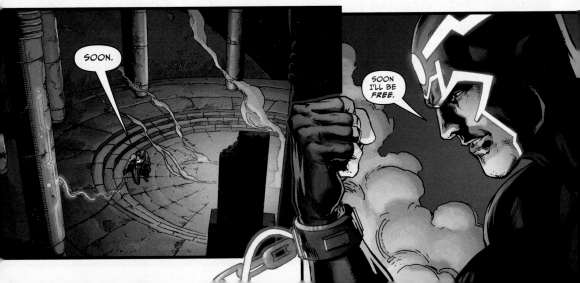

SOON.

SOON I'LL BE FREE.

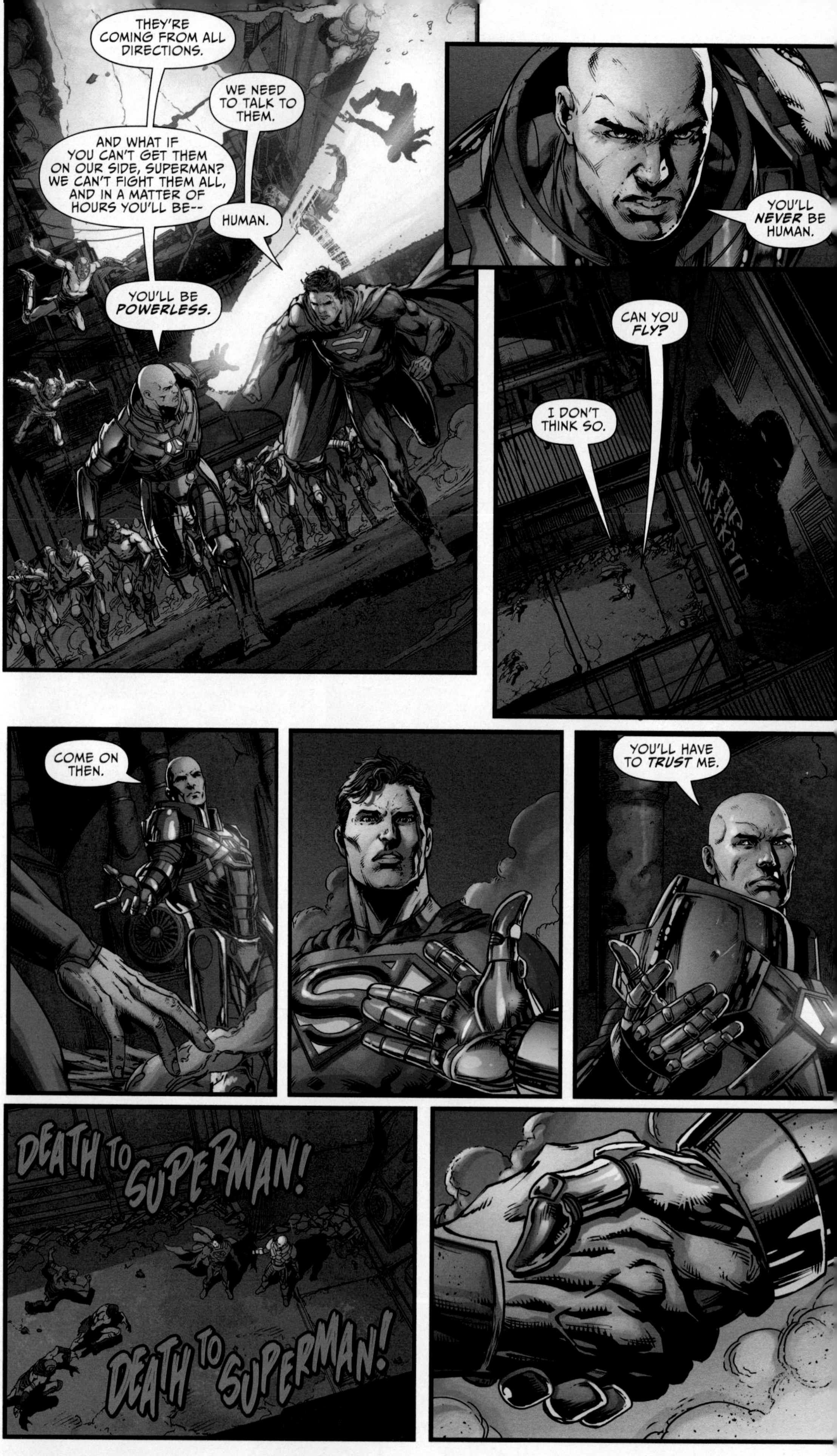
THEY'RE COMING FROM ALL DIRECTIONS.
WE NEED TO TALK TO THEM.
AND WHAT IF YOU CAN'T GET THEM ON OUR SIDE, SUPERMAN? WE CAN'T FIGHT THEM ALL, AND IN A MATTER OF HOURS YOU'LL BE--
HUMAN.
YOU'LL BE POWERLESS.
YOU'LL NEVER BE HUMAN.
CAN YOU FLY?
I DON'T THINK SO.
COME ON THEN.
YOU'LL HAVE TO TRUST ME.
DEATH TO SUPERMAN!
DEATH TO SUPERMAN!

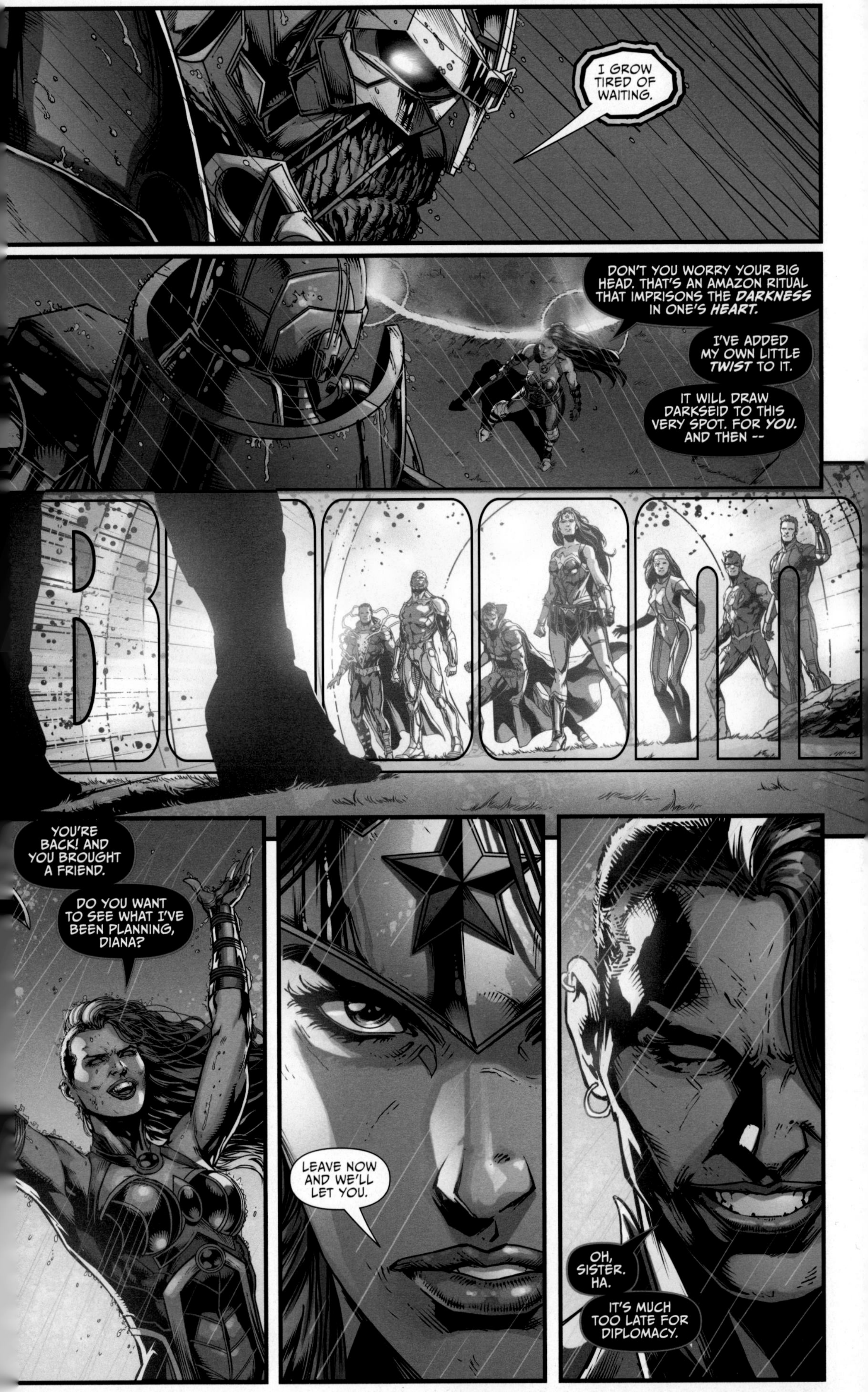

I GROW TIRED OF WAITING.
DON'T YOU WORRY YOUR BIG HEAD. THAT'S AN AMAZON RITUAL THAT IMPRISONS THE *DARKNESS* IN ONE'S *HEART.*
I'VE ADDED MY OWN LITTLE *TWIST* TO IT.
IT WILL DRAW DARKSEID TO THIS VERY SPOT. FOR *YOU.* AND THEN --
BOOOM
YOU'RE BACK! AND YOU BROUGHT A FRIEND.
DO YOU WANT TO SEE WHAT I'VE BEEN PLANNING, DIANA?
LEAVE NOW AND WE'LL LET YOU.
OH, SISTER. HA.
IT'S MUCH TOO LATE FOR DIPLOMACY.

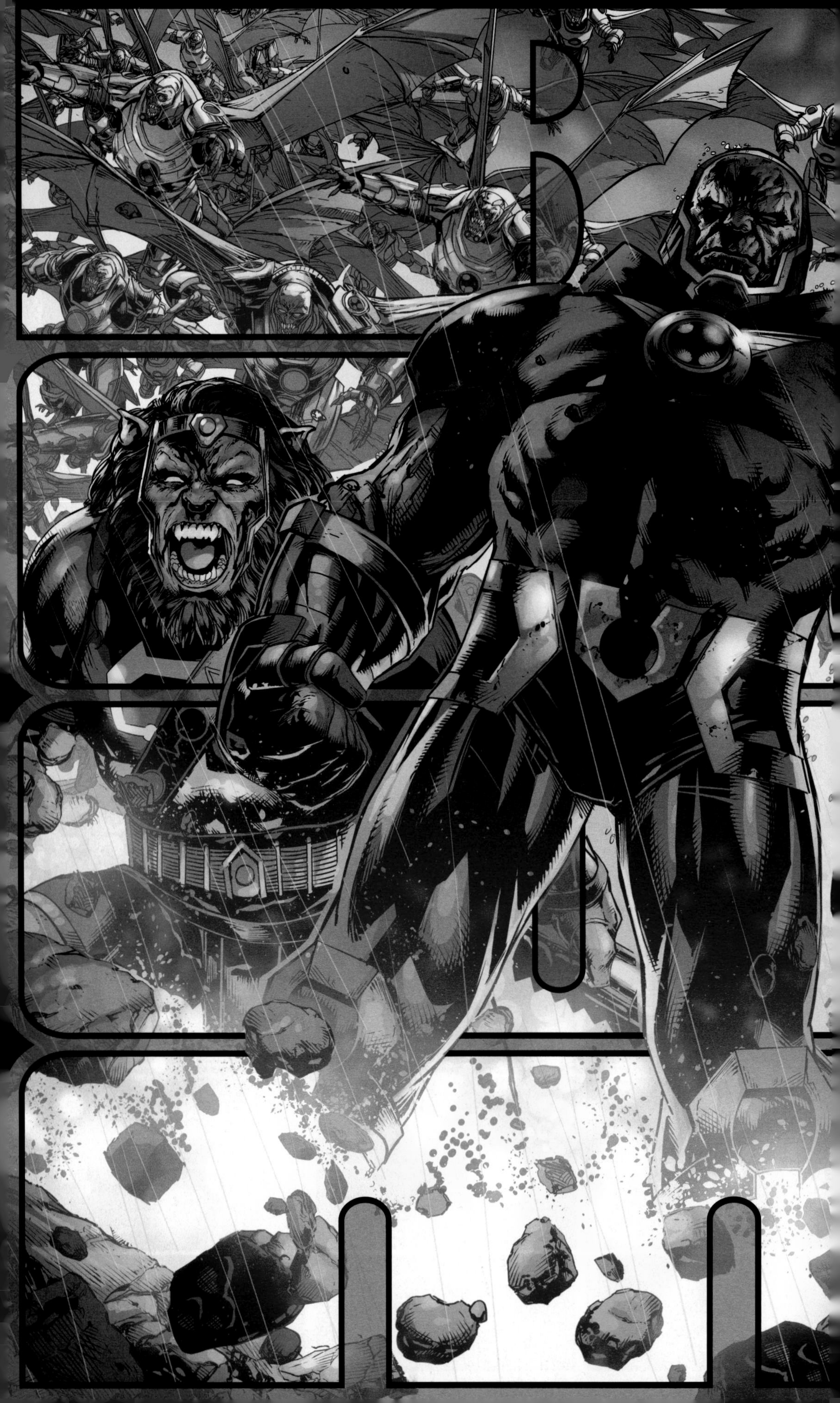

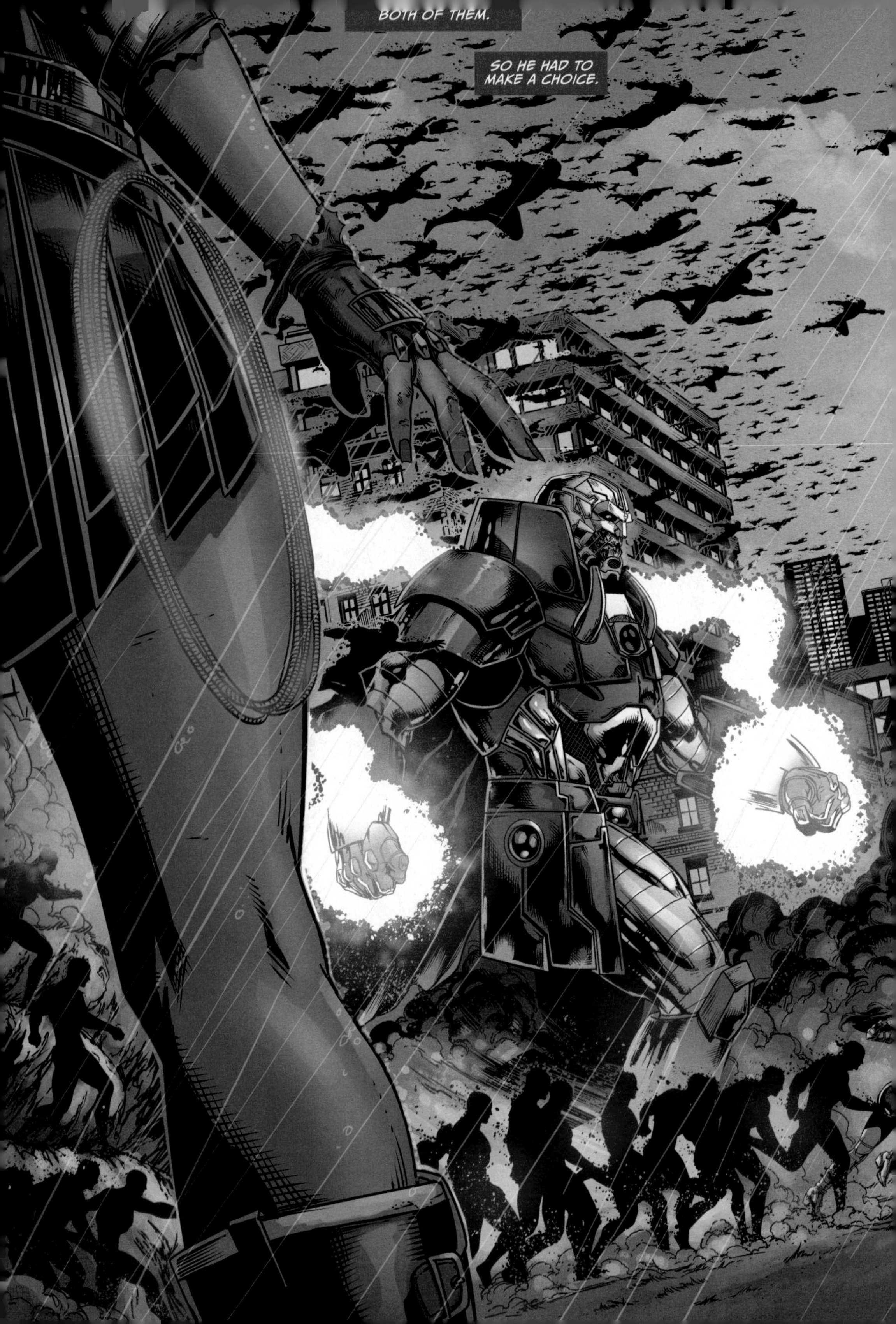
BOTH OF THEM.
SO HE HAD TO MAKE A CHOICE.

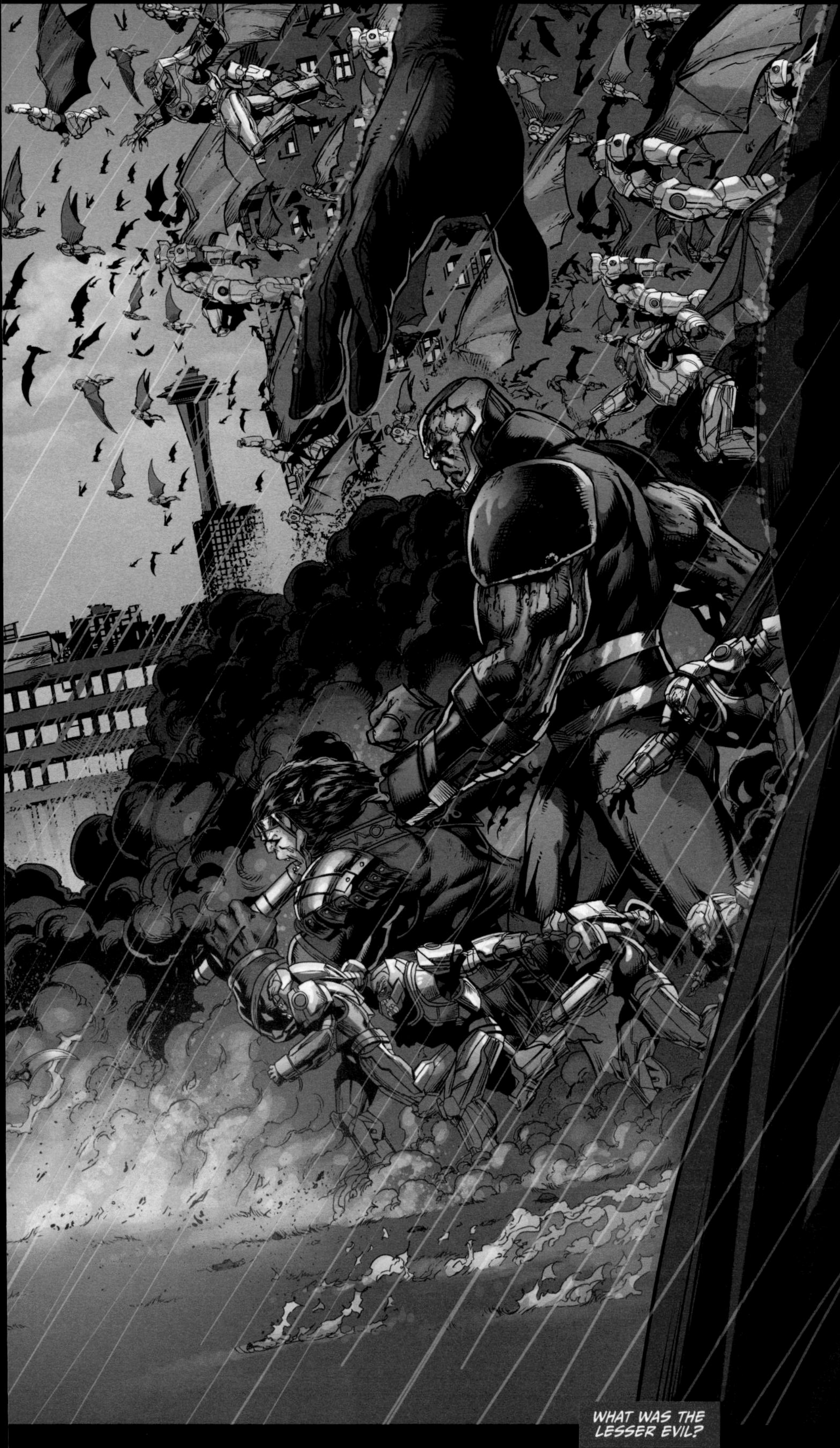
WHAT WAS THE LESSER EVIL?

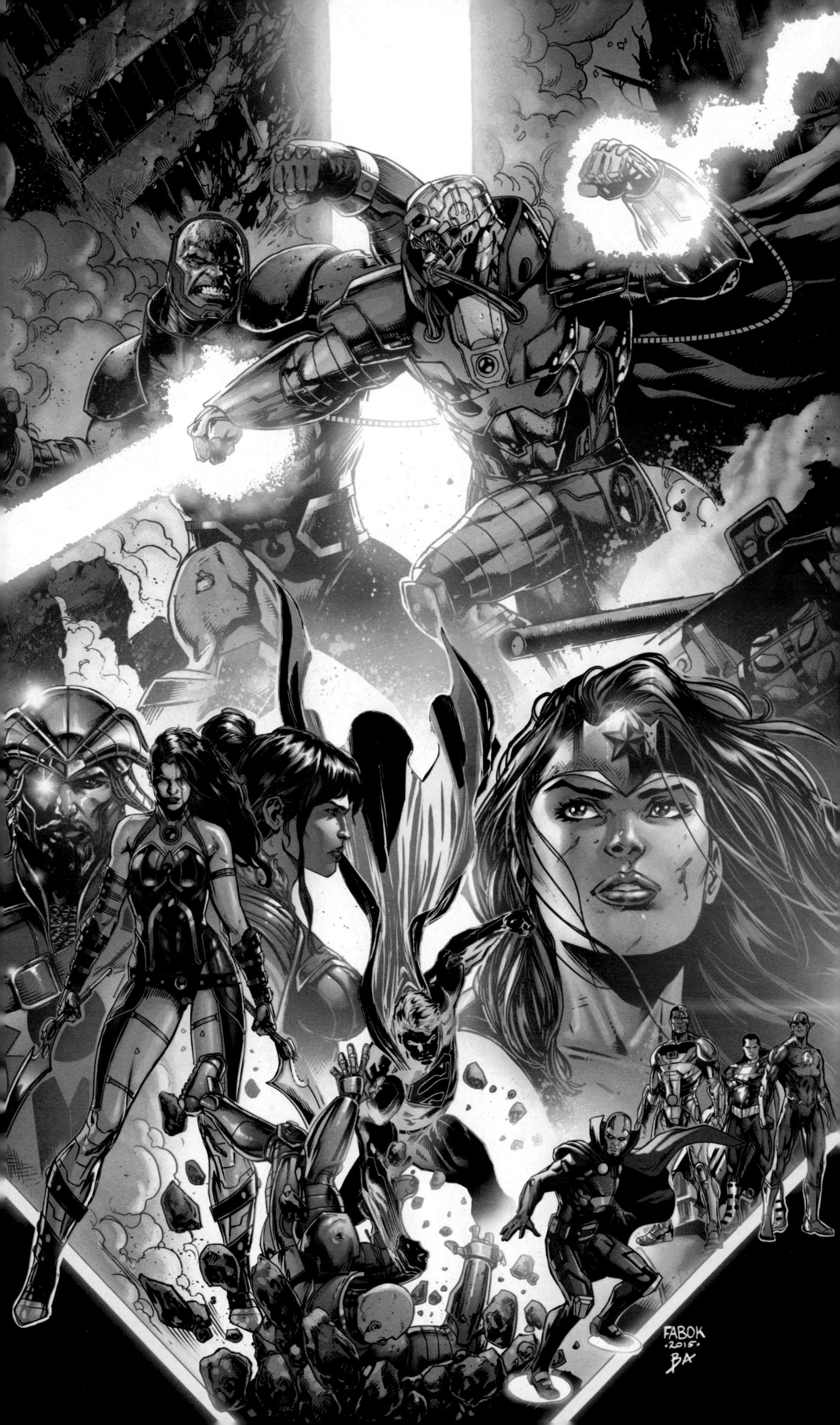
FABOK
·2015·
BA

THERE WAS ONE GOD MY MOTHER HATED ABOVE ALL OTHERS.

HIS NAME WAS GELOS.

THE GOD OF LAUGHTER.

MY MOTHER DIDN'T DESPISE GELOS BECAUSE THE AMAZONS DON'T BELIEVE IN LAUGHTER.

THEY DO.

IT MIGHT NOT APPEAR EVIDENT AT TIMES, BUT THEY BELIEVE IN JOY, HAPPINESS AND LOVE.

GELOS DID NOT.

HE FOLLOWED MY MOTHER LIKE A SHADOW ACROSS THE BATTLEFIELDS. LAUGHING AT THOSE IN PAIN. JEERING AT MEN AND WOMEN DYING.

HE WAS INVISIBLE TO US, BUT NO MATTER WHERE YOU STOOD, YOU COULD HEAR HIS CACKLING.

IT HAUNTED HER.

BRUCE?

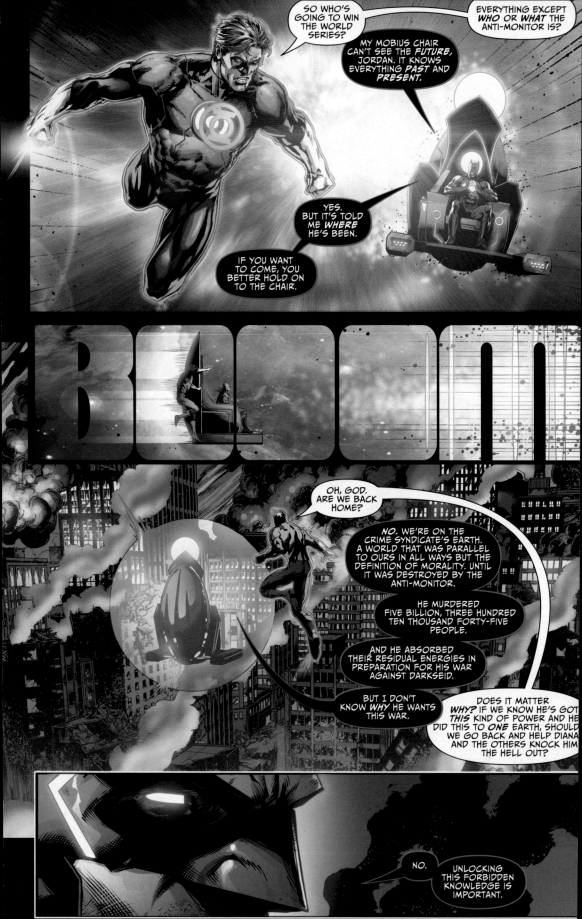

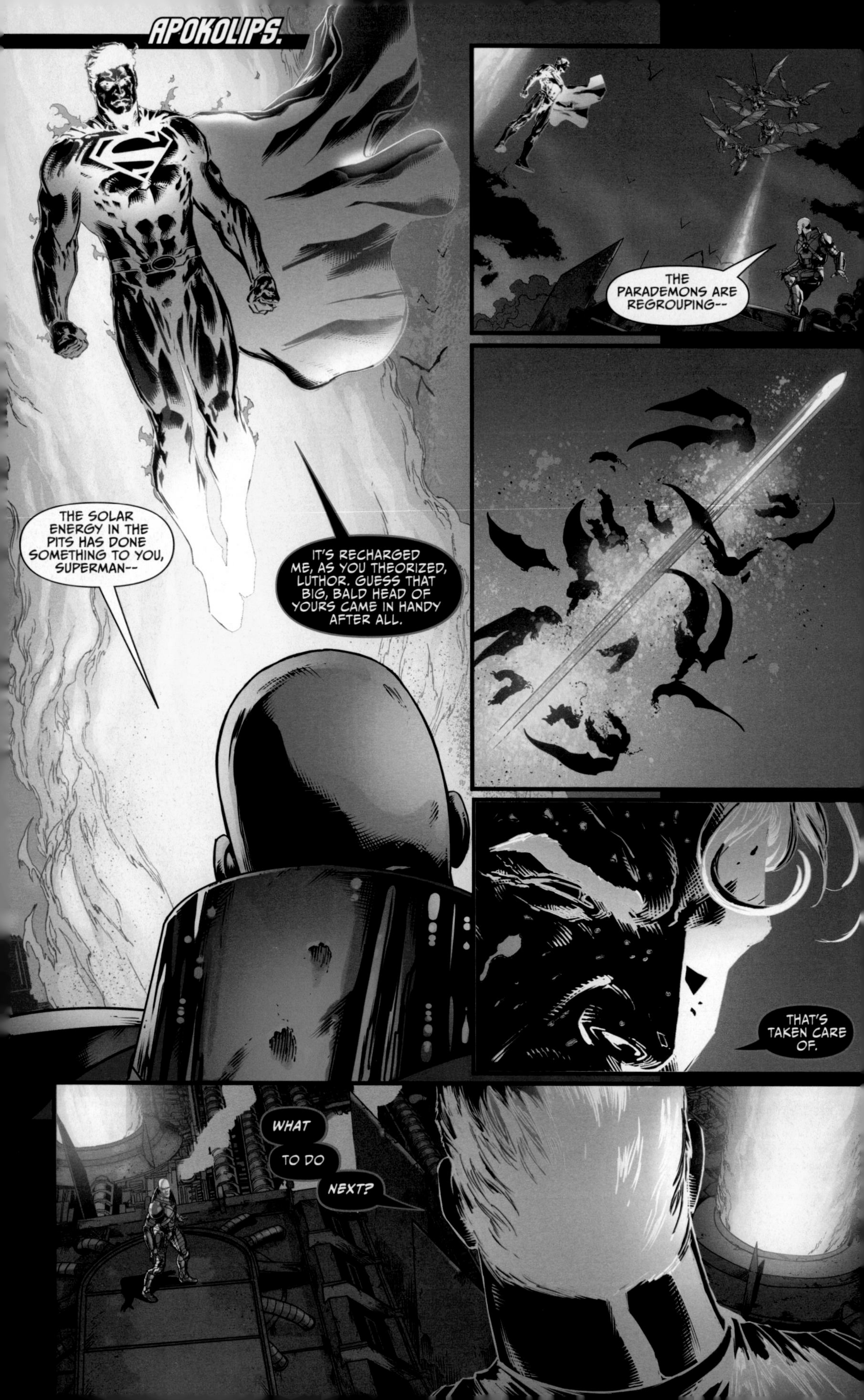
APOKOLIPS.
THE PARADEMONS ARE REGROUPING--
THE SOLAR ENERGY IN THE PITS HAS DONE SOMETHING TO YOU, SUPERMAN--
IT'S RECHARGED ME, AS YOU THEORIZED, LUTHOR. GUESS THAT BIG, BALD HEAD OF YOURS CAME IN HANDY AFTER ALL.
THAT'S TAKEN CARE OF.
WHAT
TO DO
NEXT?

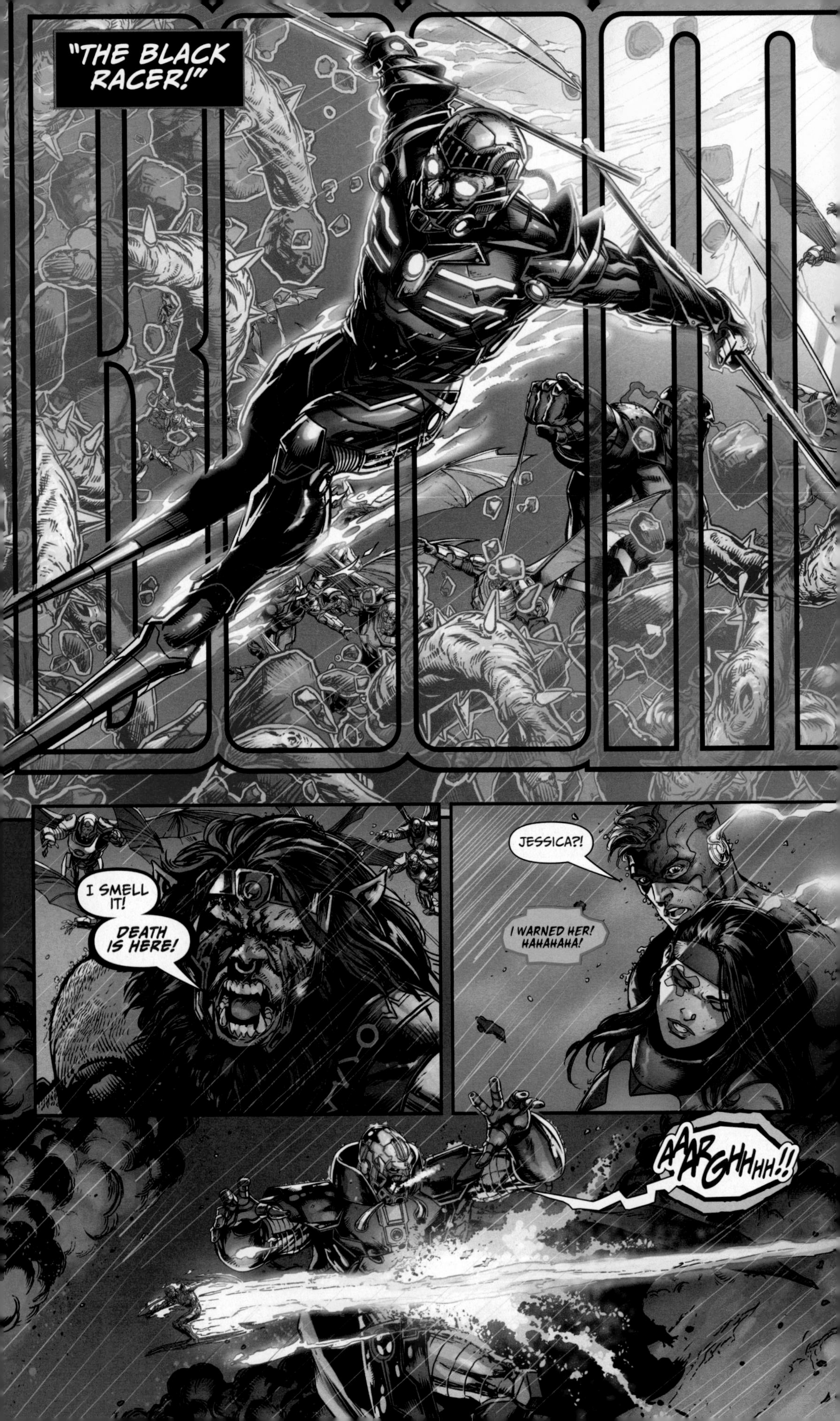
"THE BLACK RACER!"
BOOM
I SMELL IT!
DEATH IS HERE!
JESSICA?!
I WARNED HER! HAHAHAHA!
AAARGHHHH!!

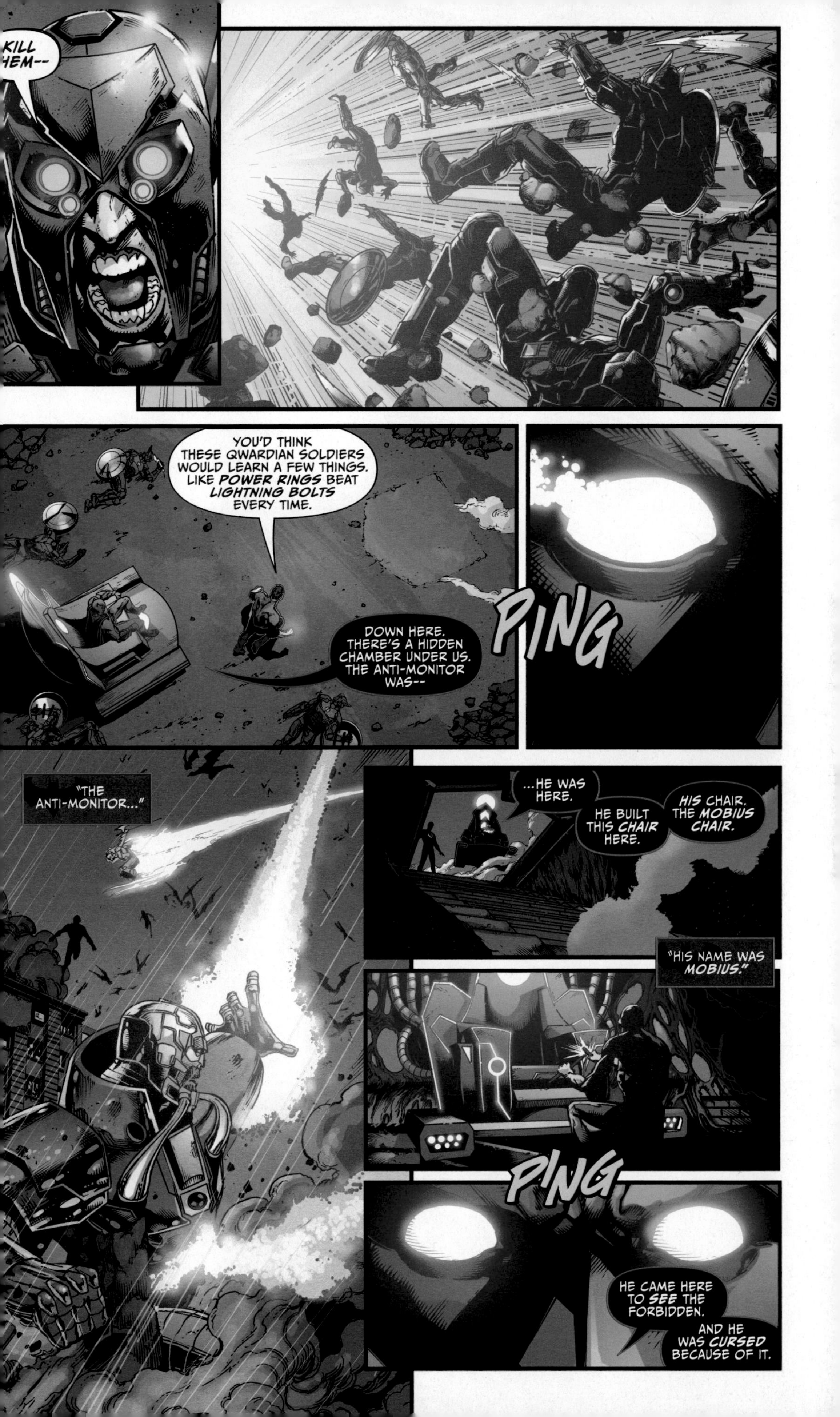
KILL THEM--
YOU'D THINK THESE QWARDIAN SOLDIERS WOULD LEARN A FEW THINGS. LIKE POWER RINGS BEAT LIGHTNING BOLTS EVERY TIME.
DOWN HERE. THERE'S A HIDDEN CHAMBER UNDER US. THE ANTI-MONITOR WAS--
PING
"THE ANTI-MONITOR..."
...HE WAS HERE.
HE BUILT THIS CHAIR HERE.
HIS CHAIR. THE MOBIUS CHAIR.
"HIS NAME WAS MOBIUS."
PING
HE CAME HERE TO SEE THE FORBIDDEN.
AND HE WAS CURSED BECAUSE OF IT.

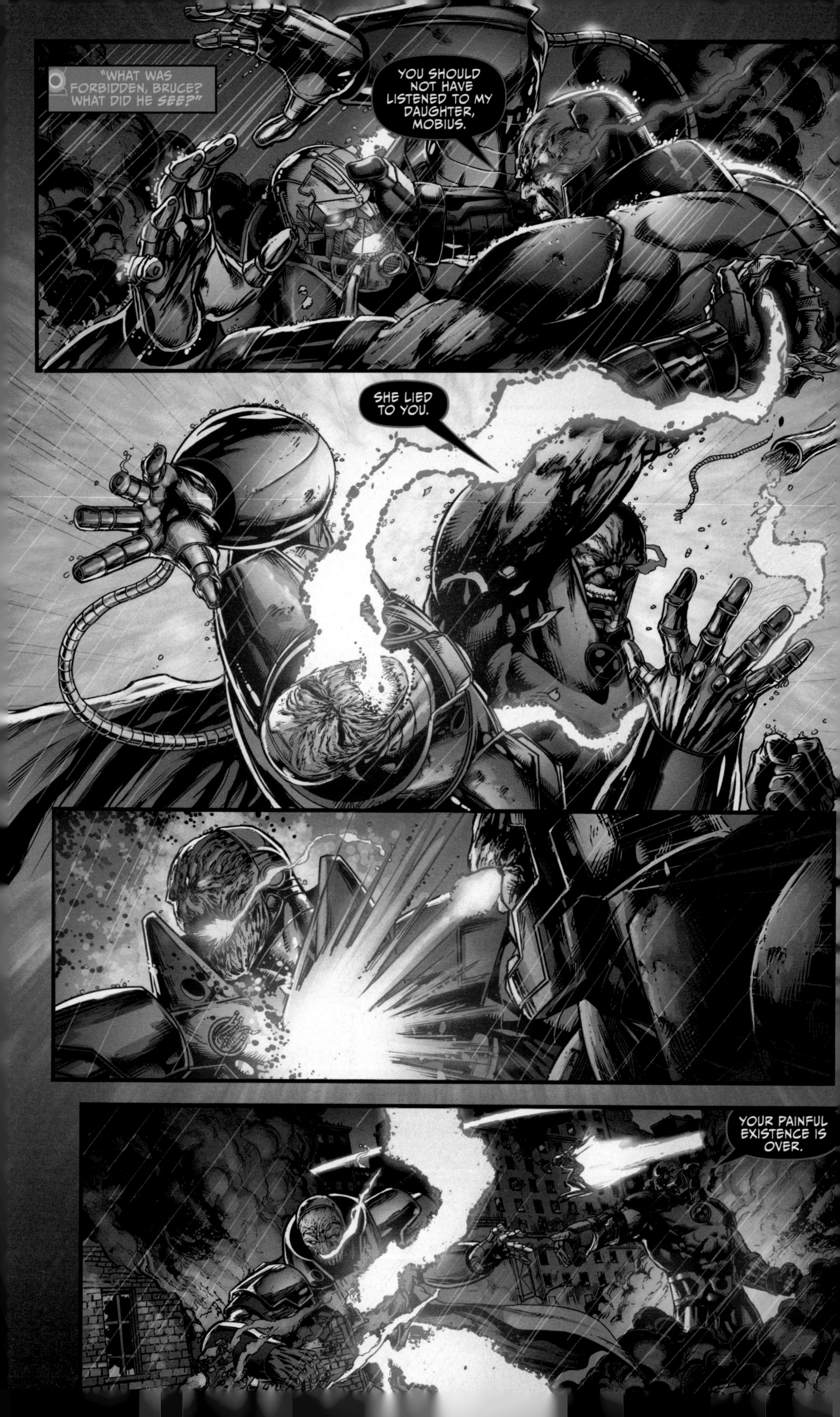
"WHAT WAS FORBIDDEN, BRUCE? WHAT DID HE SEE?"
YOU SHOULD NOT HAVE LISTENED TO MY DAUGHTER, MOBIUS.
SHE LIED TO YOU.
YOUR PAINFUL EXISTENCE IS OVER.

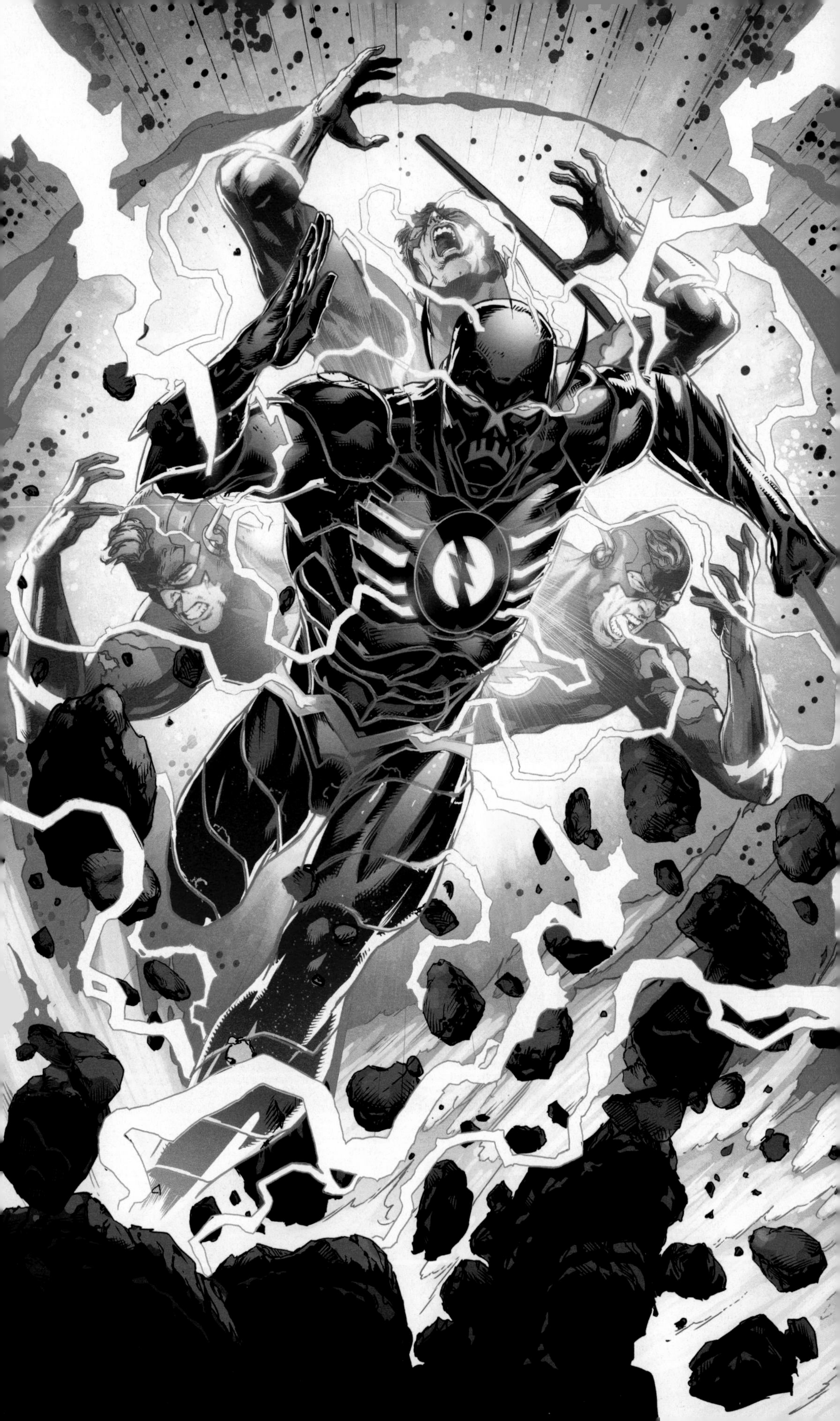

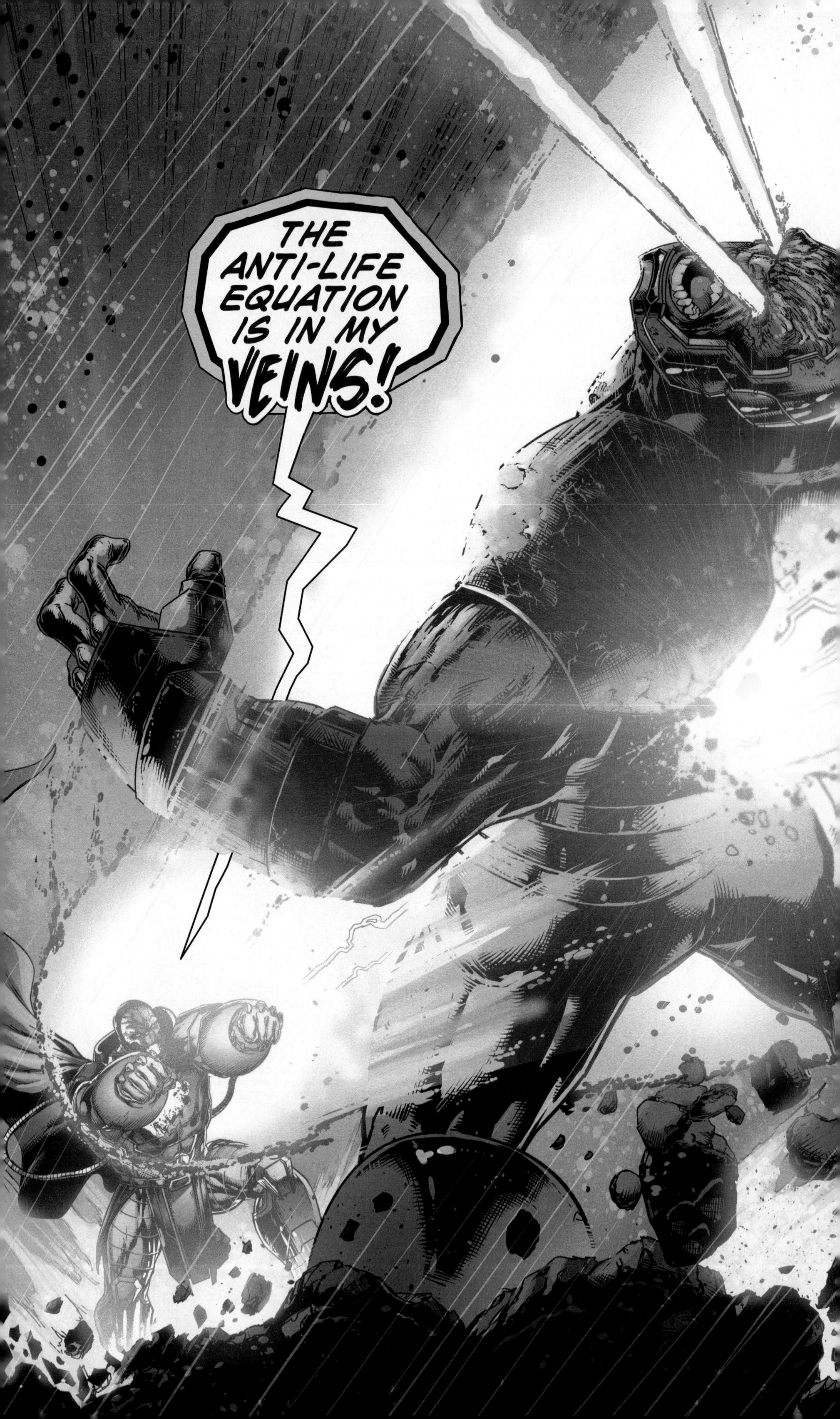
THE ANTI-LIFE EQUATION IS IN MY VEINS!

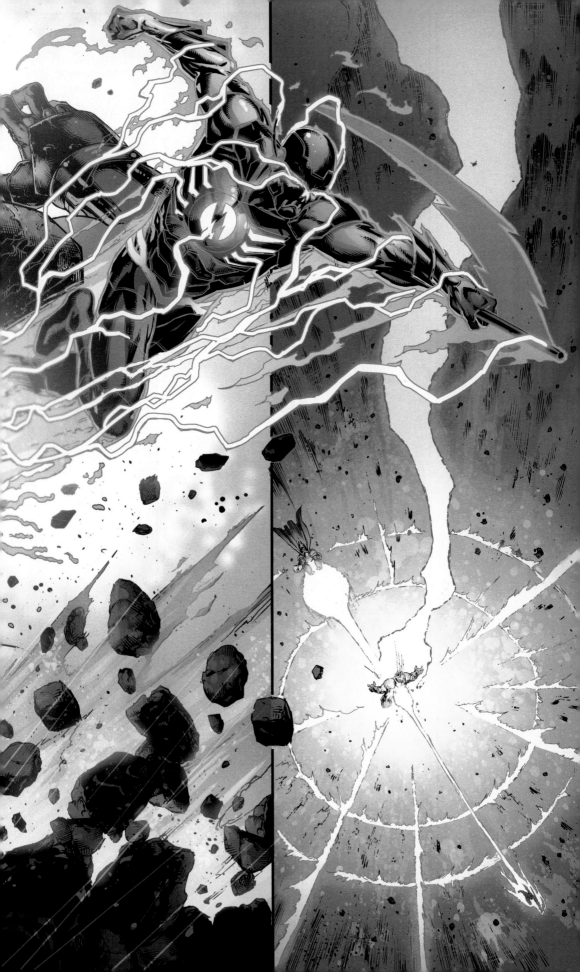

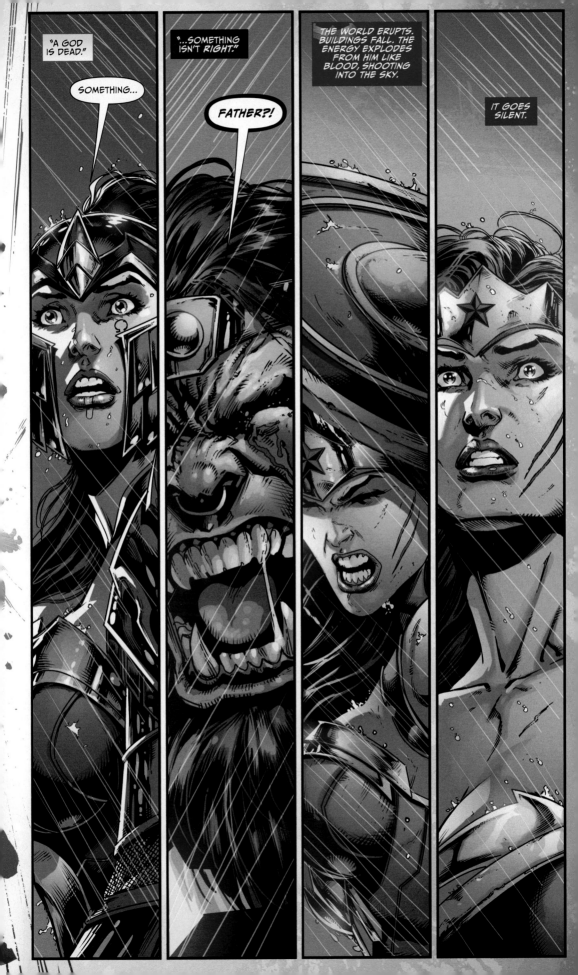

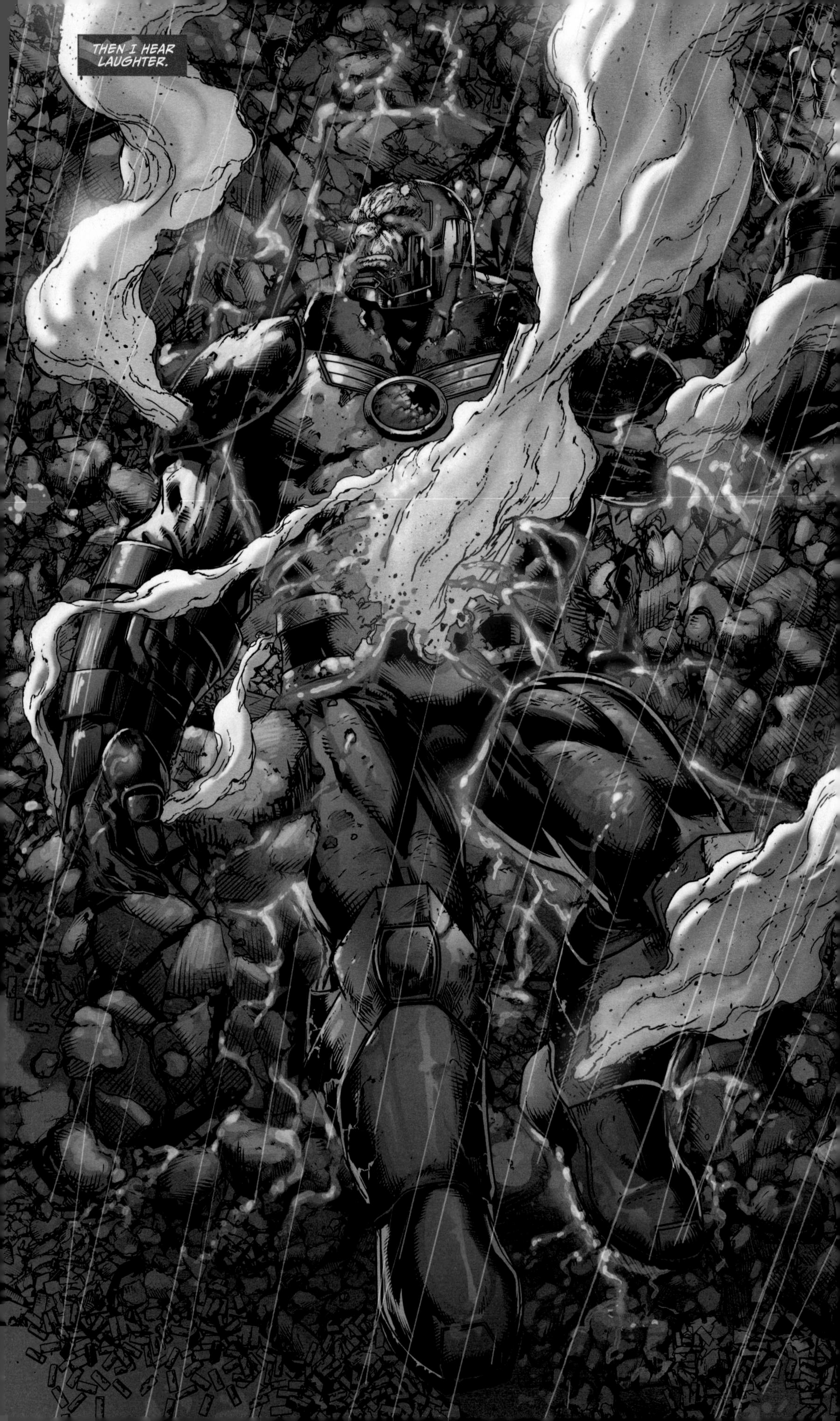
THEN I HEAR LAUGHTER.

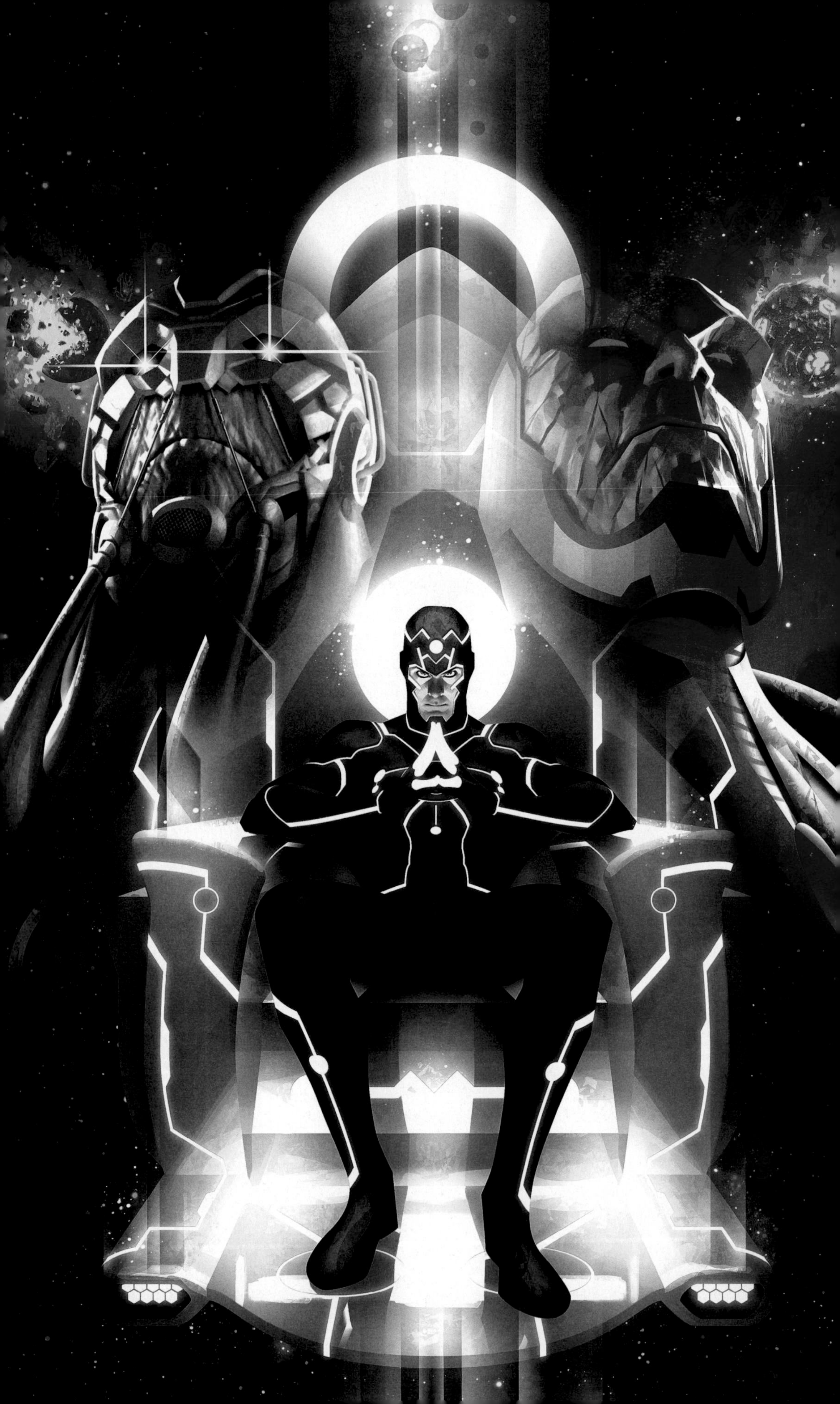

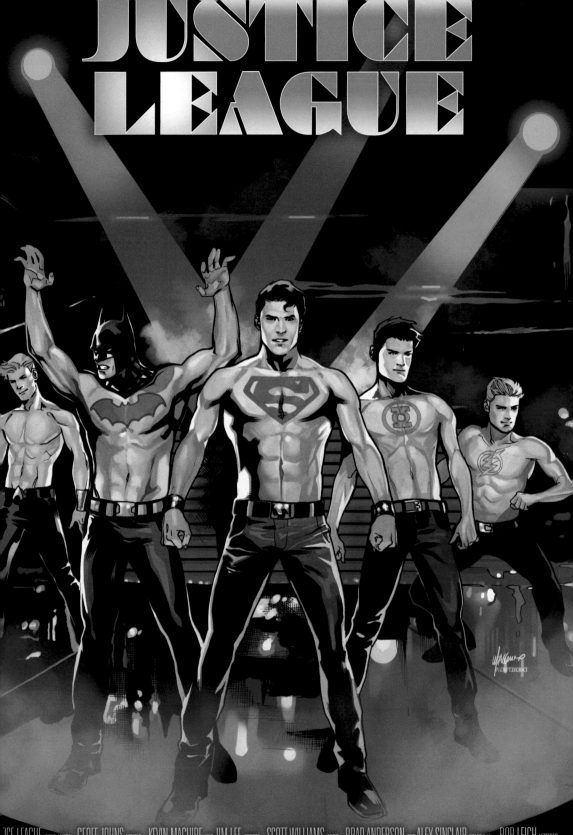

ICE LEAGUE ISSUE FORTY GEOFF JOHNS WRITER KEVIN MAGUIRE AND JIM LEE ARTISTS SCOTT WILLIAMS INKER BRAD ANDERSON AND ALEX SINCLAIR COLORISTS ROB LEIGH LETTERER
EMANUELA LUPACCHINO MOVIE POSTER VARIANT COVER AMEDEO TURTURRO ASSISTANT EDITOR BRIAN CUNNINGHAM GROUP EDITOR BOB HARRAS SENIOR VP — EDITOR-IN-CHIEF, DC COMICS
RATED T TEEN DAN DIDIO AND JIM LEE CO-PUBLISHERS GEOFF JOHNS CHIEF CREATIVE OFFICER DIANE NELSON PRESIDENT

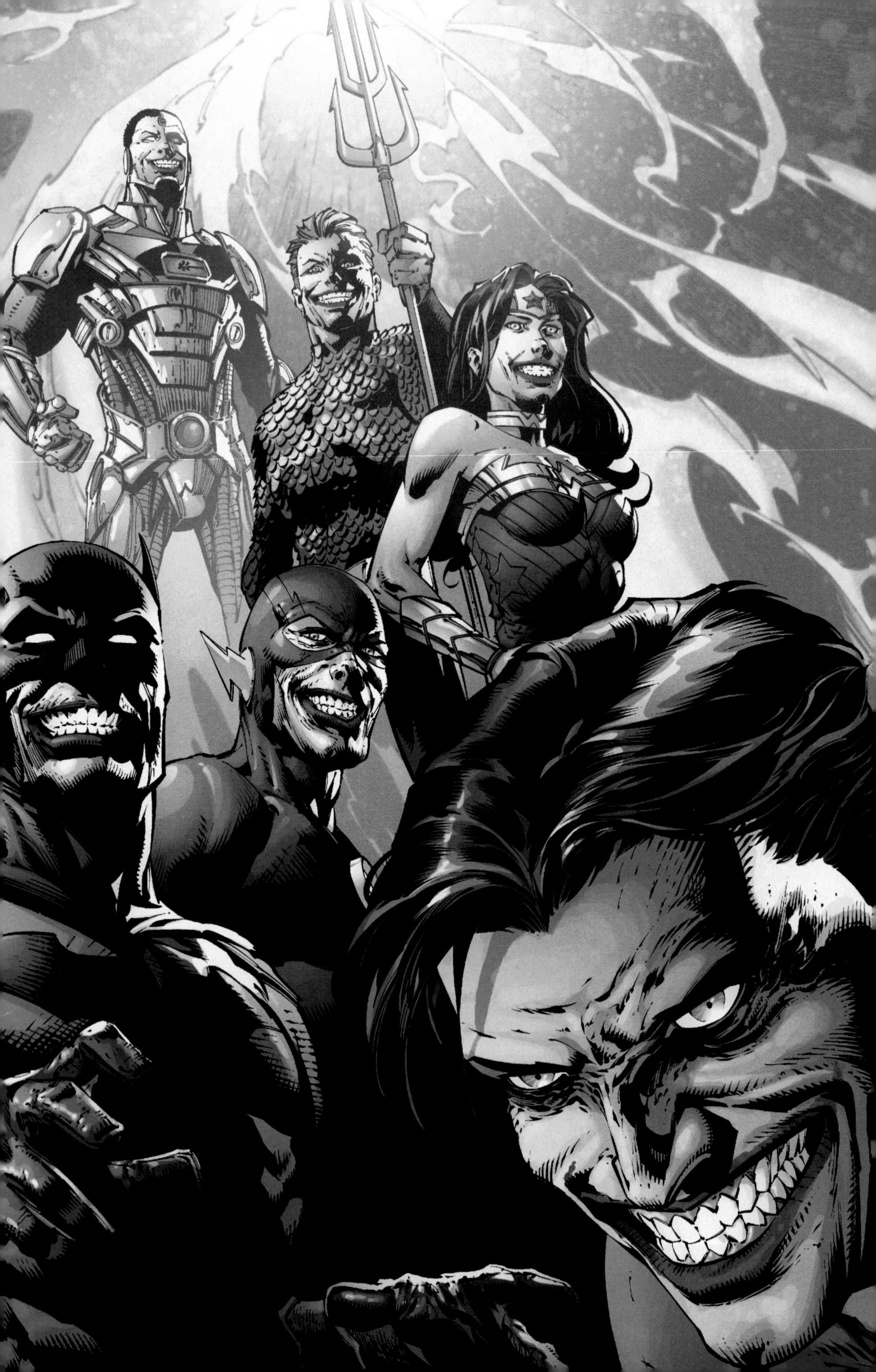

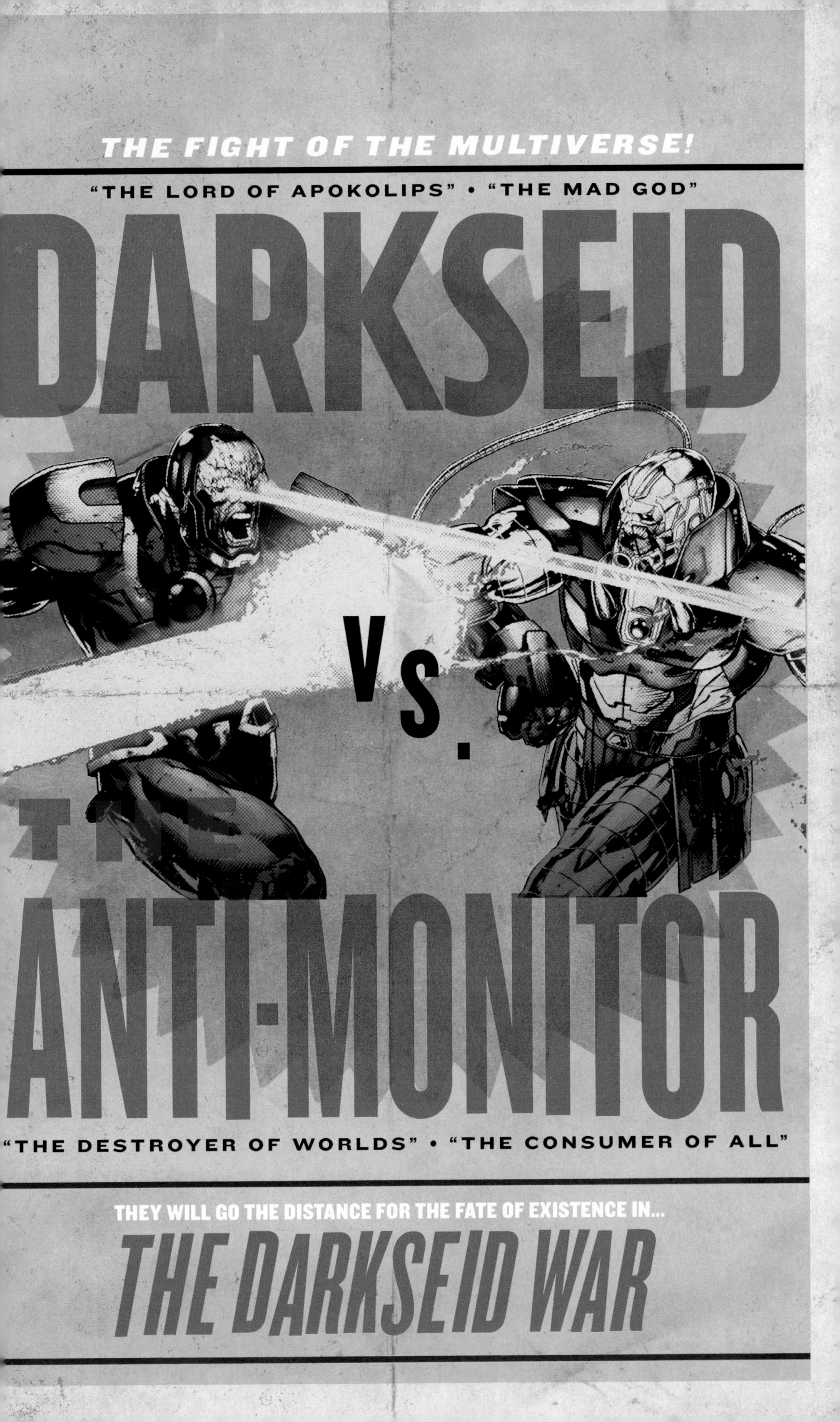
THE FIGHT OF THE MULTIVERSE!
"THE LORD OF APOKOLIPS" • "THE MAD GOD"
DARKSEID
VS.
THE
ANTI-MONITOR
"THE DESTROYER OF WORLDS" • "THE CONSUMER OF ALL"
THEY WILL GO THE DISTANCE FOR THE FATE OF EXISTENCE IN...
THE DARKSEID WAR

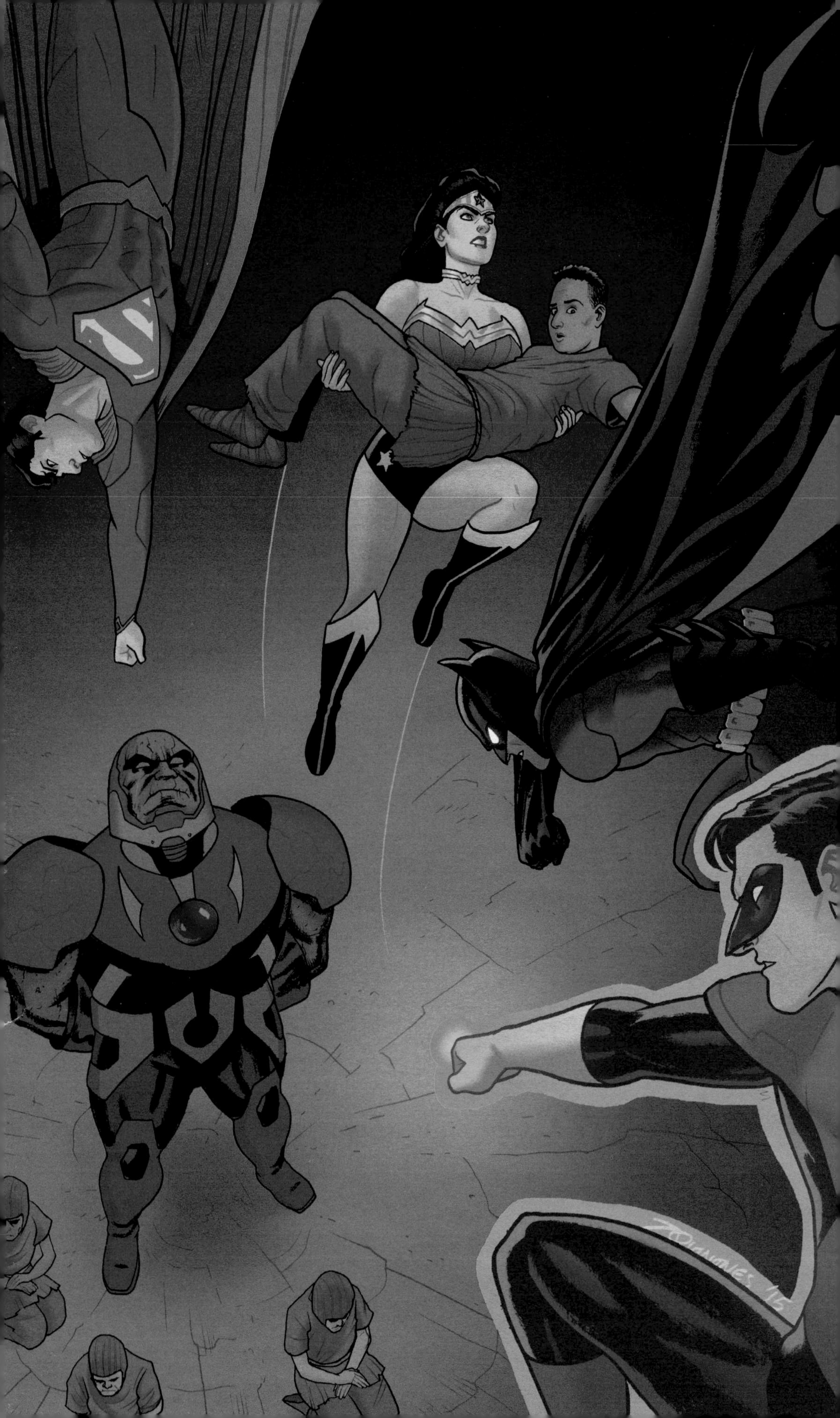

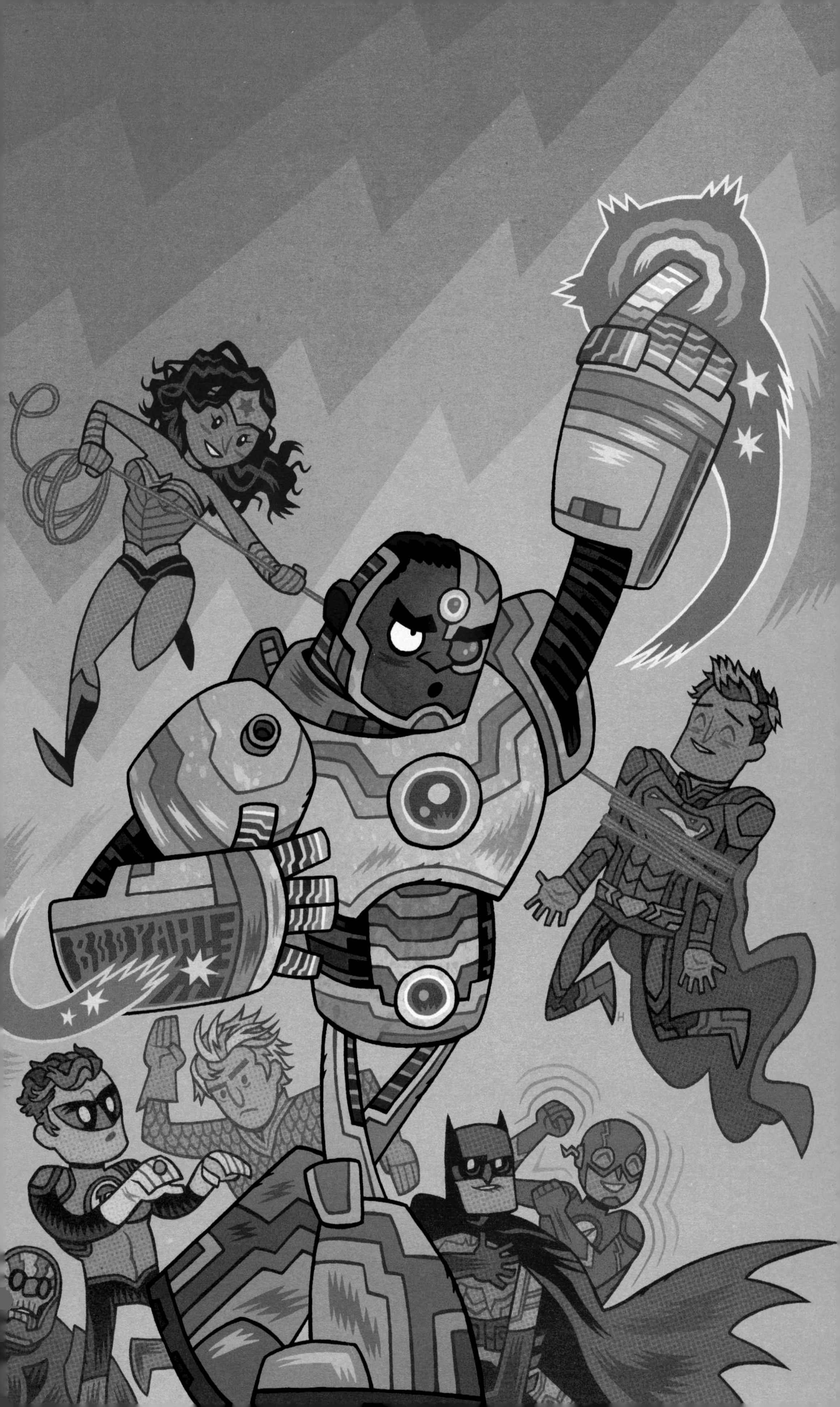

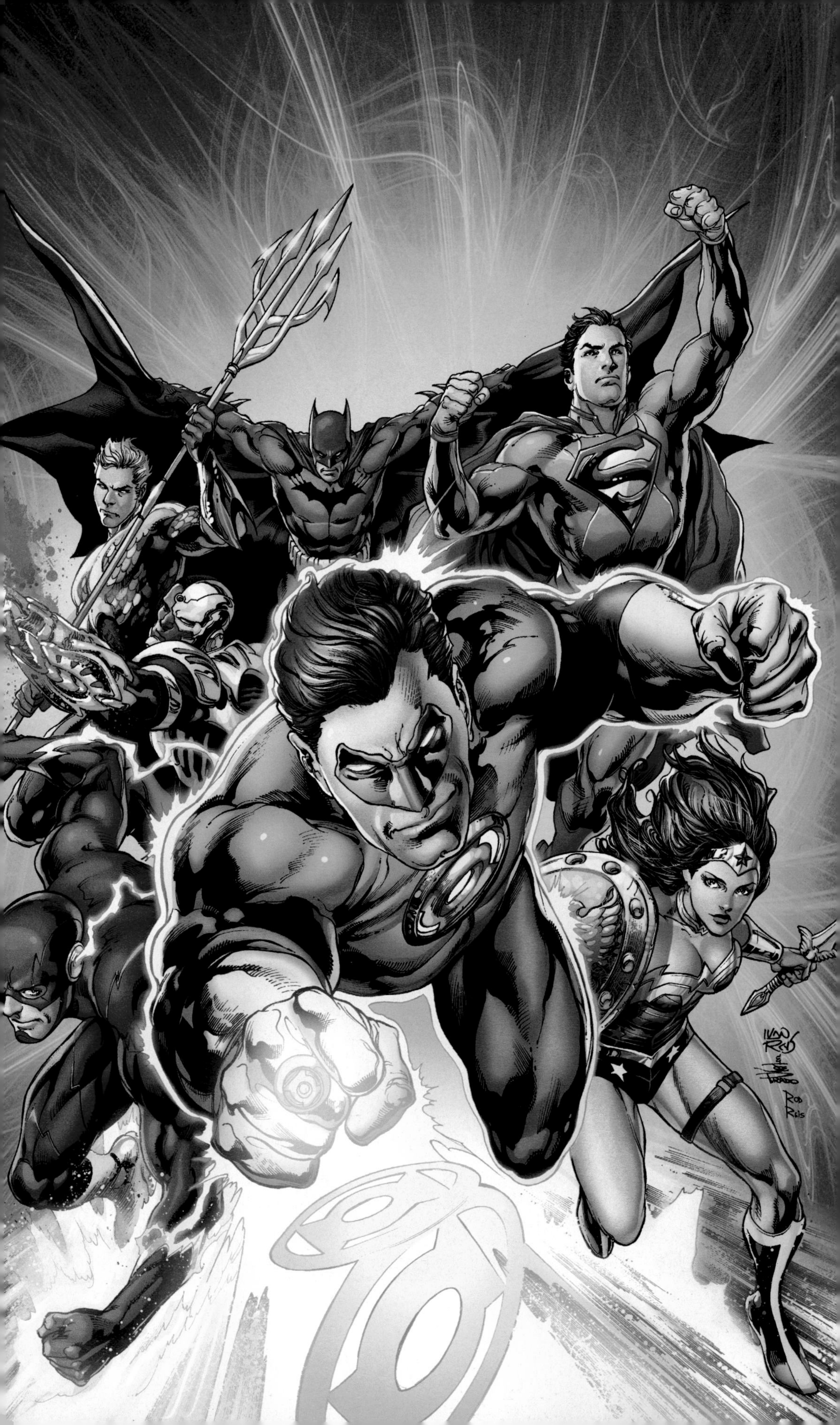
Rod Reis

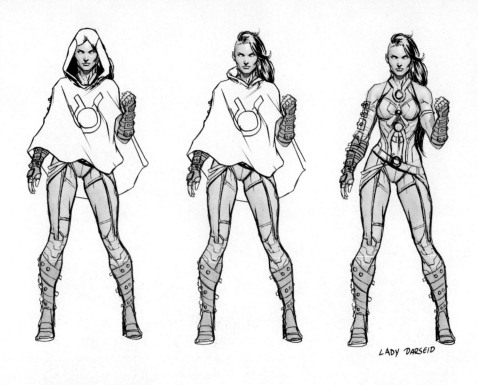

LADY DARSEID

LADY DARSEID
FABOK '14

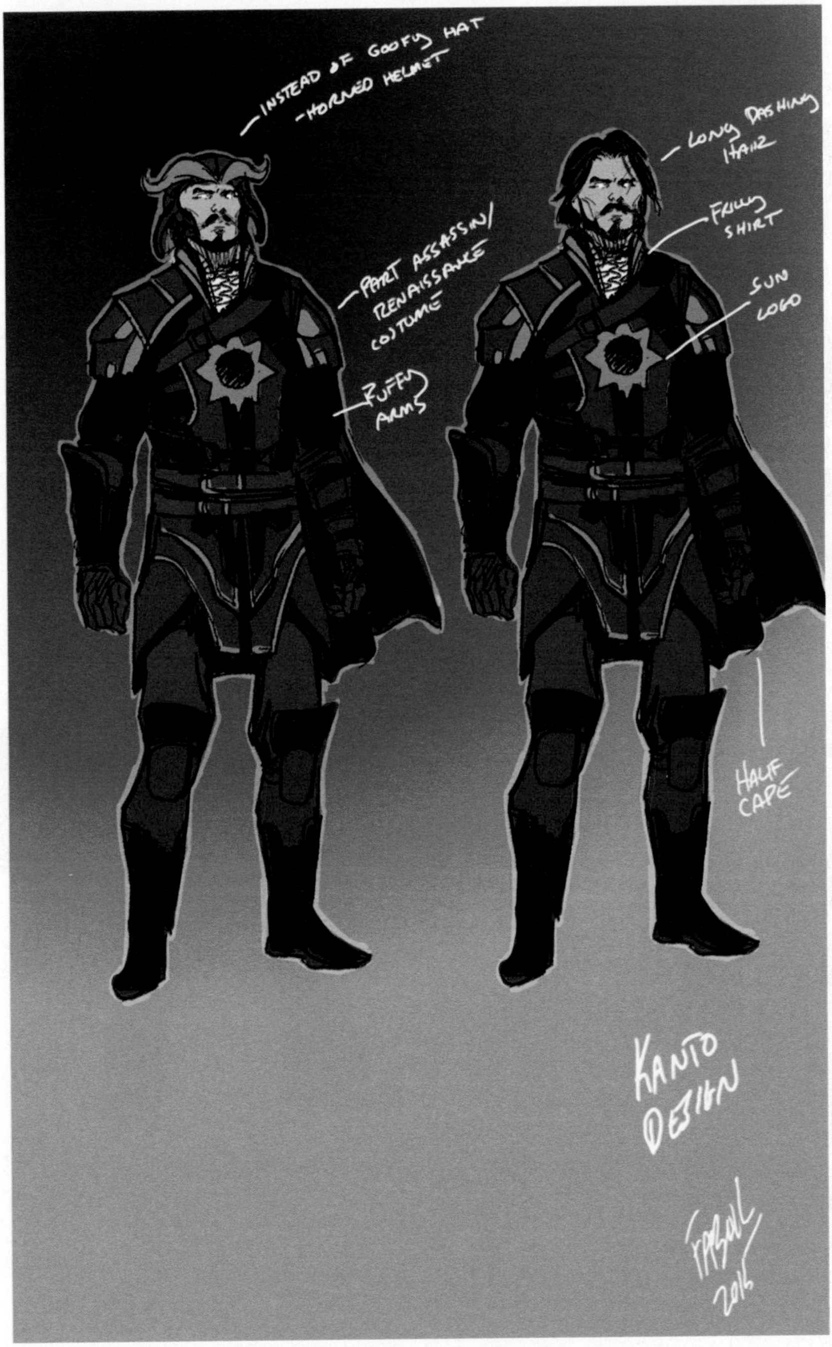

INSTEAD OF GOOFY HAT
-HORNED HELMET
LONG DASHING HAIR
PART ASSASSIN/ RENAISSANCE COSTUME
FRILLY SHIRT
SUN LOGO
RUFFY ARMS
HALF CAPÉ
KANTO DESIGN
2016

LOTS OF THESE
SHAPES

RELIEF
EDGES

COLORS:
- WHITE
- DEEP GREY/BLUE
- YELLOW

- CONTRAST THE
BLACK, BLUE,
DARK GREY,
OF DARKSEID

ANTI-MONITOR
ROUGH DESIGN
J. FABOK
2015

ANTI-MONITOR
ROUGH DESIGN
J. FABOK
2015

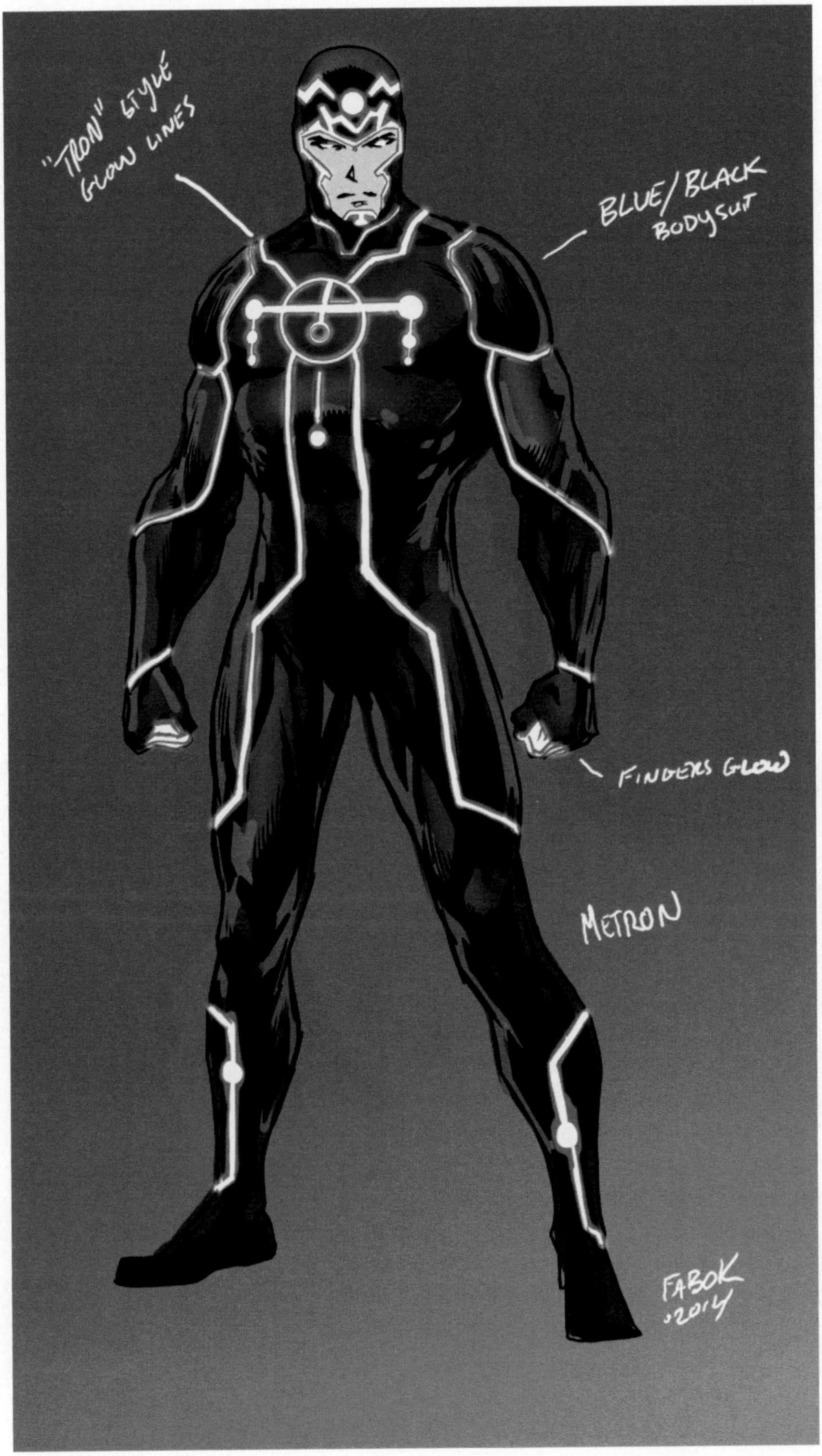

"TRON" STYLE
GLOW LINES
BLUE/BLACK
BODYSUIT
FINGERS GLOW
METRON
FABOK
©2014

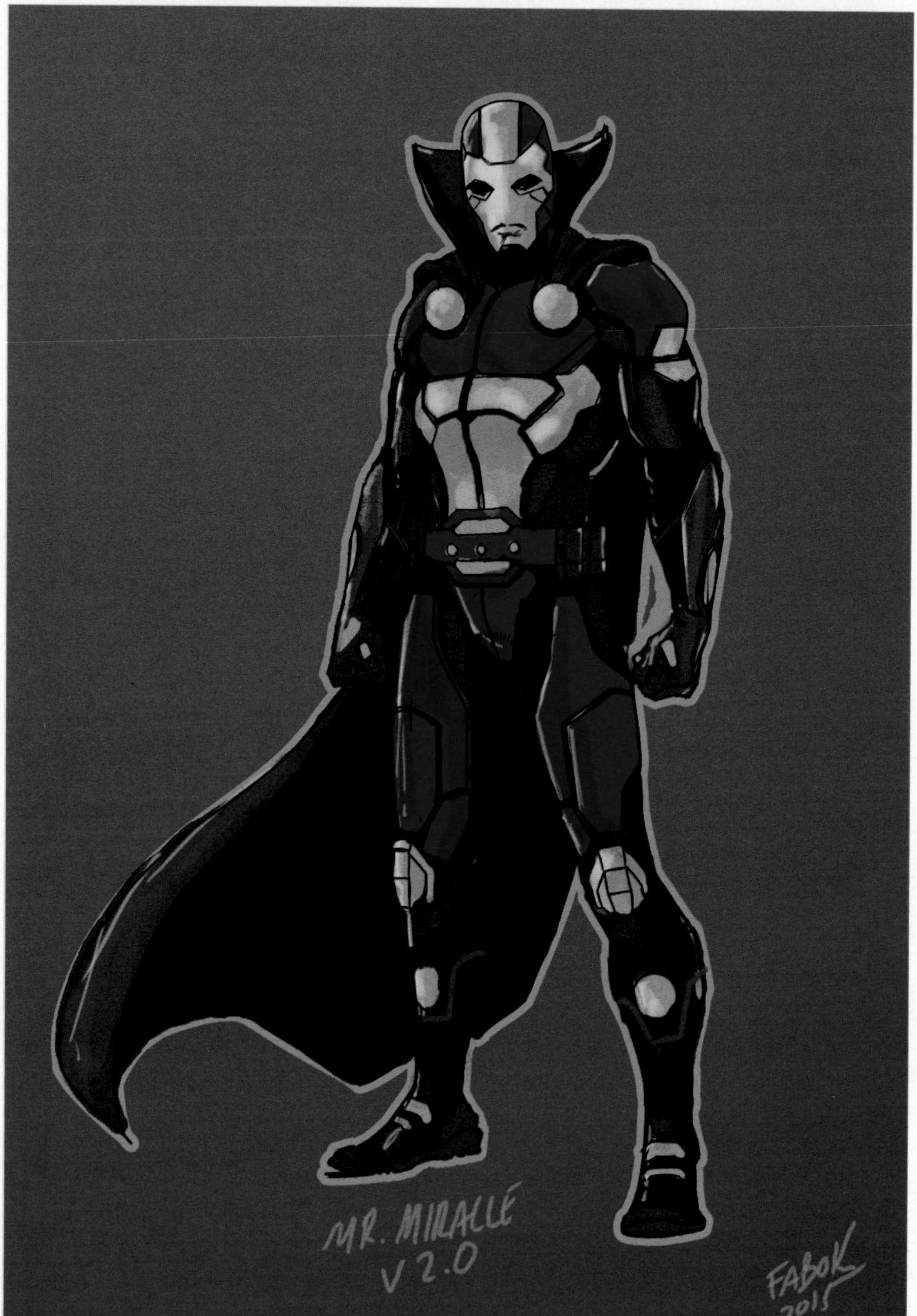
MR. MIRACLE
V 2.0
FABOK
2015

Rough panel layout for the death of Darkseid by Jim Lee, which became the basis for Jason Fabok's spread.

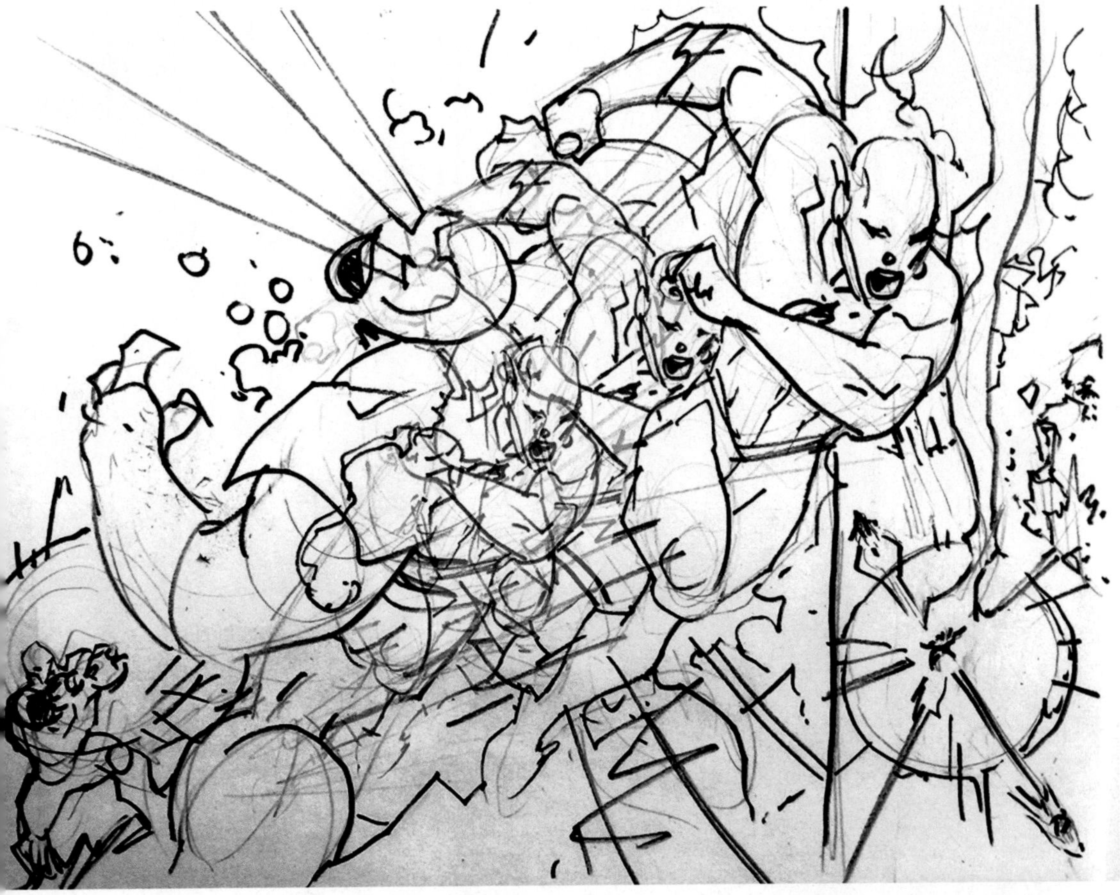

Issue #44 Pages 18-19

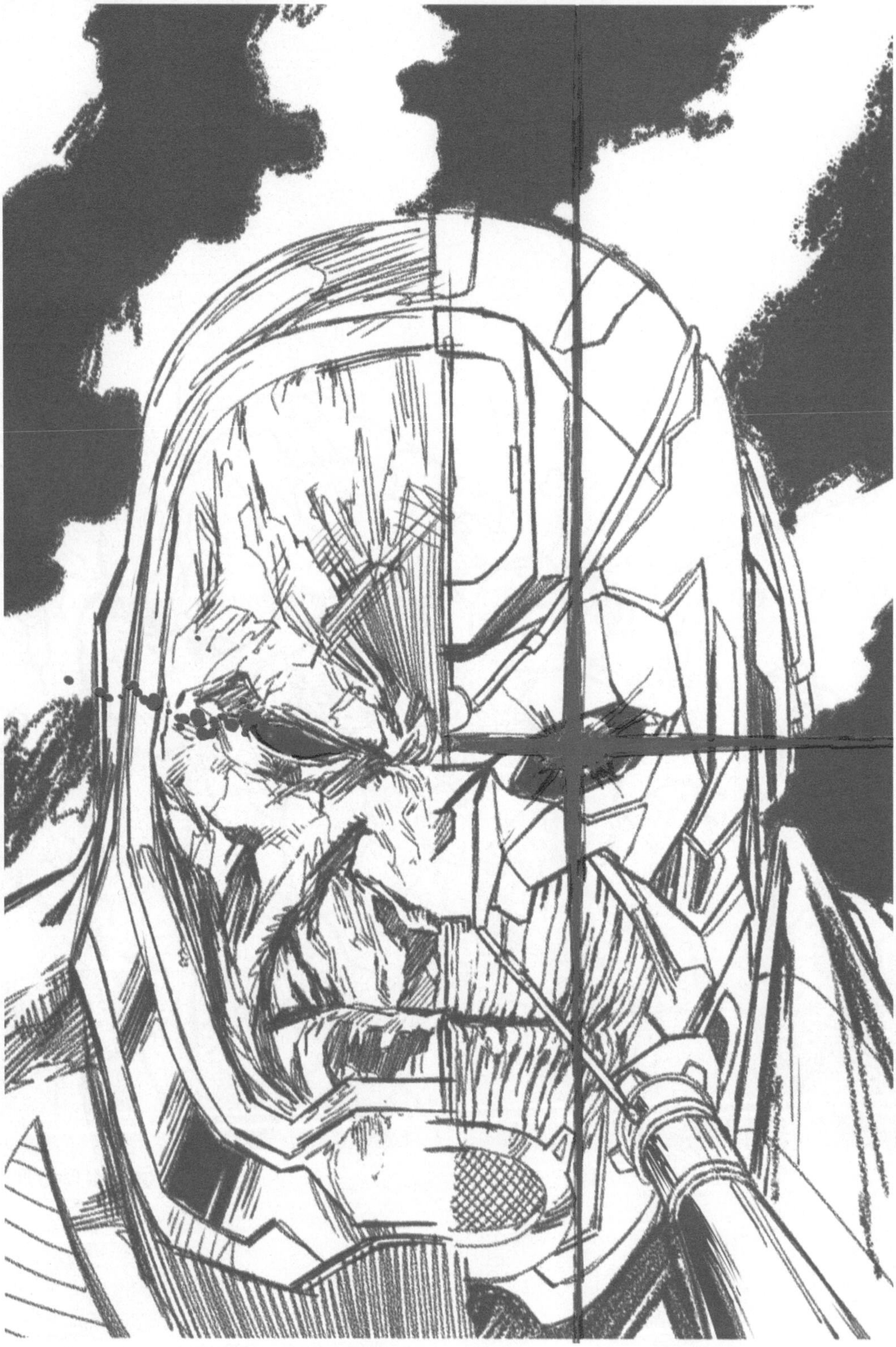

Issue #40 cover sketch

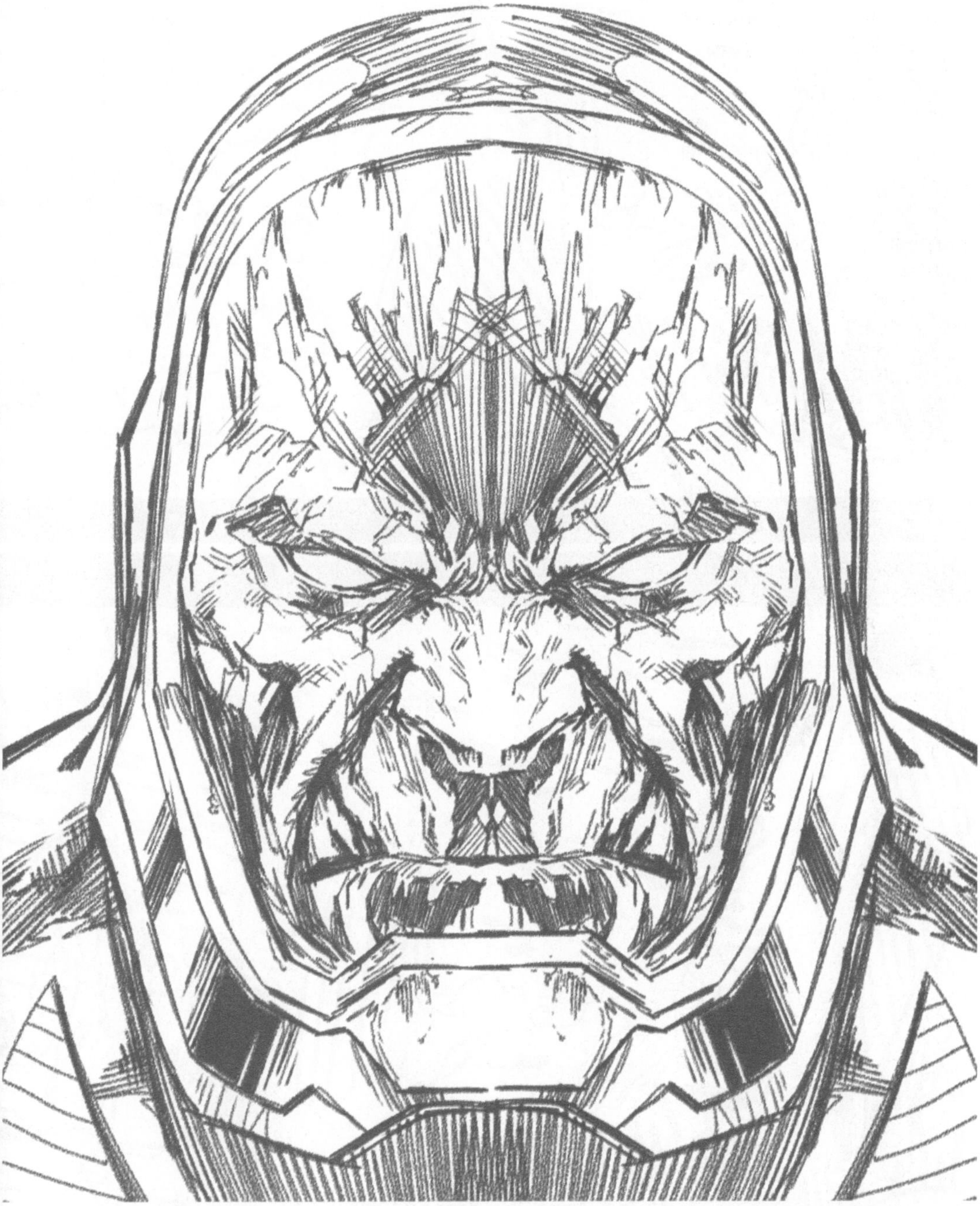

Issue #40 cover sketch

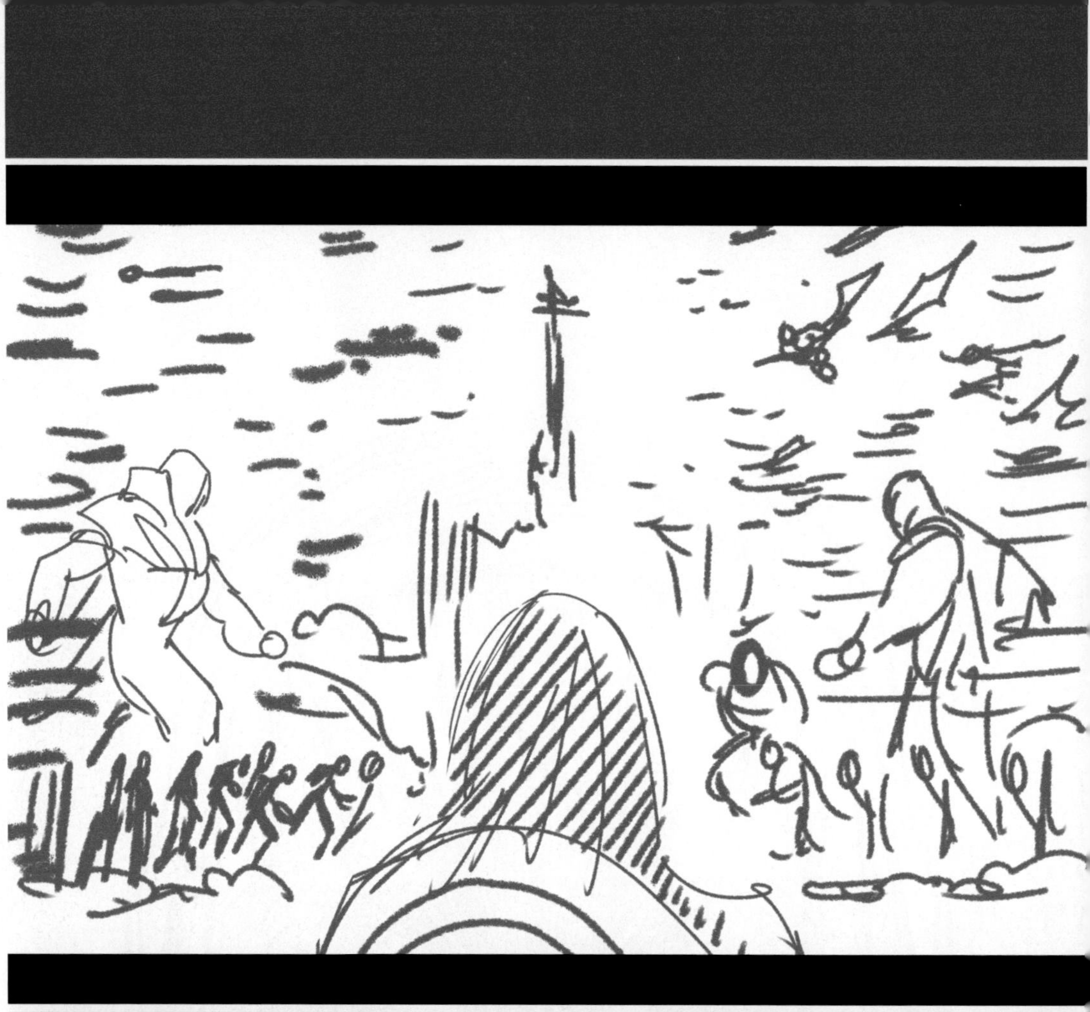

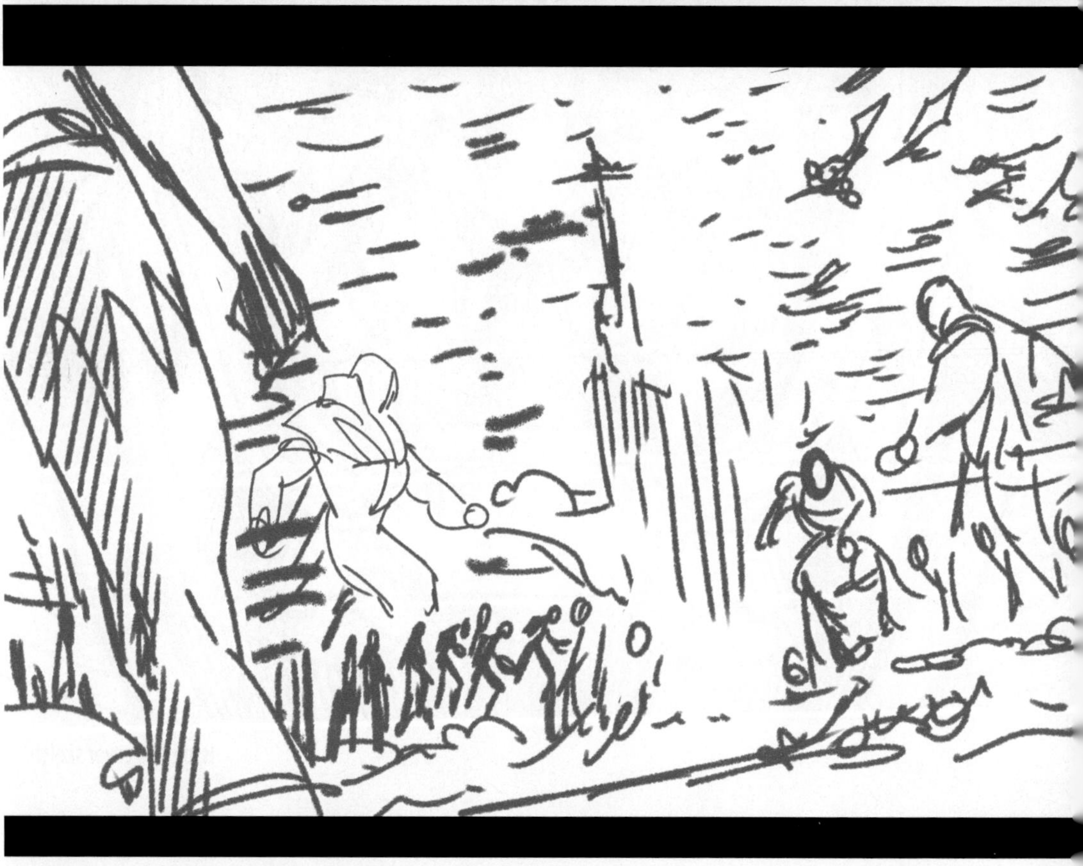

Alternate layouts for issue #43 pages 20-21

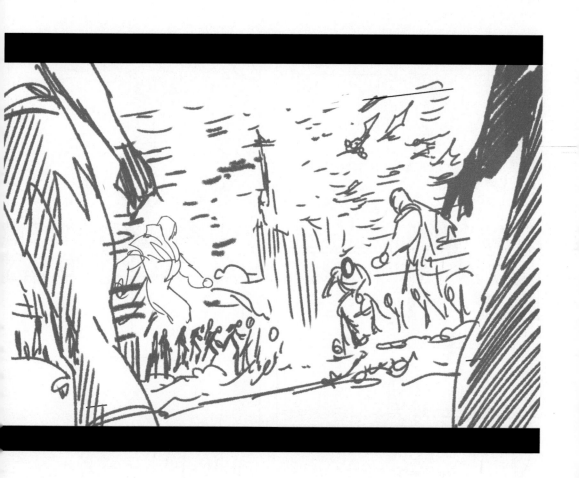

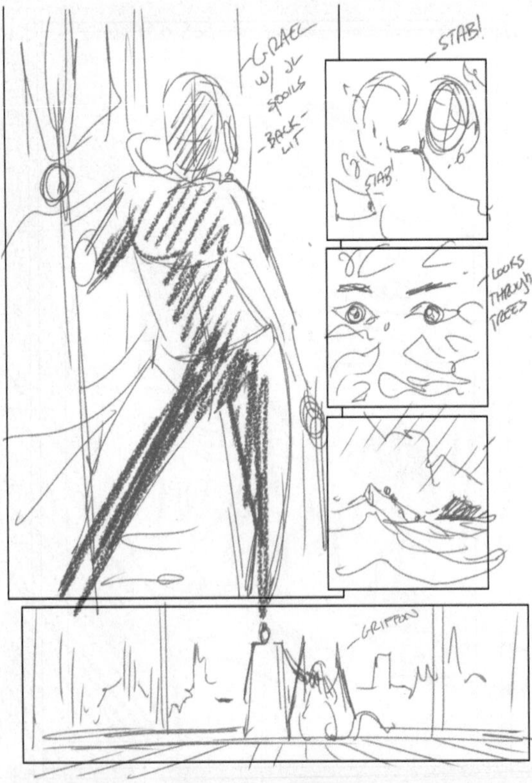
GRAEL
W/ JL
SPOILS
BACK-
LIT
STAB!
STAB!
LOOKS
THROUGH
TREES
GRIFFON

Sketch for page 8 of DC SNEAK PEEK: JUSTICE LEAGUE #1

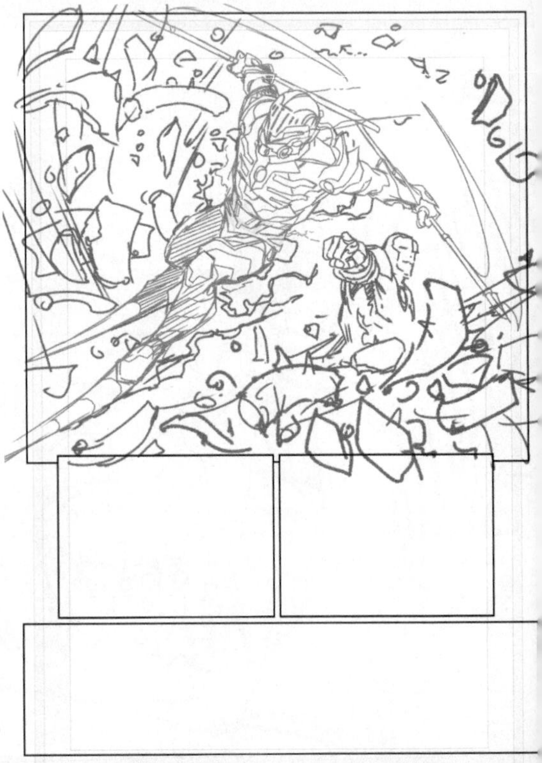

Issue #44 page 11 sketch

START AT THE BEGINNING!
JUSTICE LEAGUE
VOLUME 1: ORIGIN
GEOFF JOHNS and JIM LEE

JUSTICE LEAGUE VOL. 2: THE VILLAIN'S JOURNEY

JUSTICE LEAGUE VOL. 3: THRONE OF ATLANTIS

JUSTICE LEAGUE OF AMERICA VOL. 1: WORLD'S MOST DANGEROUS

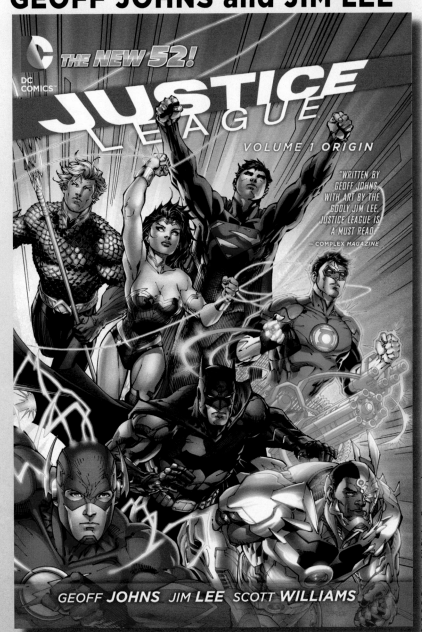

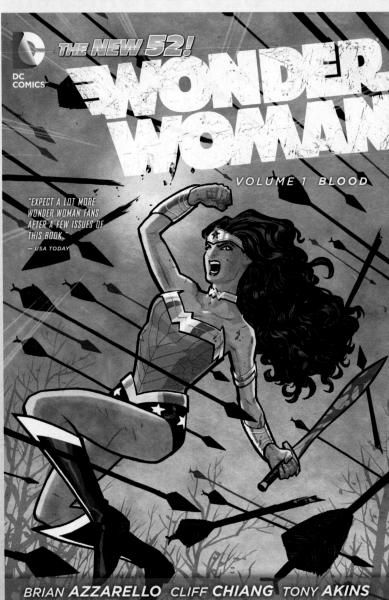

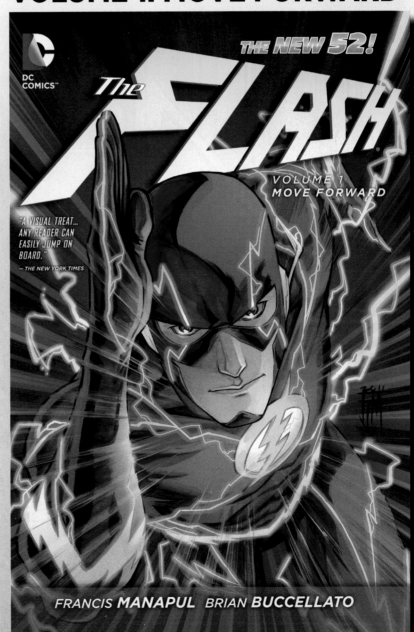

START AT THE BEGINNING!

THE FLASH
VOLUME 1: MOVE FORWARD

THE FLASH VOL. 2: ROGUES REVOLUTION

THE FLASH VOL. 3: GORILLA WARFARE

JUSTICE LEAGUE VOL. 1: ORIGIN

START AT THE BEGINNING

SUPERMAN: ACTION COMIC
VOLUME 1: SUPERMA
AND THE MEN OF STEE

**SUPERMAN
VOLUME 1: WHAT
PRICE TOMORROW?**

**SUPERGIRL VOLUME 1:
THE LAST DAUGHTER
OF KRYPTON**

**SUPERBOY VOLUME 1:
INCUBATION**

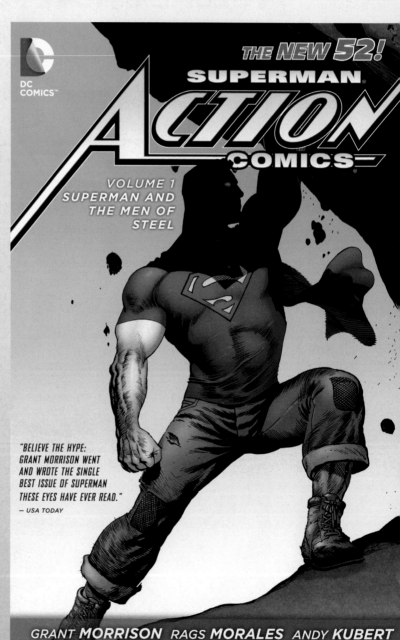

"BELIEVE THE HYPE:
GRANT MORRISON WENT
AND WROTE THE SINGLE
BEST ISSUE OF SUPERMAN
THESE EYES HAVE EVER READ."
— USA TODAY

GRANT **MORRISON** RAGS **MORALES** ANDY **KUBERT**